Commodities Rising

Commodities Rising

The Reality Behind the Hype
and How To Really Profit
in the Commodities Market

JEFFREY M. CHRISTIAN

WILEY

John Wiley & Sons, Inc.

Published by John Wiley & Sons, Inc., Hoboken, New Jersey.
Published simultaneously in Canada.

For general information on our other products and services or for technical support, please
contact our Customer Care Department within the United States at (800) 762-2974,
outside the United States at (317) 572-3993 or fax (317) 572-4002.

Wiley also publishes its books in a variety of electronic formats. Some content that appears
in print may not be available in electronic books. For more information about Wiley
products, visit our web site at www.wiley.com.

Library of Congress Cataloging-in-Publication Data:

Christian, Jeffrey M., 1955–
    Commodities rising : the reality behind the hype and how to really profit
in the commodities market / Jeffrey M. Christian.
        p.   cm.
    Includes index.
    ISBN-13: 978-0-471-77225-5 (cloth)
    ISBN-10: 0-471-77225-9 (cloth)
    1. Commodity exchanges.   2. Speculation.   I. Title.
    HG6046.C5733 2006
    332.63'28—dc22

                                                            2006003344

Printed in the United States of America.

10   9   8   7   6   5   4   3   2   1

Dedicated to Kathy Christian, my soul mate.

*To Andy Christian and Eric Christian,
my sun and moon, the coyotes baying at night.*

*To David Nelson and Jeffrey Maguire.
Jeffrey taught me to keep it simple;
David tried in vain to teach me to
look both ways before I cross the street.*

Contents

Preface

C ommodities markets are a fascinating part of the world economy and financial markets. I probably first became interested in commodities as a young boy, watching tangible assets (things) move around the United States and around the world. The clockwork that is the international commodities market, that brings molybdenum from Chile to steelmakers in Pittsburgh, wheat from Kansas to bakers in North Africa, and timber from far eastern Russia to furniture makers in North Carolina, is an incredible machine, built by mankind over centuries.

My interest in commodities expanded in college, where I wanted to study how communist countries traded internationally, and the economic relationships between developing countries and corporations in the industrialized nations. A surprisingly large portion of this trade was commodities-based, and I was fortunate enough to be able to meet Soviet petroleum experts, Chinese gold traders, and South African mining magnates as part of my education. This led naturally to a career in studying commodities markets.

I have found throughout my career that others shared my passion and interest in commodities. Some of the most prominent economic thinkers of our times have discussed the extent to which they continue to track commodities markets as part of the international economic system. Commodities are less important than they used to be, in terms of percentages of gross national output, but they still form the critical base for all economic activity. I have witnessed during this time the ability of the commodities markets to capture and inspire the imagination and thinking of investors, business people, analysts, and government leaders in ways that other financial assets—from stocks to bonds—simply cannot. The tangibility and vitality of commodities captures people's intellect.

Commodities, Not Futures

My company and I are interested in commodities, and not necessarily futures markets. Until recently, virtually all of our consulting work providing hedging and investment strategies involved dealer forwards, over-the-counter options, and non–exchange traded instruments. Futures markets are only the most visible manifestation of these commodities markets to people not involved in commodities producing or using industries. Many commodities are not traded on futures or options exchanges. Many of these non–exchange traded commodities are extremely interesting to us, and to investors. They are a lot harder to invest in.

For the purposes of this book, I focus on some of the more accessible and more liquid commodities markets. I include discussions later in this book on a number of commodities. I tend to limit discussion to those commodities that are traded on organized futures and options exchanges, since these are the most accessible to investors. However, I include uranium, which is not traded on any exchange per se. Uranium prices rose from $6.40 in early 2001 to around $33 in 2005, reflecting strong growth in demand from both nuclear power plants and investors, on the one side of the market, and some tightening of supplies on the other. Uranium is a special commodity, since it also has military uses. Even so, investors are interested in uranium. As a result of this, several uranium investment funds have been started over the past two years to offer investors easier access to uranium.

Commodities are things. They are stuff. They are the building blocks of the real economy. They are called *tangible assets* in the financial markets, along with real estate and art. These markets often are seen as more interesting than equity and bond markets by people who are attracted by their tangibility. Some of these people are investors who, as kids, dismantled radios, televisions, and other things to see how they work. In contrast to some of the work in stock and bond market analyses, working and investing in commodities can involve a person in the study of much more fundamental, tangible assets. Many investors take a much keener interest in their precious metals investments than in their other stocks and bonds, I have found.

In the 1970s and part of the 1980s, one of the major business daily newspapers had a reporter who was truly interested in commodities. He was required to do the daily roundups of major activities in the futures markets, and he dispatched this responsibility with great accuracy and thoroughness. He also went a bit further. Every year or so he would write a seasonal update on the maple sugar market, or the cranberry or blueberry markets. At one point he interviewed a commodities dealer who specialized in seeds, such as sesame and poppy seeds. The interview included a discussion of the study McDonald's had commissioned to determine whether the sesame seed market could supply it sufficient sesame seeds if it switched to a sesame seed bun. The rest is history. The point I would make is that commodities are much more than futures, and there are a lot more commodities than there are futures markets.

Who I Am

I should stop here and mention a bit about who I am and why you might want to read a book by me.

I run a company named CPM Group, which generally is seen as one of the best sources for information, statistics, intelligence, and analysis on commodities markets. I have run this company since 1986. Prior to that I ran the research department at J. Aron and Company. In addition to being a major precious metals trading company, J. Aron was also at that time the largest coffee trader in the world and a major foreign exchange and oil trader.

J. Aron merged into Goldman, Sachs & Company in 1981, and I became the head of the commodities research group within the Goldman Sachs Investment Research Department. For a variety of reasons I decided that I would rather work for myself than for a large investment bank and trading company, so between late 1984 and early 1986 I proposed several times that Goldman swing a deal in which I would take my commodities research group out of their company, set ourselves up as independent consultants, and provide research and consulting on commodities to Goldman

Sachs. At the end of May 1986 Goldman struck my offer, and we left to form CPM Group. We have been independent ever since.

CPM Group has a reputation for several things. We are seen as the smartest, best informed, most knowledgeable, and most analytical group studying the precious metals markets. We are known for our contacts around the world with major producers, consumers, central banks, governments, and investors. We are known for our expertise in what we call financial engineering—the use of options and other financial instruments to help our clients manage their exposure to commodities prices. Later in the book I describe a simple, elegant method CPM Group has developed that allows investors to invest in individual commodities, or groups of commodities, while preserving all or part of their capital investment. They even can structure these "principal guaranteed" or "principal protected" accounts in ways that allow them to make money regardless of whether the price of a given commodity rises or falls.

We take a proactive approach toward the business and general press. Our policy is that we will always speak to the press, and we will never lie to them. We might tell them that we cannot comment on a given topic, given that we might have inside information, but we will not mislead the press. It is easier to bat down a wild rumor before it is put into print than after, and helping the press separate the wheat from the chaff saves us time later. Whenever we identify new reporters being assigned to a commodities beat, we invite them over to lunch, load them down with research reports, and begin to give them basic information on the commodities markets. One of the points we always make to these reporters is that they need to study and understand why anyone in the commodities markets would be speaking to them, and that everyone "talks their book" to reporters and others; by this we mean that they tell reporters only such information as supports their particular position in the markets. The same is true for investors. Investors need to question the motives of their sources of information and trading ideas.

I have been fortunate to be in the right place to experience extraordinary events in the commodities markets many times over the past 25 years. In the late 1970s I had a ringside seat during the run-up in gold and silver prices. Later in this book I discuss some of the things that I saw in the silver market at that time. I explain that, from everything I saw—and I believe I saw just about everything—the famous Hunt brothers were not trying to corner the silver market, as is generally believed today. They were trying to ride a wave, and maybe help create it. I watched it unfold firsthand, and had direct contact with most of the important market participants on both sides of the market at that time.

Later, in the middle of the 1980s, I was involved in the ultimate disposition of the Hunts' physical silver, which was sold by a bank appointed to handle this transaction after the Hunts' silver position collapsed in April 1980. The bank sold it to J. Aron while I was there. I was part of the team that placed it with the ultimate buyers. I also watched a few other major investors become involved in silver in subsequent years, often from close range.

In the gold market, I worked at J. Aron at a time when it was developing some of the most innovative financial transactions involving gold. We were on the vanguard of bullion trading companies that were borrowing gold from or swapping gold with central banks. I watched our gold lease book bulge as increasing numbers of central banks entered into secret agreements to lend out their gold in order to generate some return on what had become an otherwise sterile asset. When we had too much gold on our books to lend to jewelers, J. Aron became one of the first bullion dealers to arrange to lend gold to a mining company for the purpose of financing development of a new gold mine. I worked on several gold loans to producers. After I left Aron and Goldman, I continued to advise on such arrangements with gold producers and others.

I was also involved in developing some of the commodities options programs still used by producers, consumers, central banks, and institutional investors. CPM Group advised numerous central banks in the late 1980s and 1990s on their gold reserve policies and programs. We were advising some large auto manufacturers in the 1980s, the 1990s, and the early part of this decade when particularly significant platinum group metals transactions occurred. There were a lot more such transactions that I have been lucky enough to be involved in.

All in all, these experiences have provided me with deep and broad firsthand knowledge about how these markets work, how commodities are monetized and traded around the world, and how these various transactions are executed. In commodities today there is a great deal of market chatter about the mechanics of some of these transactions, such as central bank gold lending and mining company hedging programs, and their effects on the markets. Much of what is said and written about these transactions is wrong, often egregiously so. We are able to sit there and listen to the rumblings. People in the market tend not to laugh over these outrageously off-centered commentaries. Rather, we tend to shake our heads in disbelief. This superior insight allows us to gauge likely market trends into the future more accurately than most other groups involved in commodities. A sizable portion of what we do that is valuable, in terms of allowing us to position ourselves and our clients to profit in commodities, tends to be taking positions designed to profit from the inevitable reaction in commodities prices when they correct for moves that were based on bad information.

Who This Is Written For

This book explores the world of commodities from the perspective of the individual investor, although a great deal of information in it will be new and valuable to other market participants and observers. One of the points I make is that fundamental supply and demand still rule in the commodities markets. There is money to be made in commodities, but you have to do your homework.

In writing this book I have tried to use plain language and to avoid the Byzantine nomenclature behind which many financial market participants hide. For example, in Chapter 6, "Commodities as an Asset Class," I speak about the usefulness of commodities to investors both as a means to make money and as a way to diversify investment portfolios to smooth out total returns that would fluctuate more if a portfolio were only stocks, bonds, or some combination of them. Market practitioners these days talk about *alpha*, meaning the ability of an asset to generate profits on its own, and *beta*, meaning that asset's effect in smoothing portfolio returns through its statistical correlation with the other assets in the portfolio (its beta to them). I have strived to avoid such market terminology as much as possible, and to make this book as readable as it is informative.

How This Book Is Organized

Chapter 1 gives an overview of the past, stormy present, and future of commodities. Chapter 2 focuses on two of the more widely circulating myths about commodities: the concept of a long-lasting supercycle in rising commodity prices and the idea that China will be a massive consumer of commodities forever, gobbling up the natural resources others need and driving prices higher. Chapter 3 looks at the role of commodities in the world economy; this is followed by a discussion of the theoretical basis for considering commodities as investments (Chapter 4). Chapter 5 reviews the instruments available to investors interested in building exposure to commodities prices, while Chapter 6 discusses some specific strategies, including the principal protected and guaranteed principal accounts.

Chapters 7 through 11 are dedicated to taking deeper looks at 16 specific commodities, grouped under the following headings:

- Precious metals (gold, silver, platinum, palladium)
- Energy (petroleum, natural gas, uranium)
- Tropical agriculturals (cocoa, coffee, cotton)
- Grains (corn, soybeans, wheat)
- Base metals (copper, lead, zinc)

Each chapter includes critical background information needed to assess the attractiveness of these individual commodities as investments. Chapter 12 looks at the future of commodities.

Acknowledgments

First of all, I must acknowledge all of the assistance provided me in the preparation of this book by Carlos Sanchez, the chief research analyst at my company, CPM Group. Carlos has been with me since the cold winter of 1999. I have put him through many paces, as he has had to deal with my distractions and sometimes nonlinear ways of thinking. He has succeeded in becoming one of the most knowledgeable persons in the world on commodities statistics and analysis, and works closely as my right-hand man. Not only did he help immeasurably with the work that went into this book, but he picked up enormous volumes of slack at our company while I focused on writing it.

Catherine Virga is an excellent research analyst. She has helped with the specific development of the statistics and analysis in this book more than anyone else, and has provided an organizational coherence when I became overwhelmed with the sheer volume of information we were seeking to distill into this book.

In addition to Catherine and Carlos, many others at CPM Group have helped out in a range of ways. Lennys Ramos is our administrator. Like Carlos, she has picked up a large number of responsibilities from me, allowing me to focus more on this book. Chris Munford worked with CPM Group in 2005 and produced much of the research on uranium that informs that section of the book. Rohit Savant is another research analyst, whose work on tropical agricultural commodities formed the basis for Chapter 9. I also must acknowledge the direct and indirect help of the rest of the staff at CPM Group, including Madhusudan Daga, Ralph Mizrahi, Doug Sherrod, and Phil Barkett. Commodities analysis, the way we do it, is a collaborative effort. Everyone has a say, everyone has input, everyone has insights that come together to form a complete and hopefully coherent view of the market for each individual commodity, as well as the global macroeconomic environment in which these market forces play out.

In the midst of writing *Commodities Rising* I was approached by two investors, Mark Hansen and Richard Hansen, who were interested in working with CPM Group and me, and interested in the exposure to commodities markets that our company provides. They became our partners in late 2005, as this book was being pulled together. I cannot express enough my gratitude to them for understanding, tolerating, and accepting my enormous distraction from my work at CPM Group while getting this book completed.

Similarly, I must thank all of my clients who sensed the tone of panic in my voice and allowed me to focus on completing this book instead of the projects I owed them.

I also must thank my editors at John Wiley & Sons, Kevin Commins and Emilie Herman. Their insights and direction have been extremely valuable to me. I simply would not have written this book without Kevin. Others at Wiley have been very helpful and patient with me, for which I am grateful. Scott Friedlander converted our rudimentary graphics into art suitable for the present volume, making our thoughts look so much prettier than they are.

1

The Commodities Rush Is On

C ommodities prices have risen sharply since 2003. The financial press attributed this to an increased use of basic commodities in China and other developing countries. Increases in actual demand—what the market calls *fabrication demand*, as opposed to investors buying for hoarding or speculative purposes—both within developing countries such as China and in industrialized nations such as the United States and Japan, has been a factor. However, an even larger factor has been the rush of investors into commodities. Several hundred billion dollars have been invested in commodities since 2003, almost all of it on the long side of the market. Commodities prices are in the midst of a speculative bubble, similar in some ways to the tech bubble of the late 1990s. From individual investors to large institutional investors, even savvy and experienced professional money managers are falling into this common trap and ignoring basic economics, finance, and logic. They go long and stay long at the wrong time.

The idea that many investors who rushed into the commodities markets will lose a lot of money quickly should not surprise anyone. It is the way that commodities investments have played out for centuries. In the futures markets, which represent the most common and visible way for investors to participate in commodities, various industry association studies show that the majority of investors who get involved in futures lose money. It is not that the futures or commodities markets are inherently designed to separate uninitiated investors from their cash. It is, rather, that investors often seem to lose their wits when it comes to commodities. They approach these markets with many misconceptions about commodities, and fail to do their homework both before and while they are involved in the futures markets.

There *is* a great deal of money to be made in the commodities markets, from oil and gold to wheat and coffee. The money will be made by investors and traders who do their homework, who do *not* get caught up in the market hype, and who keep a level head about expectations. My own experience, and that of the clients I respect the most, suggests that the investors who will do best in the commodities markets over the next few years will be those who are just as willing to sell markets short as they are to go long. Investors shy away from selling, or shorting, in almost all markets. Shorting takes more courage and savvy. It also takes a certain psychological composition. Most people want to be optimists. They want to see the prices of assets in which they invest rise. They are not set up mentally to try to make money by betting that those optimists who are long are wrong.

You see this in the broader economy as well. Investors and others accept a steady diet of inflation, which slowly but consistently eats away their buying power. Inflation of 2 to 3 percent is accepted readily and willingly. As soon as there is a whiff of disinflation, investors, politicians, and others panic. The United States has not experienced deflation since the Great Depression. There was a series of devastating bouts of deflation in the second half of the nineteenth century, as the Industrial Revolution led to massive reductions in the prices of many goods and services, and bred a wide range of economic upheavals that caused widespread dislocations and economic suffering. The Federal Reserve System was not created in 1913 out of whimsy. It was an attempt to solve some fundamental financial market problems that had contributed to enormously destructive economic fluctuations for much of the nineteenth century. Ever since then investors, politicians, and the general public have panicked at the concept of deflation, even though it is a monster rarely seen in these parts.

In the early part of the present decade the United States experienced a round of disinflation. This was not deflation, but rather a move toward even lower inflation rates than the 3.1 percent average rate experienced in the United States from 1983 through 2004 (in other words, a more beneficial inflation environment than had been experienced in the United States for many decades). Inflation fell to 1.6 percent in 2002. It was still a positive number, but the financial press was overwhelmed with articles worrying about the dangers of deflation. Most people are much more psychologically prepared and willing to accept rising prices, even if such price increases threaten long-term negative consequences for them. The same psychology limits investors' willingness to trade stocks, bonds, and commodities short.

This chapter takes you through the current commodities rush—why it is happening and where the dangers lie—to assist you to see your way through the hype and misinformation so that you can assess opportunities and exploit them.

Why Commodities, Why Now?

Commodities markets have become, over the past four decades or so, increasingly marginal portions of the world financial market. They are still very important economically, but the enormous expansion of financial markets since the 1970s has outpaced the more arithmetic growth in commodities markets. In the past few years, however, commodities have staged an almost amazing resurgence, capturing much of the center stage in international financial markets since 2003. Banks, asset managers, and others who had shunned commodities for most of the past two decades have rushed back into the market, seeking to position themselves as authorities on that which they formerly found repugnant.

There are three major reasons for the current rush into commodities. The first is that world economic, financial, and political trends and conditions have turned hostile since 2000, and consequently stocks and bonds have not done so well over the past five or six years. There were times during this period when stocks or bonds did well for a while, but overall these markets have not been returning particularly stellar performances since the turn of the century, and investors ranging from institutions to individuals around the world have been chasing returns. Alan Greenspan has spoken several times about the fact that investors are accepting greater risks for any given expected return than is historically typical. He is right. Investors have taken on greater risks in the search for investment returns, and one of those risks has been to move into commodities, which many had traditionally shunned.

Second, a recent round of academic and market research has shown

that commodities can stand up as equals to stocks and bonds as investments. Commodities traditionally were disparaged by financial markets,
which saw them as more volatile, less profitable, and too complex to ana-
lyze. They had no book value per se, compared to stocks, and no yield like
bonds. But commodities have gained new respectability and desirability as
assets, and as an asset class comparable to stocks or bonds. Fund managers
and others have realized that commodities are not necessarily more volatile
than stocks, and that investing in commodities can be just as profitable as
investing in stocks and bonds. Commodities can compete in terms of capital appreciation potential, generating profits themselves. They also are useful as elements of a diversified portfolio, helping to smooth out the risks of
a portfolio of stocks, bonds, and other assets without significantly limiting
the capital appreciation potential.

The third reason is that commodities prices have been rising, and investors chase rising prices. Investment demand is the Mount Shasta of
economics, where demand rises proportionately with prices. In any
other segment of the economy, rising prices lead to lower demand, and
vice versa. Investment demand, however, is positively correlated to
prices: Investors buy more of investments as prices rise, and less when
prices are falling. It does not make sense to
value-oriented investors like me, but it is a
fundamental reality that one must remember
when analyzing all investment markets. Commodities prices, in general, have been rising
over the past two years. As a consequence, investors have poured money into commodities.

Investment demand, however, is positively correlated to prices: Investors buy more of investments as prices rise, and less when prices are falling.

Other factors that have contributed to investor interest in commodities since 2003, such
as the decline in the dollar's exchange rate, for
example, are subsets to these three major trends.

Who Will Win, Who Will Lose

This much I can tell you with certainty: A great deal of money will be
made by investors and others in commodities over the next few years—
and a great deal of money will be lost by other investors in commodities
over the same period of time.

A lot of the money lost will be that of investors who have gone or will go long a wide range of commodities, convinced that commodities prices inexorably must rise because of fundamental changes that have altered the economic history of mankind. Those who make money will be the more nimble—or less believing—investors who buy and sell commodities based on reasoned and rational analysis of supply, demand, and economic trends.

There are marketeers abroad today who speak authoritatively about the imminent collapse of the U.S. dollar and the world monetary order. Some of these people have been making the same arguments nonstop since 1980 at least. They have been wrong for 25 years, and yet they still attract thousands of subscribers to their newsletters and thousands of adoring fans to their seminars.

I use the term *fans* knowingly, because it hints at the reality of the investing community that one must understand in order to comprehend the true nature of the current rush into commodities. These are not investors making informed decisions based on rational analyses of markets. These are people who have a gut feeling that something is wrong that will lead to economic and financial crises. They are not looking for intellectually based insights, but rather quasi-religious confirmations that their beliefs are about to be confirmed.

The marketeers riding the current commodities boom are having a heyday, after many years in the wilderness. Money is flowing into their personal coffers as never before, not even in the period 1978 through 1980 when commodities prices last rose sharply. One gold mutual fund manager I know made a tremendous amount of money for his investor clients in the period 1975 through 1980. From then onward he lost more than 90 percent of their money, over 23 years. In the past three years he has made some of it back, but not nearly all of it. Now, again, he is the hero to his investors. The rise in gold prices over the past three years has reaffirmed their belief, which they held in the 1970s and throughout the intervening decades, that the postwar world economic system cannot last.

In the early 1990s, when he was French Minister of Finance, Eduard Balladur said that a world monetary system without gold serving an integral base could not last. I pointed out that the current system was 20 years old. His response was that two decades were but a drop of water in time, and that from a longer-term perspective gold must be restored to its central role in the international currency system.

That is the attitude of many commodities investors as well: In the long run, I will be proven right. I may have lost a fortune in the interim, and I may die before my views are vindicated, but someday it will be shown that I was right.

Gold bugs, the term that is applied both to irrational gold investors and to true believers in gold's inescapable role as the ultimate, one true currency, often point out that no currency system not based on gold has ever lasted—they all have collapsed. That is true. However, it is also true that *all* currency systems *except the current one* have collapsed, including every currency system that ever used gold or silver as its base asset. The critical point is that currency systems do not last. It does not matter whether they are based on gold or not.

All of the factors that have caused commodities prices to rise and fall in the past are still in effect today. Basic economics still apply. The recent increases in some commodities prices, from oil and gold to copper and steel, have been firmly grounded in basic economics. Major changes in the world economy have increased demand for many commodities. The single most important development has been the rise of a consumer class in India, China, Russia, Brazil, and many other countries. But there has not been any major transformation that has ushered in the end of basic economic laws of supply and demand. The rise of the consumer class was well foretold by both Karl Marx and Thorsten Veblen in the nineteenth century. The fundamentals of supply and demand still dictate commodities prices, and many investors are still lured into commodities investments at exactly the wrong time by wild promises of easy riches. It is one of the oldest stories known to mankind, and it is playing out yet again in 2005 and 2006.

> *There has not been any major transformation that has ushered in the end of basic economic laws of supply and demand.*

None of that matters to many of the investors rushing into commodities. They hear stories of boundless demand for every imaginable commodity and raw material from a newly emerging China. They hear about books with titles referring to a billion new consumers seeking to buy every imaginable consumer good. They hear bond salesmen and motorcycle mechanics, turned into overnight commodities pundits, expounding about decades-long commodities price booms on late-night television, and never bother to stop and look at a commodities price chart to see that there never has been such a beast before, and there is no reason to believe that one exists today, either.

Avoiding the Pitfalls

The commodities markets are grossly misunderstood, even by many of the largest and most central participants. It is not unusual to find mining executives who do not understand even the basics of how their metal is traded internationally. In 2000 one major bullion bank almost convinced a group of gold mining companies to give it $450 million over three years to promote gold jewelry. The bullion bank told them it was the only way to get the price of gold to rise again. Some of the mining executives asked my company what we thought about this.

We pointed out that gold jewelry demand is negatively correlated to the price of gold. As gold prices fall, people use and buy more gold in jewelry. As prices rise, they use and buy less gold in jewelry. Furthermore, the use of gold in jewelry had already more than doubled since the early 1980s, and the gold price had moved sideways and lower through this enormous expansion of gold use. If you want to get the gold price to rise, you need to stimulate investment demand for gold—which, strangely, is positively correlated to the price of gold. This was earth-shattering news to many of the mining executives. They did not go with the jewelry program, but instead moved toward creating the gold exchange traded funds that were launched in various major investment markets from 2003 through 2005.

That sort of lack of basic knowledge is not unusual. In the middle of 2001 one of our hedge fund clients said that, before it invested in gold based on our market views, it wanted to meet with a senior gold mining executive. We arranged a meeting. The hedge fund manager came back and said that he would not invest in gold. While he accepted our fundamental analysis that gold prices were going to rise sharply over the next several years, he said he could not in good conscience invest in a market in which the executives were so ill-informed about their own products. He said that, although he was not in the gold business, he knew more about how the gold market worked than the president of one of the largest gold mining companies in the world. "My investors would string me up if I invested in companies so poorly run," he said, citing his fiduciary responsibility to invest his clients' money wisely.

This lack of self-knowledge is not unique to the gold market. In fact, in some ways the gold market is better known and understood than many other commodities markets. A study by the International Energy Agency (IEA) in the early 2000s showed a 67 percent spread between the low and high estimates made by major oil market analytical teams of the amount of

OPEC production over quota. Oil is by far the largest commodity market and is of incredible strategic importance to governments, corporations, and people around the world. Because of this, more money and attention are spent on petroleum market analysis than on any other commodity. Even so, the oil market finds wide disparities among its experts—not counting the lunatic fringes—as to how much is actually being produced and consumed.

A few years earlier, when oil prices were down around $10 per barrel, the oil market was roiled by rumors that vast amounts of unreported petroleum were being held in inventories around the world, in secret oil tank farms and in unused oil tankers. Now, there are worldwide directories of oil tank farms and oil tankers. This is an industry that is highly reported. And these are large objects we're talking about. It could be possible to hide a significant amount of gold, silver, or platinum, since the value to volume of precious metals is so high. The opposite is true about oil. It would be virtually impossible to hide large amounts of petroleum in unreported, secret tank farms, or to somehow slip some of the world's oil tankers out of the computerized lists of tankers that many people in the petroleum market track regularly. Even so, these outrageous rumors gained traction and were circulated throughout the market, and among oil importing governments, for months. This demonstrates the incredible degree to which basic information, such as supply, demand, and inventories, is not known about most commodities.

There are numerous reasons for the prevalence of bad information in the commodities markets. Some of the more important factors involved include the following:

- Lack of regulation that could screen out misinformation that circulates either intentionally or unintentionally.
- Questionable statistics and a general misunderstanding of these under-reported, misunderstood, and underanalyzed asymmetrical commodities markets.
- Marketing hype.

The remaining sections of this chapter aim to outline these common pitfalls and to discuss some very basic analytical tools that investors can use to avoid them, or even to profit from them.

Lack of Regulation

Many of the regulations that apply to stock and bond markets do not apply in the commodities markets. In the United States, the Commodities Futures Trading Commission (CFTC) is the government agency with regulatory oversight of exchange traded futures and options. Over-the-counter or dealer commodities trades do not fall under the purview of any governmental regulatory body and are regulated largely through corporate law. Furthermore, the CFTC has devolved much of the regulatory responsibility to the National Futures Association, an industry self-regulatory body.

Some things that investors and brokers cannot do in stocks and bonds are legal in the commodities markets. For example, there are no insider trading bans in commodities. There are no overt strictures against floating rumors, other than general corporate laws related to fraud.

Anyone can write or say just about anything about any commodity market. There are no certification procedures for analysts. Anyone can start a newsletter or a blog on the Internet and spout whatever thoughts come to mind. In 1993 I was approached by a publisher of financial newsletters, who said he wanted to enter a partnership to publish a precious metals newsletter that I would write. I told him there were dozens of precious metals newsletters already, and I did not see the market. He said, "Have you read any of them? There are a lot of gold newsletters, but they spend all their time trashing Hillary Clinton or flogging small Canadian gold mining stocks that paid them shares to write about them. There are no investor newsletters that write about the supply and demand for gold." He was right.

I took the thought to the next level, and started considering whether to produce a newsletter for retail investors. At the time my company, CPM Group, advised major mining companies, consuming companies, central banks, governments, and large investors. The lowest-priced product we had was $2,400. I met with a few other newsletter publishers who already marketed gold newsletters. We could not find common ground. As one of them explained, "You can sell gold to investors based on one of two primal urges: fear or greed. We sell newsletters based on fear—fear that the government is going to come and take your money, fear that the government is going to make men and women use the same public bathrooms, fear. You write about gold from the perspective of greed: How can you make money investing in gold? We can't sell that to our readers. These are fearful people. The thought of trying to make money by investing in gold does not enter their thinking, only the fear that someone will take what they already have away."

One basic truth is that commodities markets are largely unregulated. Another basic truth is that the commodities markets are overrun by incredibly bad information. There is so much misinformation circulating about many commodities. When I say this in presentations, people immediately begin to think of all of the gold and silver conspiracy theories. These are definitely an obstruction of truth in commodities, but they are not the only problem. There is also a tremendous amount of information passed off on the market by seemingly legitimate groups that simply do not know what they are talking about. We call it fabricating statistics.

One basic truth is that commodities markets are largely unregulated. Another basic truth is that the commodities markets are overrun by incredibly bad information.

In 2005 some of the most respected gold promotional organizations were publishing reports that Indian gold demand was skyrocketing. They were saying that gold demand in India was up an unbelievable 47 percent from 2004 levels. This was soaked up by even seasoned gold traders as gospel truth. It was, in fact, unbelievable. Gold demand was off sharply in India, meanwhile, in direct relation to the sharp rise in gold prices. Jewelers in India were worrying about the lack of business, as buyers stayed away waiting for lower gold prices. The gold promoters—we call them marketeers— knew that the gold market was so opaque and so self-unaware that they could write this stuff and most people in the market, most investors, would lap it up and run out to buy gold in the belief that Indian jewelry buyers would push the price higher. Besides, many gold investors in North America were looking for any reason to be bullish on gold at that time and would jump at any story to justify their enthusiasm.

One of the things that was happening in the Indian gold market in 2005 was that there was a large circular flow of gold in and out of Mumbai (formerly Bombay), which was distorting import data. Mumbai dealers and jewelers would import gold from Dubai, cast it into crude jewelry, export the jewelry to Dubai, and file requests for government subsidies and export credits for exporting gold jewelry. The Indian government offered these credits to encourage jobs creation in downstream manufacturing of gold and silver into jewelry. The jewelry would get to Dubai, be melted back into gold bars, and re-imported back to India, to repeat the cycle. Sometimes the gold would make the return flight on the same day it left India, flying to Dubai on a morning flight as jewelry, and coming back on the same plane that evening as bullion bars. This had the effect of sharply increasing recorded gold bullion imports into India. Anyone who did not know what was going on could honestly mistake such inflows of gold bullion as a sign that domestic Indian demand was jumping sharply higher. They would have been wrong, however. Worse, there were some people in the gold market who had every reason to know what was going on, who were told by Indian market participants what was going on, and still chose to publish reports touting the enormous increase in domestic demand for gold within India.

Faulty Statistics and the Asymmetrical Market

That leads to another crucial point about commodities. The statistics available for most of them are unreliable. In an earlier draft of this book, I said they stink. The quality and accuracy is dreadful. It is not unusual in my job to receive very well done econometric analyses on gold, oil, or other commodities, produced by economists at investment banks, fund management companies, and universities. The analytical work is of the highest caliber. Unfortunately, the data on which it is based is wrong.

The commodities markets are, in the words of economists, asymmetrical and inefficient. *Asymmetrical* means that information is not readily available or uniformly available across the market. In other words, some people know a lot more than others. The commodities markets are inefficient because they are ill reported, relatively small, populated by relatively fewer numbers of market participants, and relatively illiquid.

The flow of information in these markets is sparse and uneven. Much is not known about basic commodities supply, demand, and other market conditions, even by the major banks, trading companies, producers, and users of these goods. Much that is seemingly known, meanwhile, is inaccurate. My company, CPM Group, has hired people from the foreign exchange, equities, and bond markets over the years. As these people become familiar with the commodities markets, almost universally they go through a period of intense shock at the poor quality and obvious misinformation that circulates as fact in the commodities markets.

That said, I should add that sometimes the quality of information in other financial markets, and in the broader political marketplace, also seems pretty poor. Commodities market participants are used to beating themselves up as the poor cousins of broader financial markets. They tend to have inferiority complexes, and rightly so. However, that does not mean that equity and bond markets are without criticism and shortcomings.

As I indicated earlier, while equity and bond markets have many regulations and regulatory bodies to help assure better-quality information flows, most commodities markets in major financial market nations such as the United States and United Kingdom are largely unregulated. The

Securities and Exchange Commission (SEC) in the United States and similar equity market regulatory bodies in other countries have rules to protect companies and investors from the possibility of any layperson writing or saying whatever they want about a company. Someone cannot simply write a report on a publicly listed company and fill it with opinions without having substantive backing and reasons for those opinions. No such regulations exist for commodities in the United States, in the United Kingdom, or in most other countries.

A few years ago one of the more famous if lunatic gold market commentators wrote in his newsletter that the central bank of Brazil had written naked, or uncovered, call options totaling roughly 60 million ounces of gold, and that as the gold price had started to rise the central bank had been forced to go into the spot gold market and buy 60 million ounces of physical gold over one or two days to cover its exposure. Anyone who knows anything about the gold market knows that such a concept is ludicrous. It just could not have happened. Sure, daily turnover in the London gold market was running around 30 million ounces a day at that time, but most of that was not spot gold, and there are not 60 million ounces of physical gold bullion lying around ready to be purchased on a moment's notice. The idea that the bank, which held around three million ounces of gold at the time, would do this was equally outrageous and unbelievable. Finally, any entity caught in such a bind would be able to unwind such a position on a cash settlement basis, paying in dollars the losses it had incurred. In other words, none of this story held up to even the most superficial scrutiny. Anyone stopping to think for even a moment with even a rudimentary understanding of the gold market would have seen this as utter nonsense.

That did not matter in the market, however. The rumor sent ripples through the gold bug sector of the market and had a noticeable effect, albeit minor, on the gold price. There was an interesting twist about to happen, however. Foreign central banks are nationally chartered banks in the United States, and there is a law that prohibits slander and floating unsubstantiated rumors about nationally chartered banks in the United States. As a result, the central bank told the foreign ministry of Brazil, which informed the U.S. State Department, which notified other government agencies, and the gold newsletter writer was called down to Washington to explain himself. It seems that you can say just about anything about gold or other commodities with impunity in the United States, but you cannot make up things about nationally chartered banks. Of course the newsletter writer, an inveterate liar who had fabricated the entire story, was seen by the gold bugs as a martyr being harassed by a global conspiracy of governments.

I will take a slight detour here and provide another anecdote about this gold guru. In 1981 I was running the statistical research department at J. Aron & Company, one of the top dozen precious metals trading companies in the world at the time. We merged into Goldman, Sachs & Co., and I became director of Goldman's Commodities Research Group. I reported to the chief economist, who reported to the partner in charge of investment research, Lee Cooperman. Lee is and was a wonderful person on many levels. He is incredibly smart. Another thing I loved about him was his irascibility. I was called over to Goldman's offices to meet Lee and the chief economist, Gary Wenglowski. As we met and shook hands, Lee said, "I want you to know that I think gold is a religion and not an investment, and I was one of the strongest opponents to Goldman buying Aron." Being a brash young man, I held on to his hand and said that while I agreed that gold was a religion for many people, it also could be a worthwhile investment. I told him I thought he would be impressed by some of the quantitative research our group was doing on gold and other commodities. "I won't be," he said.

Years later I had left Goldman, and Lee was running a hedge fund. He hired this gold guru as an adviser. When I heard that, I called Lee and reminded him of his first comment to me, adding, "It's only fitting that when you decided to get into gold you did not hire an analyst, but a shaman." I cannot repeat his rebuttal to me here, but the market rumors were that his operation lost a lot of money based on this true believer's gold market bets. They were bets, not investment decisions.

One lesson I hope the reader derives from these anecdotes is that much of the rhetoric that investors are hearing today about why they should be loading up on commodities has been around for decades, if not centuries. Also, much of it is just wrong. The age-old admonishment about something sounding too good to be true certainly applies in all financial markets. In the wild western fringe of commodities, it applies doubly.

Industry Myths

While there are many myths that circulate in the commodities markets, two in particular have captured the imagination of investors in strong ways at present. One is that the commodities markets have entered into some sort of "supercycle" that will see prices rise for decades to come, and that such long periods of rising commodities prices actually have historical precedents. The second is that China will consume vast amounts of commodities, bidding up prices to unimaginable levels. The two myths are intertwined to some extent. Both are covered more extensively in the next chapter.

The arguments in favor of a supercycle in commodities prices that will last until 2015 or 2020, the predictions of insatiable Chinese demand for every commodity under the sun, and all the rest of the hype are just as convincing and just as grounded in fantasy as were the arguments in 1999 that the stock market would never fall again, that recessions had been banished from the economic cycle, and that the Dow Jones Industrial Average would hit 40,000 within months, if not weeks.

I have seen it all before and heard all of the seemingly convincing but incorrect arguments predicting a secular upward shift of historical proportions in commodities prices. The amazing thing to me is that investors, including some of the most sophisticated and experienced institutional fund managers on the planet, still believe the hype and rush headlong into bad investment decisions.

Additionally, the commodities markets are not stock or bond markets. Over the past few years, several major and minor traditional investment fund management companies have rolled out commodities-oriented investment products, from mutual funds to hedge funds and structured products. As they have tried to apply the quantitative management skills honed in equity and bond markets to commodities, they have quickly realized that these markets are not as well documented, statistically known, or regulated as equities and bonds. There are enormous differences—from the ways the markets work, to the tenure of investments, to the levels of market or government oversight and regulation.

Unearthing the Reality

The joke has been made more than once that I see my job as taking seemingly easy decisions and making them complex. To some extent, that is true. One of the things I do is show people that the world tends not to operate in either-or propositions, in black-and-white. The world tends to operate in shades of gray, along a spectrum of possibilities. The system is much more complex than many simplistic ideologies portray, and the future is not as cut and dried as such simplistic analyses suggest it will be.

Understanding this is central to making money in all financial assets. The world's economic system, its currency system, and those of individual nations all have a tremendous capacity to muddle through. Those who think in terms of do or die, of collapse or prosperity, do not understand the basic economic realities of the world, that the dismal science is dismal because it is the study of hard choices and compromises along a spectrum of possible decisions and outcomes. People who have been waiting for the U.S. Treasury bond market to collapse for a quarter of a century may be right someday. They also may be wrong. Regardless of the ultimate conclusion, they will have squandered much of their life and much of their potential to earn money by staking out a black-and-white financial position and adhering to it regardless of the evidence all around them that they may well be wrong.

This all is central to the reality of today's commodities markets. Some things have changed in the world. The single most important change has been the economic liberalization and deregulation of vast parts of the world economy, including China, India, Russia, other parts of the former Soviet Union, and parts of Africa, Latin America, and Asia. Close to 40 percent of the world's population has been let out of the cages that held them back from economic freedom for several decades. This has unleashed economic growth for a larger number of people than ever before has happened. This has significant implications for many commodities.

However, the economic implications are not simple and straightforward, and in many cases they are the opposite of what the commodities bulls would have you think. The view that China will suck in ever larger amounts of virtually every commodity known to man is simply wrong. China is using and will use more commodities. It will also increase its own production of many of them. We will discuss this in more detail later, but suffice it to say here that the reality of China's ability to use and to produce commodities is not a one-way street. In 2003 and 2004 China was a massive importer of steel, along with many other commodities. In 2005 it turned into a large exporter. Oops. Expect more of this across the spectrum of commodities, and not just with China.

> *Close to 40 percent of the world's population has been let out of the cages that held them back from economic freedom for several decades.*

The reality of commodities markets today is that the prices of many commodities are rising significantly, in some cases for the first time in decades. There are fundamental reasons of supply and demand behind many of these price increases. Investor mania for commodities is exacerbating these price increases, however, as investors, eager to get in on the easy winnings of a commodity bull rush, pour money into commodities. This has caused the prices of some commodities to rise too far. Already there are massive investments under way to increase productive capacity in a variety of commodities, from petroleum to gold, nickel, and copper. Already the signs are clearly painted, saying that it is time to shift from a shotgun approach targeting a wide and indiscriminant swath of commodities toward a rifle approach, picking those commodities for which it makes sense to go long and those for which it makes sense to go short.

I have a reputation, built up since the 1970s, based on a number of strengths. One is that I am just as willing to hold a negative view toward any given commodity as I am to hold a positive view toward it. I am not a gold bug by a long shot. I have held negative intermediate-term views toward gold (looking out two to three years) for extensive periods in my career, from 1983 into 1986, for example, and from early 1988 until early 1993. I am not a true believer in commodities. I am in no way convinced that anyone can make money in commodities simply by going long in any or all commodities in the years ahead. In fact, one of the few things I know with certainty about commodities is that this is not an accurate portrayal of the nature of commodities markets. I strive to be agnostic about commodities, both as an asset class and as individual investments.

Succeeding in the Current Climate

The reality of the commodities markets from 2006 forward is that one must carefully and accurately assess the short- and long-term prospects for supply, demand, and other market conditions and trends for each commodity in order to have any chance of accurately fathoming the likelihood that the price of that commodity will rise or fall in the future.

Do I believe that money can be made in commodities? Certainly. The histories of my career, my company, and my clients have proven that investors can make a tremendous amount of money in commodities. However, one of the keys to such success is not having one's investment decisions clouded by beliefs.

Another is finding and staying plugged into a superior stream of market intelligence. Commodities markets are full of inaccurate information. They are thin on real information and accurate statistics. What passes for analysis in the commodities markets would be criminal in the securities markets— literally! Much of what is published and circulated as market research and analysis in the commodities markets simply could not be circulated legally if it was being written about publicly listed and traded corporations.

A lot of what investors are hearing needs to be scrutinized, and then scrutinized again. Much of it is obviously wrong. Some of it is just plain silly. Just as the equity market promoters who said that the basic tenets of economics had been destroyed in the late 1990s were wrong, so too are the commodities marketeers wrong today.

When someone tells you about how the billion-plus Chinese are going to be buying cars, refrigerators, computers, and everything else, ask them what they will use to pay for these items. As I discuss later, more than 850 million Chinese citizens, two-thirds of the population of that country, survive on less than $2 per day at present, even after 15 years of the Chinese economic miracle. Are more Chinese wealthier today than they used to be, and buying more manufactured goods and food? Yes. But not all Chinese people are in that boat, at least not yet, and it will be a long time before they can climb aboard. How will they come to earn enough to be able to afford all of these new products? They will get jobs making things, in areas such as mining, oil and gas production, and agricultural production and processing—in other words, in producing commodities. In the meantime, some Chinese entrepreneurs are building boats of their own, so that by the time their fellow countrymen are ready to spend on consumer goods, those goods may well be made with metals mined in China and foodstuffs grown at home.

Where Do We Go from Here?

If my tales have not scared you away, and with my words of caution duly noted, let us start considering commodities as investments.

Commodities are very interesting markets in which to be involved. Their tangibility, the concrete nature of these markets, makes them much more interesting than stocks or bonds. Equity market analysis can often devolve into forensic accounting, and bond market research is virtually all quantitative. Commodities, however, force you to pay attention to real life—to people's consumption habits for agricultural commodities, housing, and transportation; to politics; to the economic policies of governments; and to many other aspects of human nature and world development.

Commodities are a good way for ordinary investors to make money, to create wealth. It takes hard work. There is no easy road to riches, no free lunch. I suspect this has less to do with commodities and futures markets per se and more to do with the attitudes with which investors approach the futures markets. They often fall prey to talk about rapid riches through massive leverage, overlooking the fact that the leverage offered to investors by futures and options cuts both ways: You can make a lot of money using the leverage that futures afford you, and you can lose a lot just as quickly. I have met many investors who take a methodical approach to equity investments and bond market decisions, but simply lose all of their sensibility when they start considering commodities futures, throwing money at the market based on the most spurious and unbelievable comments by total strangers. Not to disparage traditional witch doctors in any way, but relying on financial witch doctors for advice on commodities is not unique by a long shot.

History also shows that commodities have played a central role in the creation of the wealth of nations, through the effective development of natural resources. Even in this post-industrial, information age, a staggering amount of U.S. and world wealth creation is based on commodities. Finally, there are many wonderful stories about famous millionaires and billionaires who owe much of their wealth to their involvement in commodities.

There is money to be made investing in commodities, but careful research and a lot of detailed analysis are required in order to do it right. Investors also need a healthy dose of skepticism about all the hype circulating about commodities markets today. Some commodities will see lower prices over the next few years; other commodities are likely to see higher prices. Realistic analysis of each individual commodity will help investors discern which is which.

This book is designed to provide readers with a great deal of information related to commodities markets overall, and to specific commodities, to start them on the way to successful investing in commodities. It is a complex book. You should not expect to see what we call "arm waving" about the big increases and easy money to be had from mindlessly investing in this or that commodity or index. You should not expect to read earth-shattering convictions that the world is about to run out of oil or nickel or copper. You should expect to encounter complex issues related to the basics of human life on earth, because these are the factors that shape the future courses of commodities markets. Pour another cup of coffee, roll up your sleeves, and read on.

2

The Myths of the Commodities Supercycle and the Chinese Consumer Giant

As already discussed, the prices of many, but not all, commodities have been rising sharply over the past few years. Many factors have come together to cause these price increases. What has been happening, and what is likely to occur next, is easily explained in a coherent fashion using classical economic theories. One does not need to claim that all of the economic premises that have held through the history of mankind have fallen by the roadside in pieces, unshackling humanity from the rules and bindings of economic supply and demand. Even so, many people in the commodities markets today are praying at the altar of a new theory, a theory that commodities are about to enter a so-called supercycle that will last for many years. The high priests of this new religion say that this is a repeat of history. Yet the history books are strangely devoid of any references to long-lasting upward moves in commodities.

What has actually been happening over the past few years is that fabrication demand for many commodities has been rising, reflecting strong economic growth in many quarters of the world and an overall expansion in demand for basic commodities due to the emergence of new consumer economies in India, China, Russia, and other countries. Economic development conditions have increased the demand for many commodities at any given price. Investment demand also is rising. Supply increases meanwhile have been slower than the increases in fabrication and investment demand, reflecting the lagged effects of many years of low prices and structural underinvestment in the productive sectors of the commodities markets. It takes many years to develop new mines, even if you already know where to dig. If you need to undertake an exploration program before you start a new mine development, it takes even longer.

These trends, which form the basis of a classical economic explanation for the increase in commodities prices, are not particularly extraordinary. It is true that the current period of strong demand and high prices for many commodities already has lasted longer than most such increases. However, this is not the precursor of a supercycle, a new paradigm for future commodities market mechanics. It is the classical economics of supply, demand, and price, playing out in an extended cyclical peak.

It is also true, by the way, that the period of declining commodities prices that preceded the current boom went on for a lot longer time, and was a lot more severe, than past historical declines in commodities prices. This in fact partly explains the lag in supply increases: Commodities-producing industries have been starved for financial and intellectual capital for several decades, which has extended the period of time they need to ramp up production in response to the recent price increase. That long decline also makes the more thoughtful and informed managers at these companies more hesitant to commit massive amounts of capital to expansion programs based on two or three years of rising prices. They worry about the sustainability of the price increases, even as the less informed market commentators trumpet commodity price rallies that will last for decades.

The Myth of the Commodities Supercycle Theory

There has been much hoopla in the international commodities markets about a *supercycle*. Many investors and others who have never been involved in commodities, or at best have kept an eye only marginally on them, have come forth as instant experts on commodities, offering a wealth of profound, albeit inaccurate, advice as to how to profit from the coming supercycle in commodities prices. Bond fund managers have dressed up their bond funds to look like commodities funds, and then have appeared on financial news television programs to profess their deep understanding of the nuances of commodities markets. The degree of misinformation contained in some of the messages being circulated by the new gurus of commodities is astounding and appalling. In the largely unregulated commodities markets, however, these misstatements are made with impunity. Worse still, given the poor quality of information distribution in the commodities markets, such statements often go unchallenged and are accepted as true.

To be fair to the commodities markets, it is true that the equities and bond markets were similarly sucked into a massive duping with the so-called "new economic paradigm" of the late 1990s. In comparison to that mass hysteria, the current bubble in the commodities market appears as just another speculative investment bubble in a long line of such ill-conceived rushes.

The idea that informs all of the hype about supercycles is that commodities prices have begun rising sharply over the past two or three years, and now are embarking on a long-term upward trend that will take most commodities prices to historically high levels. There is talk that commodities prices may rise for the next 10 years. People talk about "another historical 17-year bull market in commodities," although there is no real evidence that commodities prices ever experienced such long periods of rising prices (with the possible exceptions of times during world wars and other cataclysmic events).

Much of the rhetoric that is stirring up investor interest in commodities in fact is strongly reminiscent of the "new economic paradigm" jingoism that surrounded the late stages of the bull market in equities in the late 1990s. At that time equity market commentators spoke of a new economic reality that precluded recessions and would be characterized by eternally rising equity values. The entire house of cards collapsed within a couple of years, as recessionary economic conditions emerged and stock prices declined sharply. The S&P 500 declined 50 percent, and the NASDAQ fell roughly 80 percent.

There are several major problems to this thesis. First, it flies in the face of economic realities. Higher prices, or price increases, tend to stimulate increases in supply and to decrease the use of a good or service. As prices have increased, there already have been some efforts to reduce use of gold, oil, copper, and many other commodities. There also has been a major increase in exploration, development, and expansion activities in a wide range of commodities, which is likely to increase supplies over time. These economic mechanisms tend to serve as a brake on rising prices.

History

The prediction of an inexorable extended increase in commodities prices supposedly rests on historical precedents, but few real examples of such historical antecedents exist in modern times. In fact, the historical record of commodities prices since the early stages of the Industrial Revolution strongly suggests that commodities prices ought not to be expected to enter into a massive long-term upward revaluation. The Commodity Research Bureau (CRB) commodities price index since 1957 shows that commodities prices, as measured by this one index, are well into one of three large upward moves that commodities have made since the 1950s. See Figure 2.1.

One of the sideshows in the current commodities investment circus has to do with extended discussions of what commodities ought and ought not be included in an accurate commodities index. People con-

Index

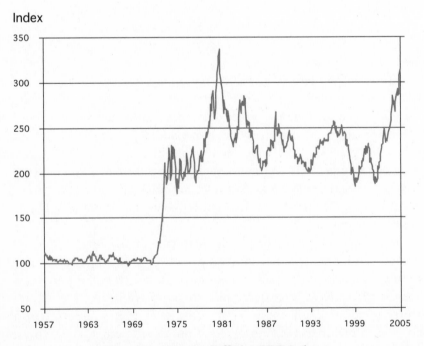

Figure 2.1   **Reuters/Jefferies CRB Index**

struct, deconstruct, and reconstruct numerous commodities indexes, trying to prove their points. An economist who worked with us at Goldman Sachs for a while in the middle of the 1980s had taken a great deal of criticism at his previous job over his insistence that inflation would come roaring back. As inflation moved from a very volatile pattern in the 1970s and early 1980s to a much more subdued trend in the middle of the 1980s, he spent an inordinate amount of time trying to reconstitute the CRB and Bureau of Labor Statistics commodities indexes—the two leading indexes of the time—in order to prove that inflation was roaring, at least at the level of basic raw materials, and that the indexes were simply ill-constructed and thus obscuring the truth. His desire to do this proved to be a great distraction. While it is important to know what the indexes are actually measuring and reporting, the impulse to build better indexes often reflects a desire to prove a point more than it does a desire to build a more representative nature of economic reality. (One should always be suspicious of people who spend too much of their energy trying to construct economic data series that will prove their points.)

Referring back to Figure 2.1, the current upward move in commodities prices had seen this index rise 70.3 percent in the 43 months from January 2002 through September 2005. This is almost as large an increase as the 78.5 percent rise that occurred from August 1977 to October 1980, a period of 39 months. It is dwarfed by the 136.7 percent rise over 34 months from September 1971, right after President Richard Nixon floated the U.S. dollar, to July 1974, right before President Nixon resigned from office. It is the third largest upward move in commodities prices since the 1950s by a very wide margin. There do not seem to be many precedents in recent history for a longer or larger upward move in commodities prices.

The two postwar increases in commodities prices prior to the current one lasted 34 and 39 months. Neither lasted 17 years, or anywhere near that. In fact, going all the way back to 1800, one is hard pressed to find any historical precedent for a 17-year bull market in commodities.

While the past is not necessarily repeated, modern commodities market history suggests that the present situation is more likely a mature upward move in commodities prices. Some commodities prices seem likely to remain strong, possibly rising significantly further, over the next several years. Other commodities are showing strong indications that the bulk of their upward move in price already has been made, and that prices are more likely to either fall or move more or less horizontally over the next few years.

This is especially true given the fundamental differences in the U.S. and world economies today compared to the previous periods of high commodities prices during the 1970s. Inflation overall is much less a problem than it was then. Monetary policies around the world seem much more vigilant against inflation and much more cautionary. Despite commentary about runaway money supply growth in the United States and other countries, money supply growth and overall monetary policies have been far less accommodating in the recent period than they were in previous periods, including several periods that never witnessed sharp increases in inflation. Other economic conditions also are much more likely to help keep inflation under control than was the case in the 1970s, including globalization and deregulation of various markets. The existence of numerous financial market innovations developed since then also assists in limiting the negative consequences of inflation.

Commodities bulls argue that the commodity price experiences of the past half century are not the historical comparisons that they are using. They argue that larger price spikes in commodities in earlier centuries and during the two world wars are more relevant comparisons to the current commodities markets. However, there are many theoretical and empirical reasons for not accepting this argument. Again, the world economy has changed dramatically since the early twentieth century, let alone since the agrarian eras that preceded it.

This argument also does not hold up to statistical scrutiny. Figure 2.2 shows inflation-adjusted commodities prices in the United States since 1800. These data were used in an August 2005 presentation by BHP-Billiton to suggest that the current upward trend in commodities has much further to go. The appearance of this chart helped ignite the commodities bulls' buying spree during August and September, as it was reprinted and circulated all over the world market.

Unfortunately for the commodities bulls, the data presented on this chart can be read either way. One could look at the data and conclude that the upward move in commodities prices since 2002 has been small, and that commodities could have a long way to go to catch up with their inflation-adjusted levels of the nineteenth century.

However, most economists who dedicate their professional lives to studying commodities markets draw the opposite conclusion from these statistics. They point out that industrialization and the move to a post-industrial service-oriented economy have led to a long-term major decline in commodities prices. Usage patterns also have shifted dramatically since

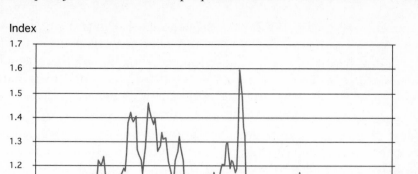

Index

Figure 2.2 **U.S. Inflation-Adjusted Commodity Prices**

then. Their analyses suggest that commodities prices should not be expected to rise back to the much higher inflation-adjusted levels of past centuries.

Partly this is due to the fact that industrialization of the industries that produce commodities, from copper and steel to wheat and cocoa, leads to sharp increases of supplies and major declines in production costs. Copper and steel used to cost several pennies per nail. Today they are a fraction of that, adjusted for inflation and in nominal terms.

What Has Actually Changed in Commodity Markets?

Commodities prices should not be expected to rise back to their nineteenth century levels. The current upward move is a natural reaction to an extended period of time in which commodities prices were depressed. For some commodities, it has further to go; for others, there are signs it is already overdone. Supply and demand fundamentals are reacting to prices already and will catch up. The period of time in which prices adjust to new supply and demand trends varies according to commodity. Some adjustments appeared in 2005 or are likely to emerge in 2006. Others will take several more years.

There have been some major changes on the demand side of most commodities markets in the past few years that have inspired the rise in commodities prices. The most significant one has been the move in India, China, and other countries toward deregulated markets. This has allowed for a more rapid expansion in industrial output and final demand. Initially much of the demand for commodities in these economies was for goods manufactured for export. As such, the demand for raw materials in these countries was not a net gain to world demand for commodities, but rather represented a shift in manufacturing location from one country to another.

Over the past several years, however, these countries have moved into a new stage of economic development, with the emergence of domestic consumer classes to buy these goods and services. This has increased total demand overall for many commodities. There has been an upward shift in the fabrication demand curve for commodities: More people want more goods at any given price than they did in the past. This has pushed prices higher.

There also has been an upward shift of the investment demand curve, as investors, including many institutional fund managers who never touched commodities in the past, have moved into investing in commodities. More investors are buying more commodities at any given price than before. (Investment demand and fabrication demand have radically different characteristics and demand curves. Fabrication demand is inversely proportional to prices: As prices rise fabrication demand tends to decline. Investment demand is directly proportional to prices: Investors buy more, not less, of an asset as the price rises, and pull back from buying as prices fall.)

The third economic curve is the supply curve. Here, there has been a major lag. While fabrication and investment demand have shifted to higher levels, the long period of under-investment in productive capacity has caused the supply of most commodities to lag. Supplies will rise. They already have in many commodities, including gold, platinum, and copper. The increase is taking longer than the rise in demand took, however. That partly reflects the lag just mentioned, and partly the lead time in finding, planning, developing, and starting new mines.

The bottom line is that commodities prices, including most of the ones covered in this book, have risen sharply over the past few years. The period of rising prices may not be over in any of these markets, as there are solid fundamental and economic reasons for prices to have been increasing. But there also has been a lot of speculative heat and misinformation contributing to the upward move in prices, especially during September 2005. Some of this speculative excess may come off of the market during the second half of 2006. If it does, the underlying fundamental and economic factors will support commodity prices. The levels at which prices find such support will bear important intelligence as to where prices should be expected to move beyond 2006.

The Myth of the Chinese Consumer Giant

Economic development has boosted overall activity in China. It has also stimulated tremendous growth in demand for basic commodities as raw materials for China's industry, for goods manufactured both for export and for domestic consumption. China has become an economic powerhouse. Its share of zinc, copper, and lead refined production has risen from levels around 5 percent or less in the early 1990s to between 20 and 30 percent today. Similar economic growth is occurring in India and in numerous other countries.

Part of the current hoopla about commodities among investors relates to the concept that Chinese demand for a wide range of goods will lead to an inexorable and irreversible growth in demand for these goods. There is some truth to this, but there is much more sizzle than there is steak in this story. Consider this: According to various sources, including IMF, World Bank, and UN statistics, of the 1.3 billion people living in China today, 150 million live on less than $1 per day. In total, 850 million people there live on less than $2 per day. That's more than twice the population of the United States. Perhaps as many as one billion live on less than $3 per day, or $900 per year. The country overall had per capita income of $1,290 in 2004 (compared to U.S. per capita gross national income of $41,400).

Separating Hype from Fact

While there is an urban consumer class emerging in many parts of China, it is not true that 1.3 billion people are rushing out to purchase cars, washing machines, computers, and other items that require copper, steel, gold, platinum, and other materials. The commodity hypesters and newsletter writers who trumpet this as the only thing you need to know before you buy commodities are practicing hyperbole, and missing a lot of very important nuances to what is going on in China.

There is tremendous income disparity within China, and it is worsening.

The vast majority of Chinese individuals still are excluded from the economic miracle occurring in parts of the country. Commodity hype has it that every household in China will want to buy a stainless steel frying pan, boosting nickel consumption to astronomical levels. The same arguments are used to promote western investment in everything from cotton to silver to copper. Most Chinese households cannot afford stainless steel frying pans, however, let alone cars, computers, cameras, televisions, and the rest of the consumer goods common in the West.

Consider this: Approximately 18 million cars and small trucks are sold annually in the United States, to a population of around 298 million people. The number of annual vehicle sales is equivalent to roughly 6 percent of the U.S. population. In China, auto sales have skyrocketed to around 2 million vehicles per year now. With a population of around 1.3 billion, that is an auto purchasing ratio of 0.15 percent, one-fortieth of the U.S. ratio. The commodities bulls say this shows how much demand will increase in China. That could prove to be true. The timing of such growth is a key issue, however—it is not going to happen overnight.

Another aspect even more threatening to the bulls' stories is the specter of Chinese production growth. Let's stay with automobiles for a moment. China has built up its auto industry and market over the past few years. It has built an auto manufacturing capacity of 5.5 million cars per year. Its domestic market has risen to only around 2 million cars per year. Some of the seemingly excess capacity is designed to meet future domestic demand, but most of it is intended to build automobiles for export.

The same pattern is repeating itself in basic commodities. The commodities bulls focus on China's textile industry growth and its need for cotton. They conveniently overlook the even more rapid increase in Chinese cotton growing in recent years.[1] They look at the fact that China now accounts for roughly 20 percent of world aluminum and copper consumption, and increasing shares of the use of a wide range of other raw materials. But they overlook the fact that China's domestic productive capacity is rising even further and faster, and China increasingly is shifting from being

---

[1] At the time of this writing, Chinese cotton production has reached a plateau and actually may decline. It will not decline due to production problems, however. Instead, it appears that authorities have come to view cotton farming as a less efficient use for Chinese farms, concluding that it would be cost effective to import cotton and use Chinese farming capacity for soybeans, corn, wheat, and other crops.

a net importer to being a net exporter of an ever-expanding list of commodities and manufactured products. Also, a big chunk of the increased Chinese demand for raw materials and manufactured components is for use in Chinese manufactured goods for export, which merely reflects the shifting of demand for these commodities from other countries, such as the United States, Taiwan, or South Korea, to China. Such shifts do not reflect net increases in total fabrication demand worldwide, but only a shift in the location of manufacturing.

China was a major importer of a wide range of commodities through 2004. It has been shifting in many of these markets to being a net exporter. The steel industry perhaps is the most prominent example, but the same pattern is repeating itself across a range of goods, from basic raw materials to manufactured products. China has roughly 260 steelmaking plants. Their capacity to roll out steel was expected to reach 390 million metric tonnes by the end of 2005 and perhaps 500 million by the end of 2007. This is up from roughly 160 million metric tonnes in 2000. China shifted from the darling of the international steel market in 2004, the largest and fastest-growing buyer, to the devil, a huge low-cost exporter competing in other markets in 2005.

On top of all of this one must remain cognizant of the fact that economic growth is not assured in China. While the reports in the western media are few and far between, there is a growing militancy across China against the rush to commercialism. Reports suggest that there were around 10,000 protests, demonstrations, and riots in China in 2004 alone. Many of these were anti-corruption or anti-pollution. Some of this unrest represents poorer Chinese people wanting a chance at a piece of the economic pie. However, some of the discontent is taking the form of a longing for a return to communist economic practices—shared poverty instead of a growing economic inequality, as many observers put it. There are still many hard-core Communists, who feel that the consumerism western tourists note in Shanghai and a few other cities is a shameful misdirection of China. There are also several hundred million Muslims in China, some of whom would like to see wars of separation (or independence, in their minds) erupt. Many things could happen to slow, halt, or even reverse the economic conditions that foster heavy commodities demand in China.

A Reason to Be Cautious

I keep in my office a report from Handy & Harman from the 1920s that always reminds me to be a little cautious regarding Chinese demand for commodities. Handy was one of the world's largest silver refiners and users for many decades. It produced one of two basic tenets on silver from early in the twentieth century until the 1990s. (The other was the J. Aron annual silver report, which became the *CPM Silver Yearbook*, published by John Wiley & Sons in 2006.) In one of the Handy silver reports from the 1920s, I stumbled across a statement that now that the Boxer Rebellion had been put down and political stability had emerged in China, Chinese demand for silver and a wide range of western goods would explode to incredible levels. Of course, political stability was a chimera in 1920s China, followed by a series of revolutions and civil wars, the Japanese invasion, World War II, and the next round of civil wars leading to the Communist victory over the Koumintang in 1949. Political stability was not necessarily found even after the Communist Party asserted control over China. Handy's hopefulness about the nascent Chinese demand for silver and other commodities was many decades ahead of itself.

A few years ago I bought a copy of Marco Polo's journals for my son Eric. He promptly left it in the living room, so I began to read it. I was stunned to read one of Polo's major conclusions gleaned from his trips to China. He said that China represented an enormous market for European goods, and that the demand for such commodities in China would be almost unfathomable. I realized that while Handy & Harman may have been 80 years too early, Marco Polo was eight centuries too early, and that in fact China has always represented a tantalizing but unrealized potential market for western mercantilists.

Yes, China is emerging as a major market for many commodities. Enthusiasm must be tempered about what this means for markets. In many markets, from steel to silver, China is increasing not only its domestic raw material requirements, but also its own domestic productive capacity.

A large amount of silver has been flowing out of China each year since around 1998. Most of this silver is metal recovered in base metals refineries and smelters, from both imported base metals mine concentrates and from domestic mine output. The refiners want the copper, lead, and zinc. They also get by-product gold and silver. As they refine the mine product, they keep the base metals to feed the demand for these within China and export the gold and silver. Since 2000, additional silver has come out of China from scrap, which had commonly been used in photographic film and paper within China. The photographic industry in China began modernizing, and in the late 1990s, concerned about purity, it stopped using the domestically available silver and began importing silver nitrate instead. Much of the silver that used to go into photographic materials in China is now exported. Thus, the large, steady flow of silver from China since around 1998 has been from these two ongoing sources and reflects the modernization and industrialization of China.

Meanwhile, the silver mining trade association in North America repeatedly asserted that the silver being exported from China has come from central bank coffers and that, since it was coming from finite government inventories, it would someday run out, at which point the price of silver would skyrocket. In fact, the silver is not coming from bank stocks but is newly refined metal coming from ongoing sources at smelters and refineries, and from scrap. It will not run out. The volumes are increasing. The Bank of China meanwhile has complained about being misrepresented in the market as the source of this metal. The silver bulls do not want to hear these protestations, however, nor have they paid much attention to the rational explanation for what is happening within China. This is important to understanding the silver market. Even more important to understand are the ways in which China's economic development is turning this country into a *supplier* of commodities to the world, and not a net buyer.

Even worse miscalculations are occurring about Chinese demand for commodities. In late 2003 a few commodities brokerage companies in London issued reports touting massive increases in nickel demand from China. "If every Chinese household wants a stainless steel frying pan, the demand for nickel will be enormous," ran the logic, referred to earlier. Remember that most Chinese consumers cannot afford such a pan. The fact that 850 million people there live on less than $2 per day removes 65 percent of this potential market right away, and a significant portion of the remaining population is not much better off.

Reading these bullish nickel reports, first one large hedge fund in London and then a few others began buying nickel. Nickel prices shot sharply higher, rising from around $11,000 per metric ton to nearly $18,000 in less than three months. (It had been below $5,000 two years earlier, in late 2001.) All of the trade press trumpeted the increase in nickel prices due to Chinese demand.

In January 2004 the first hedge fund's manager began worrying that it was not Chinese demand but hedge fund buying that was driving prices higher. He decided to sell. The price of nickel fell nearly 25 percent in one day. It was the hedge fund buying, much more than Chinese fabricators' demand, that had been driving nickel prices higher. Prices continued to slide through most of the first half of 2004, falling back below $11,000. Prices rose back, but it took until the second quarter of 2005 before they approached their January 2004 peak, and prices maintained that level only briefly. By October 2005 nickel prices were back to around $12,000 per metric tonne.

3

Commodities and the Global Economy

Many market observers have used commodities, both in general and individually, as indicators of overall economic conditions. Some have used commodity prices as a leading indicator of inflation, while others have used them as barometers of overall economic activity and health. In both cases this may not be wise, as the conventional wisdom of a relationship between commodity prices and overall economic conditions does not hold up to quantitative analysis and scrutiny.

Fortunately, sometimes the analysts get it right. For example, in late 1986 and 1987, gold was sending what could have been misinterpreted as a signal that the Federal Reserve Board should have been tightening monetary policy. Had it done so, such tightening could have combined with the stock market crash in October 1987 to push the U.S. economy into a recession. The Fed got it right, however, recognizing the rise in gold prices not as a sign of nascent inflation, but rather as a reflection of investors selling U.S. dollars and of political unrest in South Africa. By not tightening money supply in response to rising gold prices, the Fed helped avert a recession in the face of the sharp sell-off in equities in September and October 1987.

Gold is often used as a leading indicator of general price inflation. So, too, are general commodity price indexes. In reality, commodity prices, including gold prices, have never been good indicators of impending inflation in modern times. The joke in some financial circles is that gold has forecasted 13 of the past 3 bouts of inflation. So, too, with commodity indexes. Furthermore, the relationship between inflation and commodity prices, insofar as one exists, has weakened over the past three decades, as commodities and commodity-based manufacturing have become less important in terms of overall inflationary pressures, and service industries and other non-commodity-sensitive sectors have gained in importance.

Commodity prices also historically have been much more volatile than general price inflation. This makes sense for a number of reasons. While inflation at times has moved broadly in line with commodity prices, statistical evidence suggests that the relationship is not a very tight one. There have been numerous times, such as the period 1992 to 1995, when commodities indices and individual commodities such as gold have given false signals of impending increases in inflation. And, as already mentioned, the measurable influence of commodity prices on general price inflation has deteriorated in recent years.

People look at commodity prices as indicators of future inflation for several reasons. One reason is that a long time ago commodity prices were more important to the general economy, and there is a traditional view that commodity prices are indicative of broader economic trends. Another reason is that many commodities are traded on public futures exchanges, which allows price increases to show up more quickly and more prominently than in other sectors of the economy. In contrast, statistics showing employment trends or manufacturing orders, which actually are more pertinent in determining general inflation trends, often are reported with a significant lag.

Year-over-year changes in the CRB index have very low statistical correlations to the U.S. consumer price index (CPI). From 1970 to the middle of the 1990s, the relationship was 0.07 on a concomitant basis. With a one-year lag, the relationship rose to a more significant 0.42. While that is better, it still means that investors, government policy makers, and others who used commodity prices as a presage of inflation trends were likely to be wrong more often than right.

The same is true of individual commodities such as gold and oil. There is some relationship, but it is nowhere near as tight as many casual observers believe it to be. For example, gold prices rose sharply in 1985 through 1987, a time when U.S. price inflation was at an all-time postwar low, between 1.5 percent and 2.0 percent. As previously mentioned, had monetary authorities taken heed of calls for much tighter money supply at the time, as gold bugs were preaching, they would have thrown the United States into a recession unnecessarily. There are many other similar examples. Contrary to popular belief, oil and gold prices lagged the two major increases in general inflation in the early 1970s and the late 1970s. In both instances, oil prices were increased after inflation and a decline in the dollar's exchange rate had significantly eroded the value of petroleum at the expense of oil exporting nations. Meanwhile, gold prices were completely disconnected from the increase in U.S. inflation from 1988 to 1990, falling as inflation rose from around 1.7 percent to 6.0 percent.

I have written extensively about the relationships between gold prices and general commodity prices, on the one hand, and general price inflation on the other. It is clear from numerous and repeated econometric and other studies that the relationship is much weaker than many believe. Investors who buy and sell gold as a surrogate for inflation generally miss many major market moves, and often trade counter to gold price trends.

Commodities and Economic Output

Turning to the relationship between commodities and real economic activity, the same conclusion can be drawn. Clearly, there is a relationship between demand for commodities and overall economic activity levels. As real economic activity expands, people and companies are using more commodities. As disposable incomes rise, people buy more things, most of which are made out of some commodity. Thus, demand for commodities tends to rise and fall in line with real economic activity.

The relationship is very complex, however, and it is not a one-for-one move. Technological changes increase and decrease the need for individual commodities, both in individual products and industries and in relationship to broader economic activity. CPM Group regularly researches the amount of individual commodities used worldwide per capita and per unit of gross domestic product (GDP). As this intensity of demand fluctuates, changes in economic activity have a greater or lesser effect on commodity demand and prices.

The relationship between commodity prices and real economic expansions and contractions does not lend itself to any simple formula or pattern. Not only is there no clear statistical relationship, but the lags and leads between the two shift dramatically from time to time. In the early 1970s commodity prices lagged the growth in GDP, and did not really increase until the economy was moving toward the mature stage of an expansion or even a recession. In the late 1970s and early 1980s the rise in commodity prices was concurrent with the late stages of the economic expansion. Since 1980 there have been both times when commodity prices rose in line with real GDP and times when they moved countercyclically. Overall, real GDP and commodity prices have not moved in synchronization with each other.

Commodities and Economic Development

It may surprise many people who view the world economy today as a post-industrial, information-based economy, but basic commodities remain a vitally important part of economic development and international trade. This is true not only for what we now call the transitional economies (formerly Communist states in transition to something else) and developing countries, but also for countries such as the United States and Japan. Agricultural exports account for 8 percent of total U.S. exports these days. Domestic production and consumption are significant portions of GDP. Metals account for another 3 percent of exports. These basic building blocks of economic output remain central to overall economic growth, even in countries with large service economies.

Basic industries and basic commodities often are overlooked in efforts to foster economic development. That is unfortunate, because commodities are so critically central to overall economic development. Yes, economies can grow away from basic industries as they develop; nonetheless, it is clear that if a country has natural resources that can be developed and used, it is better off in the long run if it develops the resources it has.

That may seem so obvious and simplistic as to be absurd. Unfortunately, many executives and economists involved in international development actually belittle the concept of natural resource development. Some believe that countries and governments detract from their long-term development potential by paying attention to developing their natural resources. Quantifiably, that is wrong. But facts and reality often have little currency in international development policy debates.

I was glad to see in late 2005 comments by an adviser at the World Bank who said that the Bank wished to focus on mining developments in parts of Africa as a way to help develop national economies. The impression I had was that this was not a sentiment universally accepted either within the Bank or in the development community at large.

Development economists often discuss what they call the "commodities trap," by which they mean that a developing country that focuses on trying to harness its natural resources might find itself saddled with an economy that is largely dependent on basic industries with low value-added prospects. The U.S. government in recent years has advised various countries in Africa to move away from the natural resource industries and try to refocus on high-tech industries. I was in Uganda in 2002 when the U.S. government was hosting a trade fair aimed at encouraging Ugandan entrepreneurs to consider trying to compete in computer componentry and software. This is a land-locked country far from most high-tech centers. Its primary exports are coffee, cotton, bananas, fish, and cut flowers. I would never suggest that any country not try to move into information technologies, but I also would never suggest that a country ignore its well-established industries and the natural resources available for it to develop in order to move to a higher level of economic activity.

In the late 1980s and early 1990s I was engaged in various programs to help countries in Africa, Latin America, and Asia attract foreign direct private investment to their local businesses. Some of these programs were run by the World Bank, the United Nations, and other intergovernmental organizations; others were private programs run by mining companies. These efforts involved several things. Many of these governments needed to revise various legal codes to allow foreign ownership of companies and repatriation of profits, set up basic corporate laws and regulations, and establish environmental and regulatory regimes in which companies could work under the rule of law. There were many issues, ranging from importation of mining equipment to title and rights protections and many other topics. Many countries had no bankruptcy laws, for example. This sounds like an obvious and easy thing to fix, but it actually causes a great deal of political angst in many countries. It is also a killer oversight for most business: You can start a company in our country, but you cannot close it down if it does not work out.

As a result of these efforts to stimulate economic development, we saw some real gains. One of the first countries to rejuvenate its mining industry in West Africa was Ghana. Ghana saw its mining industry rise from 2.2 percent of the country's gross domestic product in 1986 to 9.1 percent in 1993, and even further over the next decade. Metals and minerals rose from

16.6 percent of exports to 44.5 percent over the same period and provided needed foreign currency for the country's economic development.

Another early entrant was Mali, where a large Australian company built what was to become of the first gold mines in the region in the late 1980s. Mine production went from less than 1.0 percent of GDP and 2.6 percent of export earnings in 1986 to 2.7 percent of GDP and 16.8 percent of exports by 1993. That meant an increase in both real GDP and foreign currency earnings from this sector from around $9.0 million to $71 million. Such growth can have very important benefits for the economy.

As the benefits to Mali of this first mine became clear, countries throughout Africa began revising their legal codes for foreign direct investments, mining development, land tenure, foreign exchange flows, foreign profits repatriation, and tax codes, in order to attract mining investments. In Burkina Faso, next door to Mali, mining went from being a negligible contributor to the economy in 1986 to providing 2.1 percent of GDP and 11.8 percent of export earnings within seven years. Mining development moved forward around the world, from Tanzania to Papua, New Guinea.

Some observers claim that mining and energy sector investments are detrimental to developing countries. Some say the earnings do the countries no good, since the money all flows to corrupt officials. Others say they cause nations to become sucked into the commodities trap mentioned earlier. Still others claim that they are environmentally destructive. None of these arguments stand up to honest evaluation.

The issue of money flowing to corrupt officials instead of being used wisely in the broader economy for the benefit of more people within a country has nothing to do with mining, energy industry activity, or business activity in general per se. It has to do with corruption in a country. There are numerous examples where relatively uncorrupt governments have allowed the economic benefits of real development to flow to those to whom the rewards ought to accrue. There are numerous examples of corrupt governments commandeering the profits. In the end, it is better to be moving the economy forward than it is to let economic deprivation continue to erode the quality of life for people. Work is certainly needed to reduce corruption, but that work has little to do with mining or developing commodities-based industries specifically.

There also is scant evidence that countries that seek to exploit their natural resources become entrapped in a commodities trap in which they are limited to industries with low value added. In fact, the opposite is evident in many countries. Remember, the United States and Canada, two of the richest countries in the world, began as natural resource–oriented countries and economies. They still are, even though they also have become homes to some of the most sophisticated, cutting-edge industries.

One of the keys to allowing the economic benefits of natural resource development to lead to more advanced manufacturing and service industries lies in assuring that the legal regulations of a given country do not restrict or limit the use of the profits of these industries. The early fur trappers who settled my hometown of St. Louis invested wisely in railroads and other industries in the early part of the nineteenth century, as they foresaw the decline of the fur trading business and were captivated by the potential of emerging technologies such as steam-powered riverboats and railroads. Oddly enough, some countries' governments still restrict how the profits from one industry can be used, reducing the efficient deployment of capital and stifling industrial innovation. For example, in some countries profits from a mining operation cannot be reinvested in other types of mines or other industries. In such case, a mining company that successfully develops a mine generating significant revenues cannot invest in, say, an electricity-generating facility, a road construction company, a bus company, or any other type of industry that may be sorely needed in that country.

The argument that allowing mining companies to develop modern mines is environmentally destructive is also not particularly well supported by reality. In many countries mining occurs on what is called an artisanal basis prior to the arrival of mining companies from overseas. I have seen small mining operations in Chile where the locals used mercury to collect gold from river deposits. They used their hands to swirl the mercury in the water, and then dumped the mercury-laden water into the river, poisoning not only themselves but also everyone who drinks the water downriver. In Brazil the *garimpieros* practiced mining with shovels and picks, devastating the landscape, dumping their waste rock and dirt into nearby rivers, killing the fish. There were a few horrific cave-ins of these artisanal mine works.

The arrival of mining companies bringing in modern techniques often leads to a reduction of these problems. The mining companies meanwhile sometimes have to clean up and deal with the legacy pollution from past small-scale operations. International mining companies tend to introduce state-of-the-art-technology and adopt international best practices for mining. In many cases this upsets local, domestic mining operators, who have successfully blocked government efforts to impose environmental mining codes by arguing that their countries could not afford to do so.

Most mining companies also undertake major development programs. They bring in clean water, electricity, and wastewater treatment facilities for the local community because they need these things for themselves and for their workers. They build hospitals, clinics, and schools, and then hire doctors and teachers. Again, their workers need them, but they bring these services to the neighboring community.

In many remote places where mining is undertaken, modern medicine is new, and no one, not even the government, has ever made a historical study of local health concerns. In some of the most corrosive examples of irony, the doctors brought in by a mining operation record a high prevalence of various birth defects in communities for the first time, only to have semi-informed observers try to use this documentation as evidence that the mining operation has caused these birth defects and ill health conditions. The high incidence of bad health may have extended back for generations. In some populations the occurrence of birth defects is taken for granted. These health problems may be related to high levels of minerals occurring in the local water supply due to natural leaching from the rocks. They may be caused by something else entirely different. Discussions with locals uncover the fact that such birth defects have occurred throughout generations. The arrival of the modern mining operation, with its attendant physicians, has not *caused* the health problems, but rather has brought them to the public's attention, and broadened the public to include people around the world. One of the most poignant examples of this was a series of articles accusing a U.S. mining company of causing health problems at a mine opened in Indonesia within the past decade. Some of the health problems were genetic conditions in people in their 60s and 70s, which obviously had occurred long before the miners had arrived.

I have known mining companies that built local textile weaving industries, to help preserve the local weaving styles and to provide an industry that the community can have in operation, ensuring jobs long after the mine is played out. The mining companies then get accused of destroying the local culture. The locals often are grateful for the health care, clean water, jobs, and chances for better lives, while outsiders fret over the loss of the culture in the area. As one wag said, "What could be more natural than dying of tetanus at the age of 18."

Much of this discussion has focused on mining, but similar arguments are made about development of other commodities, including tropical agricultural products such as cotton, coffee, and cocoa. These commodities often are not seen as environmentally destructive, although in some cases their farming can have negative consequences for the land, including increased rain run-off and soil erosion.

The major problem facing some of these markets has to do with the persistence of subsidies for farmers in the developed economies of the United States and Europe, with some subsidization problems in China. I am against subsidies, but the practice of governments supporting agricultural production against future droughts, floods, plagues, and other problems dates back to ancient Egypt at least. The vested interests make a lot of money off of the governments that provide the subsidies, and they fight hard to maintain their cash flow. This has led to situations such as exist in the cotton and sugar markets today, where the U.S. government provides a great deal of money to higher-cost producers in this country, encouraging overproduction, which drives the prices of these commodities lower on the international market. Lower prices hurt farmers in developing countries and raise the payments made through the subsidy programs. The vested interests argue that the subsidies do not lead to overproduction and lower prices, but their arguments do not stand up to scrutiny on either an empirical basis or a theoretical level, never mind the ethical or philosophical underpinnings of a system that takes money from taxpayers, distributes it to some of the wealthiest people in the world, and contributes to crushing poverty with all of its attendant woes around the world.

Old But Still Good

Commodities markets are the oldest forms of commerce. Primary commodities, from agricultural goods to basic metals, were the first goods bought and sold, and formed the basis of the earliest trade. Commodities continue to be important economically and represent the stepping-stone to economic development. They remain critical to all economic activity, even in highly developed, technologically dominated countries. The economic power of the United States, as an example, is based on many resources, including the capital built up in this country, the installed industrial capacity, and of course human resources. But U.S. output of basic commodities—especially agricultural goods but also basic metals, energy products, and other commodities—represents a surprisingly large amount of the country's basic economic output and strength. People still need to eat, to clothe themselves, to have places to live and work and vehicles to transport themselves. Basic commodities are unavoidable. Rather, they are critical to human life, and as more people seek to live more enjoyable lives the world will need larger volumes of most basic commodities.

Yet commodities have become marginalized in many economies. Some governments mistakenly neglect the development of basic natural resources and agricultural potential, fearing that these economic activities would consign them to subordinate positions in the world economy. They are wrong, as I hope my cursory discussion earlier in this chapter highlighted. The degree to which governmental leaders in many countries great and small do not understand the importance of basic commodities is indicative of the miscommunication and poor information flow about these markets.

Just two decades ago the majority of world currency flows represented trade flows—currencies changing hands based on the trade of goods and services. Today, trade flows are dwarfed by capital flows. The world tends to focus on capital flows and on the glamorous high-tech industries. The basic foodstuffs, steel, copper, base metals, precious metals, petroleum, and other commodities needed to sustain our new world economy are neglected.

This neglect has taken many forms, but to a large degree they all represent lack of investment. There has been a lack of investment in exploration for natural resources and development of productive capacity. There has been a lack of investment in the development of technology and innovation, so important to both the production and consumption of commodities. There has been a lack of investment in management: Many talented potential managers have not been interested in basic commodities industries over the past two or three decades, being attracted to other, newer industries instead.

This is beginning to change in the middle part of this decade, as the rise in commodities prices and investor interest in commodities has helped spotlight certain interesting aspects about working in these industries, and some really talented people are coming into what they see as new business areas offering them wide-open opportunities. Also, there have been some exceptional examples of highly intelligent and qualified managers within the commodities industry throughout history, including the past several decades. Overall, however, the commodities-productive industries have not been a final destination for many executive talents with imagination, wisdom, and ambition. Finally, there has been a tremendous lack of investment in information flows in, around, and out of these markets.

Information and Knowledge

Information is critical to commodity markets, as it is to all markets and commerce. Knowledge—understanding what to make of all that information—is even more critical. Both accurate information and substantive knowledge are in relatively short supply in the commodities markets.

Management scientists talk about organizational systems that *learn*, meaning corporations, industries, and markets that effectively develop and manage a set of collective information and knowledge. The commodities markets are learning very slowly and haltingly, and have not been very efficient in this regard in recent decades.

Even in the most advanced economies, there is a sharp divide between natural resource companies and other industrial concerns. Advanced management, finance, and organizational techniques that are considered standard operating procedures in most industries are viewed as exotic, radical, risky, and incomprehensible by commodity producers and processors.

One example is the degree to which basic commodity producers and handlers do not avail themselves of simple, elegant hedging techniques, which would protect them against adverse price developments. Their customers—the commodity consumers—do. Thus, coffee roasters in developed countries were able to protect themselves from higher prices when coffee prices doubled for a time in the late 1990s. Coffee growers meanwhile did not take the opportunity to lock in those high prices. Within a few years coffee prices had fallen to levels that were less than one-quarter of their peak three years earlier. Coffee growers are starving around the world. All of this was easily avoidable.

Lack of basic information is at the core of the financial devastation being experienced in the more than 90 countries that are heavily dependent on a handful of basic commodities at this time. It is not so much a lack of *access* to information, although this is important. The more critical factor is a lack of knowledge as to how to use the information that is available.

In 1998 Joseph Stiglitz was the chief economist at the World Bank. In 2001 he received a Nobel Prize in economics for his work on asymmetrical markets. Commodities markets may be the most virulent strain of asymmetrical markets available for study. In 1998, at a World Bank–organized meeting focusing on the potential to help commodities-dependent developing countries, Mr. Stiglitz commented that the commodities markets had failed to provide their services to developing country producers.

Risking everything (because I was young and naive), I pointed out that commodities markets are tools sitting in a toolbox. They are available to anyone, including developing country producers, to pick up, learn to use, and use. Markets are passive instruments, however. They will not jump out of the toolbox by themselves and go seek out users. It is up to the would-be users of markets to learn how to use them and to use them responsibly. (Like most tools, they can be used for good or bad.)

Indeed, the commodities markets are strewn with terribly expensive, destructive mistakes rooted in a lack of information, lack of knowledge, lack of understanding, and lack of analysis. The coffee market has been destroyed for many years to come by massive overinvestment in poor-quality plantations that have glutted the markets. Similar patterns occur repeatedly in other markets.

Many popular business publications were filled with chagrin when petroleum and natural gas prices rose sharply in 1999 and 2000. It should not have been a surprise. The information that growth rates for world oil demand had been outstripping supply for years was there all along. Some industry observers, analysts, and participants saw it coming and predicted it. Yet governments, energy consumers, and others ignored the information, and were distracted by other information.

Part of the problem was the poor quality of information circulating in the markets. We tend to be self-critical in the precious metals markets, citing the enormous amount of bad information, pure ignorance, and disinformation that circulates in the markets for gold, silver, and platinum. Yet in the middle of the 1990s the copper market was suffering from a major breakdown in information, when an analyst stopped to perform some simple mathematic computations of the basic supply, demand, and inventory data on which most copper market participants base their planning. It turned out that the numbers did not add up, and had not for many years. There was a large unexplained, unaccounted gap between supply and demand. The statistical reporting problem related to underreported demand and inventories, both common issues in commodity market statistics.

The petroleum market is the largest commodity market. Given the strategic importance of oil, it is also the most closely scrutinized market. Governments, producers, consumers, and others pore over petroleum market data and collect information intensely. Yet, as discussed in Chapter 1, when oil prices were falling to very low levels in 1999, the petroleum market was hit with all sorts of wild, unbelievable rumors of massive stocks of unsold oil stored around the world, in enormous tank farms that clearly did not exist and simply could not be hidden from public eyes. As preposterous and unsupportable by facts as these rumors were, they enjoyed a long life in the market and distracted the attention of many serious, supposedly informed and intelligent market participants. Clearly these tank farms and inventories did not, and could not, exist without being noticed. That did not stop the market from worrying about the supposedly massive buildup in unreported, hidden, inventories.

Similarly, the International Energy Agency in Paris, at roughly the same time, released information showing an enormous gap, on the order of 60 percent, in estimates of the amount of petroleum oversupply in the market. Even the largest, most closely studied and monitored commodity market was in fact cloaked in ignorance.

Nondiscrimination of Information Quality

Which information is important and which information is a distraction is a point overlooked in these industries and markets. The lack of ability to discern critical information versus unimportant information is a major problem.

In the late 1990s, for example, an industry group in Central America equipped the local coffee growers with satellite-fed portable information devices which supplied them with enormous volumes of information, including real-time prices in the London and New York terminal coffee markets. Most of these growers had no use for this information. They could watch prices fluctuate moment to moment half the world away, but they were in no position, physically, intellectually, financially, or otherwise, to use this information to protect themselves from the adverse effects of such price fluctuations on their livelihood. Many did not fully understand what, if anything, these price changes meant to them and their farming operations. Others had no concept of what they might do with the information, if they had the capacity to hedge their production and crops.

That may be an extreme example, but there is in fact a tremendous mismatch between the flow of information and the ability to use it. Mining companies spend an enormous amount of time worrying about their competitive cost structure, buying databases that allow them to compare, for example, how much they are paying for the replacement tires used on their huge earthmoving trucks at open-pit mines compared to what their competitors are spending. Meanwhile, they often pay no attention to the price of their products on the open market, ways to enhance that price through marketing, and ways to protect their company's profitability by taking advantage of financial management techniques available to them. Until recently, at least, it was not uncommon to hear gold mining executives dismiss such criticisms of their management style by saying, with all sincerity, that their companies did not have to worry about marketing their product, since the bullion banks to which they sold their gold were responsible for marketing the gold. In fact, the bullion banks were not responsible for marketing gold, only for buying it from producers and others, trading it for their own accounts, and selling it.

In summary, there is a lack of basic information and a tremendous amount of bad information in all commodities markets. Furthermore, there is a fundamental absence of knowledge about information within these markets—what information is, how to distinguish good from bad information, and how to use it. There is an appalling lack of analysis of basic information.

These conditions exist in large part because basic commodities industries and markets have been victims of neglect and underinvestment for decades. This is partly because many of these commodities did not offer competitive returns for investors. It also reflects misguided government policies and academic theories that significantly underestimate the importance of basic commodities even in advanced industrial economies. These problems have existed for decades, and the effects of decades of underinvestment and neglect have led to a point now where there is a compounding deterioration of the quality of markets. Conditions are growing worse, and the ability to reverse these deteriorating conditions rapidly is becoming harder to envision. Bad information, and bad use of misinformation, leads to ever more important investment mistakes, compounding past problems and making solutions more difficult and less likely. The fact that most governments, international governmental agencies, nongovernmental organizations, and corporations ignore commodities means that the collective will, wisdom, and investment necessary to implement effective reform is not present in these industries.

Efforts to Improve Conditions

That said, there are efforts under way. Some of the efforts seem well directed and may lead to real improvements in the use of information and knowledge in commodities markets worldwide. Some of the efforts appear to be poorly conceived and destined to distract scarce resources from real reform.

One set of projects of interest is represented by the collective efforts of the World Bank, the United Nations Conference on Trade and Development (UNCTAD), the European Union, the Common Fund for Commodities, and other international organizations to try to develop a bridge between developing countries' commodities producers and processors, on the one hand, and international commodity finance markets on the other. The European Union started the program in 1997 by seeking an effective replacement for the Stabex program and other commodity price support programs that were extremely costly and almost totally ineffectual. At the EU's heeding, the World Bank convened a meeting in Washington in April 1998 to explore effective commodity price risk management programs and to debate what might be done to improve these markets. This led to the creation of the International Task Force (ITF) on Commodity Risk Management, managed by the World Bank and joined by numerous other intergovernmental organizations.

The first World Bank official to head up the task force repeatedly tried to push for the creation of a new, massive "Global Commodities Corporation," which would have been funded to the tune of billions of dollars under the aegis of the World Bank to provide subsidies for developing country commodities producers and processors. Quickly (by intergovernmental association standards) it was realized that the creation of another massive bureaucracy costing billions of dollars per year was out of step with reality in any number of ways. Starting in January 2001, new management brought new directions, and the ITF program began moving forward. quickly. It has gone through numerous changes since 2001, however, and has moved much more slowly than its initial supporters had hoped. It has assisted in executing a few price risk management programs, but it has been neither as involved in the programs nor as forthcoming to the public about the nature of these hedging programs as had been anticipated.

The effort is to build an information and knowledge bridge between commodity producers and international markets. The hedging instruments that could be useful to commodity producers are passive tools, waiting to be used. Educational services, training, and information dissemination are needed to assist them in learning how to use these tools effectively. An honest broker and educational facilitator could help commodity producers learn to use what instruments are available.

But it is not that simple. Commodity finance providers—banks, dealers, and brokers—in the major commodities markets of London, New York, Tokyo, and elsewhere need to learn a lot, too. Most are unable to provide effective commodity hedging services to small producers. These companies' commodities trading operations have been decimated by the poor market conditions that persisted in many of these markets for much of the past twenty or thirty years. Many banks and brokers have closed or cut back severely on their commodities trading and finance operations. Meanwhile, traders at banks and dealers often do not fully understand what producers need in terms of hedging programs, or they are blocked from offering truly effective hedging programs by internal policies and positions at their banks. The result is that they offer inappropriate hedging strategies, which wind up costing the producers money and do not provide effective price protection. These results convince the producers that hedging is not sensible for them, perpetuating the cycle in which effective price risk management programs are not implemented.

If dealers were to offer more appropriately structured programs and services, they could help their customers thrive. This, in turn, would mean that the customers survive to trade with them in the future, that the customers would conduct more business with the banks as their financial stability and sophistication increase, and that the customers would have better credit ratings and credit facilities, which would make it easier for the commodities traders to justify trading with them in the future.

This ITF is one good example of a long-term project that may lead to some improvements, although the progress has been painfully slow until now. There are many other projects under way. As I said, some are good, and some are probably distractions. There are efforts to build warehousing facilities in producing countries. There are other efforts—misplaced—to create commodities futures trading exchanges in these countries. Such developments would not help but would hinder effective markets by fragmenting already illiquid markets.

Much more needs to be done to develop and disseminate better information, market intelligence, statistics, and analysis throughout these markets, and to provide the knowledge tools necessary to understand and use these information sources. As I said earlier, the commodities markets are prime examples of systems that do not learn, or at least do not learn efficiently. As such, they are prime candidates for investment by someone versed in informational and knowledge systems.

4

Commodities as an Asset Class

Investors have been pouring into commodities for three basic reasons, as discussed in Chapter 1. One is that returns on other investments have not been particularly attractive, and investors are searching the world over for better returns. The second is that the prices of some commodities have been rising, and investors follow rising markets. The third, which is the subject of this chapter, is that commodities have newfound respectability among investors. Commodities have become an *asset class*, in the words of the marketing departments on Wall Street.

In fact, of course, commodities have been a legitimate and valuable investment sector forever. It is just that some, perhaps most, investors have traditionally avoided them. One thing that has recently changed is that many institutional fund managers have moved into commodities, in many cases for the first time ever. Another new development has been the release of some academic and market research quantitatively discussing the validity and usefulness of commodities as investment vehicles.

Commodities traditionally have been seen as something less than full-fledged investment-grade assets by many mainstream financial market types. That is one reason why larger investment banks, brokerage houses, and others call them, even today, *alternative* assets. There are many reasons that commodities have been segregated from traditional investments, relegated to second-class status. Most of them have valid bases, but some of them reflect discrimination toward commodities by brokerage companies.

To some extent this is changing. Commodities still are seen as alternative assets, but alternative assets are becoming more acceptable in polite financial circles. The trend began to emerge in the late 1970s, when government regulators decided that gold and silver, and indeed commodities in general, could be deemed a portion of a well-constructed, diversified investment portfolio. At that time, the emphasis was on commodities as a portfolio diversifier. Little attempt was made to consider commodities' ability to stand on their own as investments.

Commodities have at least two very important roles to play in investment portfolios. First, they can generate profits in and of themselves, through capital appreciation. Studies have shown what ample empirical evidence has well illustrated, that great wealth can be generated by investing in commodities.

Second, commodities perform very well as part of a diversified portfolio of investments. Commodities generally have a very low statistical correlation to other investment assets such as stocks and bonds. This does not mean that they move in the opposite direction from stocks and bonds. It means that over time they move randomly relative to these other assets. Sometimes they all rise together, sometimes they all fall together, and sometimes they move in opposite directions. This is what you want in a portfolio diversifier. You do not want something that moves only in the opposite direction: That yields a zero-sum gain, since one asset is always losing as the other is gaining. You want assets that move randomly and independently of each other. Commodities, generally speaking, do that relative to stocks and bonds. As a result, commodities make great bedfellows for stocks and bonds in a diversified portfolio. The result of adding commodities to a portfolio generally is that it smoothes out the volatility of the overall portfolio return—the risk of the portfolio—while having little effect on the overall return of the portfolio over time.

Intermarket Disconnection

Focusing initially on the second role of commodities for investors—its place in a diversified portfolio—this lack of a price relationship on a quantifiable basis is critical to understanding the value of commodities to some investors. Changes in the monthly value of the CRB commodities index has had a 0.15 percent correlation to world stocks since 1970, and 0.05 percent with U.S. stocks as measured by the S&P 500 index. Gold has had a −0.45 percent correlation over this time, and a 0.19 percent correlation to the S&P 500. Copper had a −0.10 percent correlation to world stocks but a 0.05 percent correlation to the S&P 500, while oil prices had a −0.01 percent correlation to both world and U.S. stocks. That does not mean that there are not times when gold or commodities prices are moving opposite stocks or in line with them. It means that over the course of three decades the long-run statistical relationship has been virtually nonexistent, and that investors ought not to believe they can effectively trade an arbitrage between any of these commodities and world stocks on a purely mechanical or quantitative basis.

Similar relationships exist among various commodities and bonds, currencies, and other assets. The statistical relationship between the CRB index and Treasury bonds since 1970 has been around 15.2 percent. For gold it has been a much higher 42.3 percent (gold is money), while for copper it was 0.03 percent and oil 2.2 percent.

I have to stress that these low statistical correlations do not mean that stock market levels or interest rate levels have no effect on commodities. There is a particularly strong and fundamental relationship between interest rate levels and trends and conditions in basic commodities markets. However, the relationship is complex and is clouded by other variables, such as currency market exchange rates. As a result, there is no clear-cut, easy to use statistical relationship stating that when interest rates rise you should sell commodities, or vice versa.

There are discernable patterns but they are not regularly repeated. For example, an increase in U.S. interest rates often has an initial positive effect on gold prices and becomes negative for gold only later. This is because an increase in interest rates also tends to have a negative effect on stocks. Given the large volumes of equities now traded based on valuation models that use U.S. interest rates as the risk-free rate of return, when interest rates rise there tends to be selling in the U.S. equity market, as share prices need to decline in order to preserve projected returns on shares' comparative relationship with interest rates. The selling in equities tends to be reflected positively by gold, meanwhile, so one sometimes sees an upward bounce in gold prices when interest rates rise. This does not mean that higher interest rates make gold somewhat less attractive to interest-bearing assets, or that they raise both the direct and opportunity costs of investing in gold. It simply means that in a highly interconnected financial market, the first instinctive reaction of many investors to an increase in interest rates is to sell shares, and some buy gold as they do.

There is another entirely different set of market relationships that need to be discussed, namely that commodities tend not to move in lockstep with each other. This runs contrary to a lot of commonly accepted wisdom, but it is true and quantitatively verifiable. There are a lot of investors and traders who trade commodities based on ratios, such as the gold–oil ratio or the gold–silver ratio. Over time these ratios move all over the place, and trying to trade one against the other based on some ratio that one believes is the true relationship between two commodities is a formula for disaster.

Some investors feel the copper and gold markets are similar, yet a $1 increase in the price of gold historically has coincided with a 0.09-cent increase in copper prices. Others expect a high correlation between copper and oil, as two of the largest commodity markets and two important industrial materials. In reality, their historical statistical relationship has been rather weak. A $1 increase in oil prices has on average coincided with a slight 1.6-cent decline in copper prices.

I touch on these ratios more in Chapter 6. Suffice it to say here that these relationships do not hold up to statistical scrutiny. The gold–silver ratio has ranged from 16:1 to 100:1 over the past 35 years, since gold prices were freed. The gold–oil ratio has ranged from 8:1 to 38:1 over the same period. One can use these ratios and say that the relationship between two commodities' prices has changed from what it used to be. Whether that reflects a fundamental change or not has to be explored through detailed analysis. Whether the change that caused the price ratio to shift is temporary, cyclical, secular, or permanent similarly involves detailed research. Concluding that a ratio is carved in stone and that the intermarket price relationship must revert to the mean or average of what it was in the past is a recipe for financial losses.

In late 1980 the price of platinum dropped below the price of gold. Platinum had traded at a premium to gold for most of the previous decades. (Gold prices did move to a premium to platinum in late 1974 and hold it until late 1975.) In December 1980, however, investment demand for gold was high. The world was beset with high inflation, higher interest rates, moribund stock markets, treacherous political crises, American hostages in Iran, Soviet troops in Afghanistan, and much more. Iranian and Soviet assets had been frozen in the United States, Europe, and Japan. In this environment, a lot of investors still wanted to buy a lot of gold, even though the price had risen to record levels in the first quarter of the year. Platinum meanwhile was on its back and headed lower. Platinum prices also had spiked to record levels, in April 1980, but had come down sharply. The major uses of platinum at that time were in Japanese jewelry and auto catalysts. The auto industry was plunging into its worst postwar recession, while few people could afford platinum jewelry in Japan at the time.

In this environment, I felt that platinum prices might move to a discount to gold for a sustained period of time, and maybe even drop to a deep discount to gold. The chief metals dealer to whom I reported at the time saw platinum dip below gold and was prepared to buy platinum and sell gold, as an arbitrage trade, convinced that platinum would revert to its historical premium to gold. I suggested that given the weak platinum fundamentals and strong gold fundamentals we do the reverse trade. Tradition aside, I said, there were real-world reasons for gold's price to remain strong for a while even as platinum prices might weaken. In the end, platinum moved to a discount of around $130 to gold, by early 1982, and did not recover to a premium until 1983.

Conversely, in early 1997 platinum prices began rising while gold prices actually were weakening. The Russian government had moved to revise the way it sold and exported platinum, along with palladium, rhodium, diamonds, and other items, in December 1996, and had halted sales while it considered how to restructure its program. This caused a shortfall in platinum group metals supplies in the international market. Gold meanwhile was not particularly attractive to investors, with large increases in mine production, heavy central bank sales, and extremely attractive alternative investments available in stocks and bonds. By April of that year platinum's premium to gold had risen to around $30 to $35. Traders were advising their futures-oriented clients that platinum was overvalued relative to gold, at a spread greater than $30. Our view was that platinum prices could break out of a trading range that had held since 1990, while gold actually could fall. We advised clients to buy platinum and sell gold. Platinum moved to a $100 premium later that year, a $350 premium in 2000, and a $500 premium in 2005.

Ratio trades can be lucrative, but the concept of fixed relationships among commodities that forms the basis of some investors' approaches to such trades is ill-conceived and inappropriate. The best ratio trades I have seen have been those, such as the two I just discussed, that were based on the theory that such concepts of fixed price ratios among commodities are not accurate and should be ignored.

Commodities' Role in Portfolios

The lack of correlation with other assets makes commodities excellent for portfolio diversification purposes. Some of the larger institutional investors that have been moving into commodities over the first half of this decade are in fact interested in commodities primarily for their effect in reducing overall volatility, or risk, across their portfolio, and not for any capital gains potentially available from investments in commodities.

One large pension fund, as an example, found that it was doing very well in private equity investments in the early 2000s. As a pension fund, however, it needs to match its projected returns, and the risk/reward profile of its projected returns, to its long-term anticipated payouts of pensions. Private equity can be volatile, so the fund's position in private equity reached a level where the risk managers said further private equity investments ought not be made. The quantitative analysts at the fund noted that if the fund added commodities investments to its portfolio it would reduce the volatility of returns on the total portfolio, which would then allow the fund to increase its private equity holdings. As a result, the fund embarked on a program to place a few percent of its assets into commodities-oriented investments. The ensuing reduction in volatility allowed it to increase its allocation to private equity.

There is a body of evidence showing the effects of adding commodities, either individually or in baskets, to portfolios. Besides the results and returns of existing, real-life portfolios that do and do not include commodities, there is also an extensive body of portfolio modeling by many economic research groups, university professors, portfolio managers, and investment bank marketing departments that illustrates how commodities benefit overall portfolio performance.

CPM Group has run innumerable such model portfolios itself. We have run models of portfolios using various time periods extending back to 1968, 1984, or 1991. We have run portfolios that have added gold, silver, platinum, the CRB basket of commodities, and various combinations of the precious metals. The possible portfolios that can be run are innumerable.

Typically, the average returns and average risks are calculated for these portfolios, to compare them to a baseline portfolio. The baseline portfolio can vary, but typically it is 60 percent stocks, using something like the S&P 500 or the Financial Times World Stock index as a surrogate for equities, and 40 percent Treasury notes or bonds. Economists, strategists, and others can debate forever as to what ought to constitute a baseline portfolio. I try to avoid such discussions. Most models add 5 percent or so in commodities to the portfolio. Some investment banks use 10 percent or higher figures; typically they are selling commodities investment products.

In order to be fair, the returns are calculated on a 12-month moving average basis. Otherwise, one could pick a good or bad starting time, a high or low for a given asset, in order to skew the results and make the point that the asset is good or bad. For example, if you wanted to show that gold was bad for a portfolio, you could measure the results with early 1980, when gold was at its record peak, as your starting point. Gold would show terrible returns. If you wanted to promote the view that gold made sense for a portfolio, you could start at the middle of 1982, March 1985, or March 1993, all of which were cyclical lows. But if you wanted to be fair, honest, and accurate, you would use a series of returns on a moving average, which is what we do.

The risk is defined as the standard deviation of the returns over any given 12-month period. Some models only measure capital appreciation. In the past several years some economists and investment banks have added in the forward carry inherent in various commodities, arguing that sophisticated investors would use forward futures contracts to enhance their yields.

Generally speaking, most portfolio modeling exercises show that adding some commodities exposure to a portfolio of stocks and bonds helps reduce the variability of returns in the portfolio—that is, reduce the risks. Typically the overall returns are roughly the same as they were without the commodities; sometimes they are slightly higher and sometimes slightly lower. The bottom line is that adding various types of commodities investments into a diversified portfolio generally helps the overall performance by smoothing out returns over time without foregoing yield.

There are many weaknesses to relying on such model portfolios in assessing the relative values of assets. For one thing, the weightings used are purely arbitrary. Studies have shown that shifting the mix of assets just 1 percent can have dramatic effects on returns. Second, it is extremely prejudicial to compare the returns and risks of an index of 500 stocks to those of individual commodities. Individual assets, be they stocks, commodities, or corporate bonds, have much greater volatility, and consequently much different reward/risk profiles, than do indexes. Considering the addition of a single commodity to a portfolio of a stock index does not portray the commodity in a fair light.

Third, most modeled portfolios have fixed weightings throughout their lives, which is equally unrealistic. It would be highly unlikely that one would hold a fixed basket of assets for that long without shifting among the assets based on developments in the various asset markets and perceptions of likely future trends in these markets. The essence of investment management is to use analysis and intelligence to select assets and modify portfolios accordingly, shifting the mix as economic and financial conditions dictate. The selection of individual stocks, commodities, and bonds and the changing weightings of each individual asset over time are critical—and all of this is lost in such a mechanical model. The expertise of the fund manager—the manager's timing, selection process, and asset portfolio mix—is critical in determining the ultimate return and return/risk ratio of any portfolio.

Commodities on Their Own

The ability to perform well as part of a diversified portfolio and to assist the overall performance of that portfolio is only one of the two key services commodities provide investors. The other is the ability to general profits by themselves.

Commodities were seen as bad investment choices for many years, and many of them were. For long stretches of the 1980s and 1990s many commodities did not make sense as investments, unless you were either very facile at short-term trading or willing to go short the commodities. One of my favorite clients came to me in 1991. He had been watching the gold price fall for three years and had decided to turn bullish. A friend of his, who was also my client, suggested that he call me first. He retained CPM Group as advisers. We laid out the five reasons we were still bearish on gold, and outlined a list of four or five developments that we said were required before we would turn bullish. He took our advice, went short gold, and made a lot of money over the next two years.

In August 1992, after the Republican presidential convention, we issued a report to clients saying that many of the bearish factors that had caused us to be negative toward gold had passed, and most of the positive ones we were waiting for in order to turn bullish were starting to emerge. Specifically, we saw large increases in investor buying of gold coins and small bars in the United States, Europe, and the Middle East. There were storm clouds gathering above the European currency complex, and the

European economy in general looked bad. The newly independent nations of the former Soviet Union were not doing well, with real economic activity contracting sharply. These and several other factors made us think that gold prices could rise. We had heard of large central bank gold sales in the forward market for delivery in early 1993, so we stated that we thought gold prices would remain low into March 1993, but that if the other factors remained positive for gold at that time we thought prices could pop sharply higher. The client that had done well by shorting the market based on our earlier analysis went long, and did very well over the ensuing two years in commodities. He was a rare investor, however, willing to go short a commodity and hold the position.

We had other clients who did well in commodities during the 1980s and 1990s by trading ranges back and forth. One client, we used to joke, made the same $20 in gold, buying at $340, selling it back and going short at $360, and reversing his positions once again at $340. He kept us around to tell him when the fundamentals or the macroeconomic environment was changing in ways that would lead to a breakout in either direction.

Apart from such rare instances, however, commodities were not good assets for the typical buy-and-hold investor for much of the 1980s and 1990s. This started to change in the early 2000s.

If one compares the returns and the risk/reward ratios of various commodities to other assets during these years, it is hard to make a case for many commodities. Platinum did pretty well but gold faired terribly, especially over the course of the 1990s. Again, one of the problems with traditional comparative return studies is that they tend to compare individual commodities to baskets of 500 stocks. That is not fair—nevertheless, we do it along with most others. That said, if you did compare gold, silver, oil, copper, or other commodities to individual equities, depending on which commodities you picked and which stocks you picked, the commodities would have a fairly good chance of comparing favorably to the individual equities.

The real key comes when you take a long-term view. Comparisons of the returns and risks of various commodities and commodities indexes to stocks, bonds, bills, and stock market indexes over the long run show that commodities stand up very well in comparison. This should not be a surprise. Stocks generally speaking did extremely poorly in the 1970s but soared in the 1980s and 1990s. They have not done so well since 1999, again. Commodities did well in the 1970s, partly because of the inflationary pressures of the times, partly because stocks did so poorly, and partly because the prices of many important commodities, from gold and silver to oil and gas, were heavily regulated, controlled, fixed, or managed by governments. These practices ended with the 1960s, and the 1970s saw a lot of commodities prices playing catch-up with a few decades worth of inflation. As a result of these trends, if you compare commodities to equities in the 1980s and 1990s, commodities have some tough work to look good. If you include the 1970s and the current decade so far, commodities start looking a lot more attractive compared to stocks.

For example, the Dow Jones Industrial Average had an 8.15 percent average 12-month return from 1968 through June 2005. Its average risk—the standard deviation of this return—was 8.90 percent. The S&P 500 was roughly the same, with an 8.33 percent average 12-month return and a 9.07 percent average risk during that period. These compared to a 10.10 percent return and a 10.91 percent average risk for gold during this time, and a 9.42 percent return and 18.47 percent risk for silver (you have to love volatility to invest in silver). The CRB index had a 3.88 percent return and 6.10 percent average risk during this period. The trade-weighted dollar had a −0.76 percent return and a 3.47 percent risk.

Over the long run, then, commodities can make sense as stand-alone investments. One has to be careful to invest wisely, but commodities clearly can compete head-to-head with stocks and other more traditional investment assets.

I have mentioned several reasons why commodities did not fair well in the 1980s and 1990s. One was that many investors had found better fishing in other waters during those years and had acted accordingly. As investors did well in the broader stock market, technology stocks, consumer industries, and a range of other asset classes, they neglected commodities and natural resource equities. This reduction in investment demand contributed to the price weakness, which in turn accentuated investor disinterest in commodities, further fueling the decline. It was a self-feeding cycle well known to all financial market participants.

Even as this was occurring, there was emerging a strain of investment philosophy that was leading a number of investors, including some very wealthy and prominent individual and institutional investors, to begin building positions in gold, silver, aluminum, petroleum, timber, and a host of other commodities and commodity-producing industries. We first started to see this trend of thinking emerge in the middle of the 1990s. In many cases these entrants have been extremely quiet, although a few have come to the public's attention through either required regulatory registrations, the annual reporting process, or other public pronouncements.

My company has seen this process firsthand with a steady expansion of the institutional and high-net-worth individual clients we advise. Throughout the 1990s, the amount of services we provided to precious metals specialty funds declined, as many of these funds were contracting. Their managers were focused on net withdrawals of investment funds and net sales of assets during this time and were not interested in the fresh investment ideas and strategies we provide. While this was happening in that sector of the institutional investor market, the number of clients and the amount of research, consulting, and advisory services we were offering fund managers and investors in other sectors rose sharply. This is not self-promotion, but rather is mentioned to emphasize the degree to which managers of diversified portfolios, both public and private, have been moving into natural resource assets—from commodities and structured notes to mining company stocks—in recent years.

Many of the investors moving into natural resources are attracted to these assets based on fundamentals of the industries. They tend to look into the long-term supply and demand conditions, and consider these to be industries that were experiencing cyclical lows but now are recovering. There is a strain of thought in the investment community that natural resource companies are a good complement to high-tech stocks, leading some wealthy technology entrepreneurs to become large investors in timber, energy, mining, and agricultural companies.

5

Commodity Investment Vehicles

Having decided to invest in commodities-oriented assets, the investor must then determine how he wishes to buy this exposure. There are many approaches providing various degrees of exposure and leverage, both directly investing in commodities and indirectly buying exposure to commodities prices through the stocks of commodities-producing companies, special investment vehicles, and commodities-oriented investment funds. One can purchase physical commodities, futures contracts traded on organized exchanges, and forward contracts that look like futures but are not traded on exchanges. There are also options, both simple puts and calls, and compound options strategies. There are the equities and equity options of commodities-producing, processing, and consuming companies. There are natural resource and precious metals mutual funds, hedge funds, and other funds. There are commodities funds and commodities pools. And then there is a growing pool of commodities-linked investment vehicles such as indexed accounts, indexed notes and bonds, structured investment products, and exchange traded funds.

Each of these investment vehicles has advantages and disadvantages compared to others. Some offer more leverage, some offer more protection against adverse price moves. Different investors are attracted to various investment instruments based on who they are and what they want. Some prefer futures because of the enormous leverage that futures provide them. You often only have to deposit around 15 percent of the value of the gold you are buying as a futures contract. If prices move in your favor, this is a much more powerful strategy than if you have bought physical gold. Other investors do not like the open-ended risk of financial losses that comes with futures, so they prefer buying options, the risk of which is limited to the premium you paid up front, which is a sunk cost. Others prefer gold mining shares. Still others want bullion, for any number of reasons, including a desire for secrecy, security, and protection against the idea that a given brokerage company could default or go bankrupt while holding one's futures contracts.

For example, most gold equity investors like the fact that gold shares have betas, or relationships to gold bullion prices, closer to 3.0, meaning that they are much more volatile than the underlying physical gold price. Gold shares are expected to rise more rapidly than gold prices, when gold prices are rising. (They fall faster, too, a point that some of these investors repeatedly tend to overlook in their pursuit of the greater leverage to gold price increases that gold shares give them.)

Many traditional gold-shares investors have found the new gold exchange traded funds (ETFs) that have been rolled out since 2003 attractive, but others find them unattractive because they are seeking the leverage offered by gold shares. The gold ETFs are designed specifically not to offer this leverage to investors, but to track gold prices as closely as possible. Market analysts say that the ETFs are designed to have a beta to gold prices as close to 1.0 as possible, meaning that a given percentage rise or fall in gold prices should be reflected in a similar change in the price or value of the gold ETF. These gold ETFs were actually designed to be attractive to fund managers who formerly did not invest in gold or gold equities directly because doing so seemed cumbersome to them or otherwise did not fit neatly into their operating systems.

In Chapter 6 I discuss various strategies built using these instruments. One of the most popular approaches we have found among investors in recent years has been to develop positions that have guaranteed principal or principal protection over a three- to five-year time horizon. These strategies allow investors to buy exposure to rising and/or falling commodities prices while protecting all or part of their initial investment. Originally created as structured bonds or notes indexed to various commodities, this same strategy now is mimicked in managed accounts. For now, let us examine the more conventional instruments that are available for investors wishing to build exposure to commodities.

Physicals

The purest and most straightforward approach is, of course, to purchase the commodity outright. This often is done with gold, silver, and platinum, the precious metals that also serve as financial assets. It is relatively easy to store precious metals, as they have a high value relative to their volume. They are also relatively more available in physical form for investors than are other commodities. For other commodities, buying the physical commodity outright is much more difficult and cumbersome and is far less regularly undertaken, though there are some exceptions. My company sometimes arranges for large hedge funds, other institutional investors, and wealthy individuals to purchase physical metals in some of the more esoteric markets, for metals like rhodium, iridium, ruthenium, bismuth, and cobalt. More often than not, however, we will advise investors not to invest in such markets. Buying these metals may be relatively difficult but doable, but selling them at some future time, when the market has either risen in your favor or fallen at your expense, could prove much more difficult and sometimes simply impossible. It takes a special breed of investors to be willing and able to understand and take on the sorts of risks inherent in such investment vehicles.

One also has to be physically careful. In the early 1980s there was a wave of investor interest in strategic metals. This was at a time when the Reagan administration had stirred up Cold War fears to their highest level. One book advised investors to buy osmium, the sixth platinum group metal. It has a few uses, as a catalyst in making some medicines and steroids, for example. But the author of the strategic metals investment book failed to warn people that at room temperatures osmium gives off a toxic tetraoxide gas.

Millions of investors around the world own some of the major precious metals, especially gold and silver, either in coin form, as medallions, or in larger bars. Some of this metal is stored in personal safes and safety deposit boxes, or in larger bank or security firm vaults.

In India, Pakistan, Bangladesh, China, and other parts of Asia the metal often is stored at home, sometimes hidden in the framing of a house or literally buried in the backyard. When a major earthquake hit one part of

India in early 2002, leveling a large section of a city and forcing officials to bulldoze over entire neighborhoods without either attempting to recover bodies of the dead or allowing former residents to retrieve personal belongings, the government had to recompense people for their life savings in gold and silver that had been hidden in their houses and yards.

In India and much of the Middle East, other people invest in gold and silver in the form of jewelry. Some sects of Islam and the Hindu religion proscribe women owning anything but what they can wear, and further state that a man's possessions revert to his parents rather than to his wife in the event of his death. People who subscribe to these beliefs will purchase gold and silver jewelry as a form of savings and insurance for the women of their households.

That is a bit afield for most investors in the United States. Here and in many other countries, investors will purchase gold, silver, and sometimes platinum in physical form. Most of it is held in bank safety deposit boxes, at home, or in bank or brokerage accounts. The banks and brokers in turn have contracts with vaulting companies, such as Delaware Depository Service, Brinks, or major banks such as HSBC, Scotiabank, or JP Morgan that operate bank vaults.

At the end of November 2005 there were 117.6 million ounces of silver suitable for delivery against the New York Comex silver contract which were being stored in the four depositories that are registered for use with the Comex: Brinks' vault in Brooklyn, New York; Delaware Depository's Wilmington, Delaware, facility; and two bank vaults in New York managed by Scotia Mocatta and HSBC Bank USA. Of this total, 52.1 million ounces were not registered against Comex positions. Most of this amount of silver is believed to have been being held by investors interested in owning physical silver. These stores are reported to the Comex, since they meet the exchange's grade, size, quality, brand, and other specifications and can be delivered to the Comex Clearinghouse against futures contracts. Other unreported amounts of silver are held in these same vaults in the form of 100-ounce bars, silver bullion coins, and other forms that are not deliverable against Comex contracts. Almost all of that silver, along with several million ounces of silver held in bank vaults in London and outside Zurich, is held by individual investors.

There are additional stocks of silver held in bullion and bullion coin form around the world. We estimated that there was probably around 400 to 500 million ounces of silver in bullion form held by investors as of the end of 2005, including the metal previously described. Another 500 million ounces were held in bullion coin form. Finally, perhaps three or four billion ounces of silver are held in quasi-investment holdings in the forms of jewelry and sterling silver decorative objects. Much of this latter treasure is held in India, Pakistan, Bangladesh, and the Middle East.

Similarly, there are large volumes of gold and smaller amounts of platinum and palladium held in physical form by investors. In the 1970s several wealthy individual investors bought sizable positions in palladium, convinced that the price would rise. Most of this metal was stored for these investors in Zurich. There are bonded warehouses outside of Zurich, at the Kloten airport, run by both banks and securities firms. These warehouses hold money, precious metals, works of art, exotic automobiles, and other valuables. For more than two decades there were a couple million ounces of palladium stored in these vaults, on the accounts of investors who had bought the metal when its price was below $80 for most of the time. Much of this metal was sold by these investors during the late 1990s, when palladium prices marched to higher levels.

Palladium is not an uncommon metal, but investors still need to be careful about expecting to be able to sell this metal when the time comes. In the late 1980s there was a wave of investor interest in palladium, when news reports told of two scientists having discovered cold fusion, or unlocking energy from water at room temperatures, using palladium electrodes. We universally advised investors not to buy palladium at that time because the quotes would be disadvantageous when the time came to sell. This was even more the case for options. At that time there was only one major bullion bank that would even quote palladium options. Some of our larger investors wanted to buy some, but we advised against it. Our reasoning, based on experience, was that if the market moved in the investors' favor, at the expense of the bullion bank, the quotes to sell back those options would not reflect the change in the value of the underlying palladium.

Another anecdote perhaps better reflects the illiquidity of the markets for palladium and less common metals. In the late 1980s my company helped prepare some market documents for Manfra, Tordella, and Brooks (MTB), one of the major U.S. coin dealers of the time, which was launching a Platinum Ballerina medallion. The platinum medallion—like a coin, but not legal tender issued by any country—was a big success, and MTB began to consider a Palladium Ballerina. We were hired to help with the market documents for this coin, too. I purchased a prototype Palladium Ballerina, since it was pretty unusual. The price of palladium was around $140 at the time. The medallion went into my safe.

Around 12 years later the price of palladium shot to record levels. It got to $1,080 at one point in early 2001. When it was around $860 in late 2000, I decided the price was high enough. Christmas was coming, and the profits would come in handy. I called MTB and told the salesperson I had a palladium medallion that MTB had made, and that I wanted to sell it. He corrected me, graciously telling me that there was no such metal as palladium, and I must have a platinum medallion. I corrected him, but he refused to believe me. I asked to speak to one of the executives, who knew me and had worked on the project in the 1980s. He said that of course they would buy the medallion back, but he cautioned me that, due to the sharp rise in price, tight supplies, and volatile market, they could only pay me around $800, about $60 below the spot market price. I said that was all right, since I knew that the market had a negative carry at the time and that the spot price was higher than the forward price. (The market calls this a backwardation, in one of the more colorful terms used in commodities.) He pointed out that a lot of investors get upset when they hear the size of discounts they will receive in some metals when prices rise sharply, a fact I knew to be a long-standing problem for retail precious metals sales companies.

MTB's office is just a block down Broad Street from mine, in New York's financial district. When I finished the phone call I walked down the street to sell the coin and found about eight people waiting to see what a palladium medallion looked like. If that is the level of illiquidity I find in the Wall Street area, with a one-ounce palladium medallion, you can imagine how much more difficult it can be to try to sell larger positions of this and even rarer metals away from Wall Street.

Let's return to those four vaults that are registered as silver depositories usable to deliver silver against Comex silver futures. Investors hold large volumes of gold, silver, platinum, and other metals in these vaults, as well as in vaults in and around London, New York, Hong Kong, Toronto, and other major financial market cities. The metal that gets reported as being registered against Nymex and Comex positions, or eligible to be registered, only represents that portion of the metal that meets the exchanges' specifications, such as 1,000-ounce silver bars or 100-ounce gold bars. Other metal is held in coin form, in small bars, or in bars and powder form, which do not meet the exchanges' delivery specifications. Perhaps one of the most notable such holdings was the 129.7 million ounces of silver bought by Berkshire Hathaway in 1997 and 1998. Berkshire Hathaway, run by Warren Buffett, chose to take delivery of this silver in physical form and hold it in allocated accounts, away from the major bullion banks. Initially it stored the metal at a major metals fabricating company's facility in the United Kingdom. The metal was relatively visible at the plant, as 129.7 million ounces of silver takes up a fair bit of space. Berkshire Hathaway does not discuss the disposition of its metal holdings, but it appears to have moved the metal to a private warehouse a few years ago.

Other investors, especially some hedge funds, have purchased other precious metals on a physical basis over the years. My company sometimes buys, holds, manages, and sells metals for investors, as well as for producers, refiners, and industrial users that do not want to be seen in the market. In the middle of the 1980s I was party to the sale of the Hunt brothers' silver, when I was at the J. Aron division of Goldman Sachs. Much of it went to a single investor. This investor was interested in precious metals and later purchased some platinum and palladium. It then came to us with the idea that it might buy some ruthenium and iridium, minor platinum group metals that a bullion banker had mentioned to it. I advised the investor against buying these metals, as these are extremely illiquid and small markets, populated by highly specialized companies that know each other and tend to see outsiders coming and going. Seasoned market professionals call markets like these "roach motels"—you can get in, but you cannot get out of a position. I felt that the investor might be able to buy significant positions in ruthenium and iridium, but it might not be able to get a fair price when it wanted to sell. Eventually we heard that the investor had gone to another investment bank that had no metals trading operations to speak of. There was a bond trader that handled precious metals trades when clients wanted to buy some gold or silver. The bank purchased the platinum group metals for the investor and arranged storage for it at a major precious metals vaulting facility. We later heard that our concerns were borne out, and that the investor did not get a fair price when it decided to sell the metal.

Some investors are able to muscle their way around the minor platinum group metals markets, but usually the market has the upper hand. When we were selling some rhodium for a hedge fund client in the middle of the 1990s, we managed to sell the metal over a period of time while the rhodium price was rising. We also managed to sell the metal at a premium to the prices being quoted in the dealer market for rhodium in virtually every sale we made. That was because we had Russian rhodium, which commanded a premium at the time, and we were extremely slow to dribble the metal out. Also, we were selling directly to fabricators that needed the rhodium to convert to plating salts to use in auto catalysts. The ability to beat the market that way is rare, and is largely unheard of with smaller investors' positions.

Other commodities are harder to own directly on a physical basis, as one needs to arrange storage at an industrial-strength vault, warehouse, silo, oil tank farm, or similar facility. That said, some investors do invest in physical commodities.

There are many reasons why investors, generally speaking, do not go to direct purchases with other commodities. Primarily these are issues related to storing the commodity, and also related to the exposure one receives to the investment through straight purchases of physical commodities.

Futures

Most investors focus on exchange-traded futures as the way to invest in commodities. Physical purchases are good for precious metals, but for most other commodities they do not make sense. Also, as previously mentioned, many investors prefer the leveraged exposure to commodities prices that futures offer.

A futures contract is an agreement to later buy or sell a commodity in a standardized amount, quality grade, and so on, under the terms and conditions of an organized futures exchange. U.S. futures exchanges trade standard-sized contracts. They have a clearinghouse established to assure creditworthiness of all registered market participants. The trades occur through the clearinghouse and not on a principal-to-principal basis. Futures are offered on a wide range of commodities, although not on some of the more esoteric commodities.

For any given commodity for which a futures exchange contract exists, there is a series of contract months in which interested parties can trade. There is a spot contract month, representing a commodity available for immediate delivery. The meaning of "immediate" varies from market to market, but in most commodities markets it is a one- or two-day delivery process. Any entity that has sold the spot month has the right to deliver warehouse receipts for that good to the exchange's clearinghouse. The clearinghouse then allocates the delivery notices and warehouse receipts to those entities that are long the spot month, using a formula to spread the deliveries among the longs.

One of the common misconceptions about commodities futures among investors still is that if one stands for delivery, the commodity is physically delivered to one's address. There are even urban myths about people waking up one morning to find a flatbed truck full of copper or a hopper truck full of grains parked at their home. In fact, the delivery process occurs through a network of delivery sites registered with each exchange. The four precious metals vaulting facilities used for gold, silver, platinum, and palladium were listed previously. It should be noted that none of them are owned by the exchange. These are independent companies that supply storage facilities to interested parties. The same is true for other commodities. Someone taking delivery of petroleum through the Nymex oil contract will be issued receipts that demonstrate that he owns oil in a given tank farm in the west Texas market area. For any commodity, an investor or other market participant taking delivery of a contract is handed a receipt for the amount of commodity covered by that contract in a warehouse, bank vault, grain elevator, petroleum tank farm, or other depository or storage facility that is registered and recognized by the exchange involved as a qualified storage facility for that contract.

Very few trades occur in the spot contract month, and a major activity each month is the process by which the longs and shorts in a given contract month roll out of that month. Almost all of the contracts are closed out before the first delivery date. In most commodities futures markets, around 1 percent or less of the contracts traded are delivered. Most participants in these markets are using the futures markets for financial reasons: to hedge their financial exposure to commodities prices, or to invest or speculate in the price of that commodity.

The key month in U.S. futures tends to be the nearby active month, which varies from commodity to commodity. In gold February and April are active months, for example, while in silver March and May are active months. In platinum it is January, April, July, and October. In palladium it is March, June, September, and December. There usually are historical reasons for these trading patterns, reflecting the seasonal patterns of supply and demand in the underlying physical markets. In Japan the most actively traded months tend to be one year in the future.

Investors can see which contract months are active in a given commodity by looking in a newspaper that lists the futures contracts or by going online to the exchanges' web sites or other sites that list futures. The open interest, or number of outstanding contracts, is listed for each month.

Some months will have very large open interest compared to others. Those are the actively traded months.

Each contract month will have a price. Typically, the prices for nearby contract months are lower than for forward months, and the price rises proportionately with the distance in time into the future for any given contract. This reflects the reality of what these futures contracts are. In the final analysis, they are commitments to buy or sell a commodity at a given time in the future at a given price. The price is based on the spot price at the time the trade is initiated. The future price reflects that spot price as well as the interest rate or cost of money during the time from inception to maturity, insurance, risk, and a few other factors. These costs reflect the fact that the merchant that is agreeing to purchase or sell a commodity at some point in the future has to protect itself against price fluctuations in the interim. It is in essence lending its financial firepower to the buyer or seller of that futures contract. Thus, the difference between spot and future prices typically is close to the cost of money during that period. This difference is known as the spread between nearby and forward contracts. The market also calls this forward spread a *contango*. This colorful word was made up by commodities traders in Liverpool in the nineteenth century. Its origin is lost, but it looks like a British term made up jokingly from the Spanish phrase *con tango*, "with the dance," indicating that the buyer is paying for the dance with the dealer as well as for the underlying commodity.

Another misconception that one often hears is that the forward price bears with it a great deal of information about what the market believes prices will be in the future. By and large, the forward price contains little information about market price expectations. The forward price is essentially the spot price plus the interest rate.

However, the futures prices do contain some information about market expectations. In early 2005, for example, spot oil prices rose sharply to what at the time seemed very high levels, around $40 to $45 per barrel. The futures prices were much lower than this. One year out was around $39 per barrel, and three years forward prices were around $33. This suggested that the market saw the current supply of petroleum as very tight but did not expect the tight supply situation to continue into the next few years. Thus, the market was commanding a premium for spot or nearby oil but was willing to accept lower prices for future delivery. Intuitively, this makes sense. The physical market was tight and buyers were scrounging for oil, pushing prices for prompt delivery higher. They did not care about locking in prices down the road, because the crisis they were facing was here and now. The cognoscenti of the oil industry almost universally were of the mind that oil prices were way too high to be sustainable at $40 to $45 per barrel, and that prices would have to decline over the next few years.

Later in the year, however, attitudes shifted. Buyers of physical oil began to believe or expect that oil supplies might stay tight for a much longer period and that prices consequently might remain high or move higher over the next few years. The spread between spot and forward oil prices narrowed. Even as spot oil prices resumed their rise, moving to $70 later in the year, the forward contract months were rising at a faster pace, narrowing the discount for future delivery compared to prompt delivery.

So the future prices of commodities as listed on futures contracts on exchanges do contain some information about expected price movement. They do not, however, suggest what the market expects the price to be in the future. They only indicate whether the market expects current market conditions to remain as they are in the future. In the case of oil prices, none of the industrial experts buying or selling oil one, two, or three years forward were suggesting that the prices they were paying or accepting were the prices that would be in effect when those contracts matured. They were merely indicating their expectations about the relative tightness of supplies between the time they bought or sold those contracts and the contracts' maturity dates.

Similarly, for much of the 1980s and 1990s there was a wide spread between spot or nearby silver prices and forward silver futures contract prices. This reflected an overabundance of spot silver at these times. Silver was being mined and refined from scrap at a pace far in excess of the pace at which industrial users were buying silver. Furthermore, from the 1960s through the silver bull years of 1979–1983, investors had bought hundreds of millions of ounces of silver, some of which was now being sold. As a result, there was a lot more silver wanting to be sold than there was interest in purchasing it. The dealers, bankers, and merchants that serve as middlemen in this market, marketmakers, stood to buy the excess silver for their own accounts. They did; that is their job. However, in locking in the prices at which they would agree to purchase this silver, they insisted, through their quotes, on a wide enough nearby-to-forward spread to cover their interest rate and other costs for holding this silver for the broader market for what would likely be an extended period of time.

The mechanism here is the same as the yield curve or forward spread in interest rates. If you wish to borrow money for a short period of time, you typically can expect to pay a lower interest rate than if you want to borrow it for a longer period. Interest rates are the cost of money. Merchants who offer to lend you money will usually charge a lower rate for shorter periods of time, partly because their risk in lending that money to you is lower than it would be if they were lending it to you for a longer period. The same financial calculations go into determining the forward spreads in commodities.

This touches on another basic reality about commodities futures markets and forward markets, and on another misconception. Futures and forward commodities trades are interest rate transactions. The quality of the credit risk of a given buyer or seller is central to the transaction. If a mining company has many mines, a well-respected management team, and a proven track record of producing copper, gold, or whatever profitably, it will be able to sell more metal forward to merchants than would a small company with only one mine and no record of stable performance. Many observers of the markets, at least in gold and silver, believe that there are secret stockpiles of metals that are sold in the spot market whenever a forward or futures transaction is executed. This is not the case. What happens is a financial merchant accepts the credit risk of the counterparty to that trade. In the case of a futures contract, the clearinghouse handles these risks. There is a potential for physical commodities to be available for exchange in the future, but no actual physical commodities are present or involved in the transaction at the time of the trade's inception.

Forwards

A forward contract is basically similar to a futures contract, except that forwards are not traded on any organized futures exchange. Forwards are principal-to-principal contracts between two parties—a dealer or bank on one side and an investor, user, or producer on the other side. Forward transactions can be customized to meet an individual client's specific needs in terms of delivery points, grade, volume, type of metal, delivery periods, and so on. A forward contract is a cash market transaction. Producers and others can sell on a forward basis, while consumers and others can buy on a forward basis.

Many institutional investment funds trade primarily in the forward market through major commodities trading banks or dealers. The banks or dealers in turn lay off their risks on the futures exchange. This is one reason why the closely watched government reports on the commitments of traders are frequently misread by the market: Major funds often do not show up in that data. Instead, the commercial counterparties to their trades show up. Thus, a large long position on the part of commercial hedgers in a Commitment of Traders (COT) report actually may be a reflection of a large forward long position on the part of funds. The market would never know.

Until a few years ago, certain regulations required funds that traded on U.S. futures exchanges to register with the National Futures Association. Since many hedge funds did not want to do this, they tended to trade forwards. Forwards also tended to be cost-competitive and sometimes more liquid than the futures markets. In addition, they can sometimes offer greater discretion. There were several advantages to the hedge funds to using forwards rather than futures, and the ability to avoid another layer of regulation was only one of them. Following some reforms in the U.S. regulations in the early part of this decade, there has been an increased willingness on the part of many hedge funds to trade directly in futures. This has led to a shift in the positions reported in the COT. Since 2001 there have been large increases in the long positions reported as being held by large noncommercial entities funds. Part of this increase reflects the rise of institutional investor interest in commodities; part of it reflects a migration by some funds from the forward markets to the futures exchanges.

Forwards exist for many commodities, including commodities for which there are no organized futures markets. They are the workhorses of the commercial or wholesale markets, representing the ways in which producers sell most of their products to intermediaries, and those intermediaries move the commodities on to industrial users. Forwards come in a variety of forms. The basic forward is an agreement that a producer will deliver its product, whether it is gold, copper, oil, or wheat, to a merchant either on a specific day or in a given month, at a predetermined price. That price, like the forward prices in the futures markets, reflects the spot price of the good plus the cost of money over the time period involved in the forward, plus insurance, a risk premium, and some other costs.

There are many permutations to the basic forward sales agreement. In some cases the forward will have no agreed-on price at the outset but will instead be a supply agreement: We will sell you a given volume of a particular commodity at a predetermined time in the future, or perhaps monthly over a year or two. This is a basic supply agreement, with the price either to be determined in the future, or the future price to be that which is used in the industry. A lot of supply contracts will specify parameters like "the spot price of platinum in the New York dealer market, as published by *Metals Week*," or some such arrangement. In other cases a forward can be *prepaid*. With prepaid forwards, the buyer will pay the seller for the commodity to be delivered in advance, at the time of the inception of the forward contract. The price paid is the forward price, based on the spot price plus the forward carry or spread, discounted for the cost of money. For example, at the time a prepaid forward sale is agreed on, spot gold prices might be $450 and the price of gold one year forward may be $464. The cost of money imbedded in the prepaid forward might be 6 percent, equivalent to $28, so the buyer may agree to pay the seller $436 today ($464 less $28) for gold to be delivered a year from now. Prepaid forwards are a form of loan. As with other forwards and futures, the ability to undertake such a deal is based largely on the creditworthiness of the counterparties.

Most of my work has been in the forward markets. It is rare that producers, consumers, or other industrial concerns get involved in futures markets directly. The forward markets offer them better terms and conditions. The futures markets then become the domain of the dealers that offer these forwards, and retail investors and speculators.

Options

Options are contracts that give buyers the right, but not the obligation, to buy or sell a given commodity. Options are sold both on organized exchanges and over the counter by dealers and banks. A great deal of market nomenclature surrounds options. Additionally, many salespeople involved in options marketing try to cloud matters by layering on more jargon. It is no wonder that investors getting involved in exchange traded options must sign a paper that says they understand options.

Options fall into three broad categories. The buyer of a *call* option has the right to buy, or call for, a commodity. The buyer of a *put* option has the right to sell that commodity, or put it to the market. The third category is *compound* options, which consist of combinations of puts and calls. The potential combinations, and their revenue impacts, are endless.

Of course, it is much more complex than that. There are European options, which can be exercised only on their maturity date. Then there are American options, which can be exercised by their buyers at any time between the time they buy them and the maturity date. Most exchange traded options are American options. Many dealer or over-the-counter options are European options. Asian options are based on the average price of the month of maturity, as opposed to the closing price on a single day.

The key difference between options and futures or forwards is the flexibility the option buyer has. If an investor buys a call and the price moves against him by falling, he has lost the premium he paid for that option, but he cannot lose anything more than that premium. With a futures or a forward contract, the investor is financially committed to buy that commodity at that price. He can thus incur very large losses and very large calls for margin to be deposited with a broker or dealer to cover the investor's potential loss.

I mentioned a premium. With options, the buyers pay a premium for the rights they are acquiring. That is a sunk cost, typically paid up front. That amount is the maximum potential loss the option buyer faces.

The seller of an option is financially committed to buy or sell the commodity in question, depending on whether he sold a put or a call. He is financially exposed to much greater losses. The banks, brokers, and dealers that typically sell options hedge this exposure, because they are bright enough to understand that they do not want to take that financial risk unprotected. At my company we have a policy that we will never have a position for a client that is net short an option—that is, one that has this sort of open-ended risk of financial loss.

In Chapter 6 I discuss some options strategies in further detail. I like to use compound options strategies, in which we box in a minimized maximum loss that any given position can have, which is predetermined and known at the time the investor or hedger puts that options position in place. This allows the parties involved to sleep at night.

Exchange Traded Funds

I mentioned ETFs at the beginning of this chapter. These are relatively new investment vehicles for commodities. Exchange traded funds have exploded in the equities market (see Figure 5.1), where they consist of baskets of stocks that investors can buy into. In the early part of this decade some gold market people came up with the idea of creating a gold ETF that would invest solely in physical gold held in allocated accounts and would be designed to track physical gold prices as closely as possible. The

Ounces

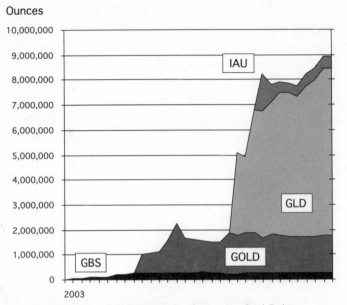

Note: IAU—IShares Comex Gold Trust traded on the American Stock Exchange.
IAU as of 14 October. GLD—Street tracks Gold Shares traded on the New York Stock Exchange.
GLD as of 17 October. GOLD—Gold Bullion Securities traded on the Australian Stock Exchange.
GBS—Gold Bullion Securities traded on the London Stock Exchange.
GOLD and GBS as of 3 October. Central Fund of Canada holds 619,591 ounces as of 17 October.
GLD from JSE holds 92,054 ounces as of 2 September. Central Gold Trust holds 118,326 ounces
as of 17 October.

Figure 5.1 **Exchange Traded Funds' Physical Gold Holdings**

concept was based on the reality that a lot of investors, including many institutional investment fund companies, did not invest in gold bullion because it was too unusual, or cumbersome, compared to their typical equity
and bond investments.

The creation of a gold ETF took several years to execute. By the time
the concept became a reality, there actually were several gold ETFs. Two of
these are listed on U.S. equity exchanges. One is listed in London. There
are also gold ETFs listed on stock exchanges in Toronto, Sydney, and Jo-
hannesburg. The first gold ETF was launched in 2003 in Australia. The
London and U.S. gold ETFs took longer to bring to market but were
rolled out in 2004.

The gold ETFs appear to have been initial successes. The amount of
gold that has been acquired by investors through gold ETFs totaled
roughly nine million ounces by the end of 2005. The vast majority of this
gold was held against shares in the gold ETF listed on the New York Stock

Exchange. Information on the nature of the investors holding the shares backed by this gold is limited, but it appears that the gold ETFs have succeeded in attracting some larger institutional investment firms that formerly did not invest in gold.

Given the initial success of the gold ETFs, producers and other promotional groups involved in other commodities markets have considered the potential for other commodity-based ETFs. It would be possible to create such commodity ETFs but they would need to be structured differently from the gold ETFs in such a way that there was not the requirement of physical commodities held in storage facilities against their shares. They would need to be indexed to commodities but not backed by physical commodities.

The gold producers that were behind the gold ETFs wanted these shares to be backed by gold held in allocated accounts in bank vaults, so that these equities would require the locking up of physical gold. That can be accomplished in the gold market, given the roughly one billion ounces of gold bullion lying around in investor inventories. No other commodity has such physical inventories though.

Silver used to have such stocks but, as discussed in Chapter 7, much of the silver bullion that existed in inventories in the past has been used in manufactured products over the past 15 years. Silver bullion stocks today appear to be extremely low, by silver market standards. Furthermore, regulators may have been reluctant to approve a silver ETF given the silver market's history of sharp price movements based on the investment practices of one or a handful of investors. Regardless, in the middle of March 2006 a silver ETF proposal was approved by the U.S. Securities Exchange Commission. At the time of this writing this silver ETF was being prepared to start trading on the American Stock Exchange.

Equities

Investors often use the equities of producing companies to build exposure to commodities prices. This works for oil and gas companies, coal companies, and mining companies. It is not a pure way to invest in commodities, however, as there are a number of complications. Investing in a commodities-producing company involves taking risks related to the company's management, the quality of its properties and deposits, country risk in the places where it operates, geological risk, and more.

Additionally, many mining companies are not pure plays. As mentioned in the section on palladium in Chapter 7, some investors buy Norilsk Nickel shares as a way of investing in palladium, even though this Russian company, the world's largest nickel mining company, actually is primarily a nickel producer. Similar problems occur with other mining companies. Many of the largest silver-producing companies actually are gold, copper, lead, and zinc mining companies, or they are large mining companies that produce everything from coal to iron ore, aluminum, and base metals.

Within the mining and energy equity markets there is a vast range of companies, from major global producers to exploration companies, as well as smaller producers and companies that are developing their initial productive capacity. Investors seeking to invest in energy or metals through producing companies must wade through a wide range of issues to determine how they should invest. My preference is to invest in a spectrum of companies, including the large producers and some smaller exploration or development companies. The large companies tend to be stable producers and provide some exposure to commodities prices through their share price. The exploration and development companies tend to offer greater potential capital gains, although they also carry much greater risks of loss of equity values.

Beyond mining and energy producers, the ability to invest in commodities through the equities of producers is much more limited. There are few, if any, publicly traded companies that produce most commodities. Some investors will short the stocks of commodities-using companies if they expect commodities prices to rise. For example, they might sell shares of bakeries short if wheat prices rise, or chocolate manufacturers if cocoa prices rise. Here, too, investors run into the complications caused by diversification. Many bakeries are part of diversified food processing companies, as are many candy manufacturers and others.

Mutual Funds

Sector-specific mutual funds are available, but I have tended to avoid these for a variety of reasons. Primarily, sector-specific funds tend to be too rigidly managed, often due to restrictive charters. They tend to be long-only, not allowed to short these markets when prices seem too high or likely to fall. They are often limited to investing in equities and equity options. About four dozen precious metals and natural resource mutual funds are listed in the United States. Around three dozen of these have charters that allow them to buy physical precious metals, but only around four of them actually do this. It is not that they are not allowed to invest in precious metals, but simply that they do not, often because the managers do not feel comfortable doing so.

Commodity Funds

There are several thousand commodity funds, commodity pools, and commodity trading advisers registered with the National Futures Association. (My company, CPM Group, is one.) Most of them spend most of their time and attention on financial futures. Most are also technically oriented funds, trading based on price charts, momentum indicators, and so-called "black box" computerized trading strategies they have devised. Again, these approaches to investing tend not to appeal to me. I like fundamentals and macroeconomic factors. I use technical analysis for market timing, once I have reached an investment conclusion based on market fundamentals and a view of the macroeconomic environment.

Hedge Funds

There also are several thousand hedge funds. Again, most hedge funds do all sorts of things and, generally speaking, commodities represent a small portion of their portfolio, if they use commodities-oriented investments at all. The best hedge funds have total discretion as to which assets and markets they invest in, and they are allowed to be both long and short.

There are a few hedge funds that specialize or focus on mining, energies, or commodities. These strike me as an oxymoron. The essence of a hedge fund is that it is a diversified investment fund with nearly total discretion to invest in a range of assets and markets. The advantage of a hedge fund is that, if it is properly structured, it is a long-short fund—it will buy and sell, go long and go short, various assets. Hedge funds are not what they used to be, and a wide range of investment funds are being established that are called hedge funds but are much more focused and limited in their mandates.

6

Commodity Strategies

There are countless ways to manage commodities investment positions in various price scenarios. Chapter 5 discussed various instruments that are available to investors interested in buying exposure to commodities. This chapter discusses some ways to use those instruments. I cannot and should not attempt to discuss all possible strategies. There are many to which I do not subscribe, so while I touch on a few of these, I am partisan in my description of them. I leave it to people who think they are wise approaches to defend these strategies and investment practices.

Let me start by outlining what I do think are wise approaches. At my core, I am a value investor. I like assets that are undervalued and show fundamental or economic reasons to expect a price increase. One must always be cautious about purchasing an investment simply because the price is low. How many investors bought Enron in the early days of its collapse, assuming prices would respond? Similarly, I looked at a bakery stock a few years ago, at the peak of the anti-carbohydrates diet fad, with the view that bakeries would come back in favor as that diet fad faded. The company I examined had its own problems, however, which suggested to me that its fortunes and share price might not survive and revive with Americans' taste for cake. That analysis, for one, proved correct.

So value investing is a start, but one has to make sure that there is a reasonable basis for assuming an asset's price will rise in the future. Any such analysis ought to be based on facts: the commodity's supply and demand fundamentals and outlook, and the economic environment's likely effects on that commodity's market fundamentals. Technical analysis should never be considered a reason to expect a commodity to rise or fall. It is good for pacing moves, but the moves are based on fundamentals and economics.

Related to value investing, but importantly different, is the concept of contrarian investing. Value investing is buying low and selling high. Contrarian investing is betting against the market consensus. That often means buying low and selling high, or rather buying assets when they are out of favor in the market and selling them when everyone else wants them. As my idol Bernard Baruch said, he made money by buying straw hats in September and selling them in May. Contrarian investing is somewhat different than value investing, however. I try to be careful about it. While my personality tends to favor contrarian thinking, and while I tend to find many people in the market underinformed, mal-informed, or misinformed, I need to restrain myself from investing merely for the purpose of being contrary. There are at least two reasons to avoid this. One is that sometimes the market can be right, even for the wrong reasons. The other is that you never want to stand in front of a racing train or a thundering herd. If the market is racing into an investment, or running for the door, you do not want to be the noble contrarian who stands up to beg to differ, only to be trampled by the stampede.

Another problem with contrarianism is how you deal with this proclivity to bet against the market when it swings around to agree with you. Sometimes you are right and the market is wrong. Then the market consensus shifts and aligns itself with your views. That does not mean you should reverse your opinions. It does suggest that you should revisit your analysis and question your assumptions, but it does not mean that the market move you anticipated has been cancelled.

For example, I turned very bullish on gold in November 2000, around the time when most experienced bullion banks and brokerage companies were closing their gold trading operations and gold was generally viewed as being dead as an investment. For six to nine months I felt like a prophet in my own land. Very few people agreed with me, and many thought I was dead wrong. By September 2001 that changed. The price of gold had barely changed, having risen from around $270 in November 2000 to around $283 in September and October 2001. I still felt that the price had to rise to levels above $320, and possibly to $400, on a longer-term basis. Suddenly, however, I found myself in the midst of the consensus. In April 2001 I had agreed to organize a roundtable discussion, scheduled for November 2001 in New York, on "The Future of Gold." The meeting was postponed until June 2002 and moved to Miami, due to the terrorist attack of September 11. By the time we got to Miami in June the following year, gold prices had risen to $325 and everyone was bullish. Some people wondered aloud why we would bother to have such a meeting, given the obvious future that lay before the gold market. Had I been a contrarian, the impulse to reverse course would perhaps have been overwhelming.

Another core aspect of my approach to investing is hedging positions. Some investors use stop-loss orders to protect themselves against adverse moves. I do not like stop-loss orders so much, although I do use them in markets where more attractive alternatives are not available. More often, I will use options to hedge a position, or I will build a core position in options and use futures or forwards to hedge it. Most commodity trade advisers, pool operators, and other investors tend to invest in futures and use options to hedge their positions. If they are bullish on corn, they purchase a corn futures position, and then buy some put options below the market to protect themselves if the price of corn falls. That works. It also works to buy corn calls and then, if the price rises, sell some corn futures to lock in your profits in case the price falls back.

A third core aspect is diversification. Earlier I mentioned my propensity to buy a range of types of equities in a commodity that I find interesting. Let's look at uranium as an example. Uranium prices have risen sharply over the past few years, but one cannot easily invest directly in uranium. It is not traded on any exchange, and purchasing physical uranium can be difficult. A few uranium investment funds have been started, but most investors buy uranium exposure by investing in uranium stock. There only are a few major producers of uranium around. Most uranium is produced by diversified mining companies, and their share prices do not accurately reflect changes in uranium prices. There are a couple of companies that are in production whose shares can be purchased, such as Cameco. Additionally, there are dozens of uranium exploration companies. An investor interested in uranium could buy some shares of a producer and also shares of some exploration companies.

Ascertaining the likelihood of success for the exploration companies is extremely difficult. I rely on information from people knowledgeable in a given market whom I trust, if I can find such people. I also pay a lot of attention to the quality of management. You can have a great mine or deposit, but bad managers can prevent the company from being a good investment. Conversely, I have seen companies with no deposits whatsoever but excellent and trustworthy management, who have been able to raise money from investors based on their obvious competencies and then go find or acquire world-class deposits to develop or mine.

I have outlined three main tenets I follow: value investing, hedging positions, and diversification. There are many more issues to consider, such as the maturity or tenure of investments—that is, whether you invest long-term or short-term. I say yes, do both. I tend not to be much of a short-term investor, although sometimes I suggest or take futures and options positions expecting to hold them for five days or so. But most of my investment decisions are longer term. I always tell prospective asset management customers that we are not traders but investors. We do not make a lot of trades in any portfolio that we manage, but rather seek to profit from longer-term trends in markets.

That said, we will trade around a longer-term core position. If we have a long-term long position in a given commodity and the price rises sharply, we will seek to capitalize the gains, to lock in profits. We may still be expecting higher prices, but we also may expect prices to fall back in the interim. Given this situation, there are a variety of hedging strategies one can use. Simple options are one approach. Butterfly spreads, call spreads, put spreads, and various other options strategies can be used as well. These strategies allow investors to buy exposure they want to a given commodity while limiting the potential for losses.

People ask us why CPM Group does not publish explicit trading strategies and concepts in its reports. The reason is that our clients range from mining companies and industrial users of commodities to governments, central banks, and institutional investors. Any given strategy will be irrelevant to the vast majority of our clients. Our reports contain our market views. How individual clients seek to protect themselves financially or profit from that market view coming to pass depends on too many individualized variables to warrant publishing strategies. Such information is provided on an advisory basis to individual clients.

For example, in late November 2005 the price of gold rose sharply, from $460 on November 7 to slightly above $500 on December 1. Much of the impetus for this increase had to do with short-term congestion moving toward the December Comex options expiration date, on November 22, and the first delivery date for the December Comex futures, on December 1. By December 1 the short-term congestion was behind the market. The gold market, meanwhile, was full of bullish froth, with gurus and others talking about gold rising to $550, $850, even $1,000. The market was ripe for short-term profit taking and a pullback in prices, but the overall economic and financial environment, including the speculative circus in gold, suggested that the price might rise further. More critically, much of the large short position that had been hanging over the December contract had rolled into the February Comex contract. This suggested that the same price pattern had a high probability of repeating itself in January, leading up to the February contract delivery period.

While many investors stood their ground, holding their unhedged gold positions, there were numerous strategies that could have been used to protect against, and profit from, any short-term pullback in prices. Perhaps the easiest approach for an investor that had purchased gold earlier, at $460 or even lower, would have been to sell the gold, locking in the gains. It could then take a small portion of those profits, less than 10 percent of them, and purchased out-of-the-money calls with strike prices above $500. In this way, the investor would profit if prices continued to rise, but would have capitalized its gains if prices indeed declined.

Commitment of Traders Reports

One tool that has been used increasingly by commodity markets participants over the past few years has been to watch the Commitment of Traders reports, published weekly by the Commodity Futures Trading Commission. These reports divide the number of futures and options contracts outstanding each Tuesday among large hedgers, large noncommercial trading participants, and smaller traders. The definition of *large* and *small* varies by commodity.

These reports contain a great deal of information and can provide important insight into market conditions. There are some quirks about the data that need to be understood, however. First, much of the institutional investing in some markets, notably gold, petroleum, copper, silver, platinum, and palladium, is not included here. Much of that investing takes place in the over-the-counter or dealer market, in forwards and dealer options. The COT only covers exchange traded futures and options. Thus, involvement by many institutions does not appear in this data. This has changed somewhat since 2001, when regulations shifted in the United

States. Prior to that time almost all hedge funds avoided exchange traded futures and options, since to invest in them would require the hedge funds to register with the CFTC and the National Futures Association. With the modernization of commodity exchange regulations at the end of 2000, some hedge funds began investing directly in futures and futures options.

Many of those forward and dealer options are hedged by the dealers in futures and exchange traded options. Thus, a large long position taken on by a hedge fund or other institution in the dealer market would not appear as a long position in the COT data. It would, however, be reflected in the data as a large long position taken on by a commercial trader. Some market observers wonder at the large short positions that commercial dealers have in some markets, such as gold. The answer is that these are hedges against forward market positions.

Another quirk is that the CFTC fades out-of-the-money options in calculating these figures. The commission has a formula whereby puts and calls that are in the money are counted contract for contract, but as the strike price of a given option gets further away from current market prices, the options are counted as something less than full contracts. There could be enormous positions that are far away from current market prices, but the COT statistics will discount the importance of those options to the market. This can be important since one interesting strategy is to buy deep out-of-the-money options. These tend to cost very little and often rise in value at a faster pace than do closer-in options, should prices move in an investor's favor.

Finally, *whose* trading is reflected in these statistics needs to be understood. One often hears market commentators referring to these positions as being those of commodity funds. That used to be the case, more or less, prior to the change in market regulations in 2001. It is much less the case now. Today commodity funds, which focus on exchange traded futures and options, are joined by other institutional investors, including hedge funds, in trading these contracts. Additionally, it has never been clear where proprietary trades executed by banks and brokers show up. There is a great deal of discretion in the collection of this data. A major bank or brokerage company ostensibly is a commercial participant in these markets. If it is hedging a position it has taken on as part of its brokerage or trading operations, that is a commercial position and should be reported as such. But much of the trading by these companies is proprietary. The bank or brokerage company is trading its own positions, or trading managed accounts for investor clients. These are not commercial trades per se.

However, there is some overlap at some banks that run unified books, and it sometimes is difficult to say what is a commercial trade and what is an investment position. The data collection system used in pulling these statistics together allows for a lot of leeway in counting these trades, and it is never clear whether proprietary trades taken on by banks and dealers are showing up as investment positions or commercial positions.

Figures 6.1 and 6.2 show the positions of large noncommercial market participants in gold and copper. (I am not bothering to show the positions of large commercial entities.) Figure 6.1 shows the large noncommercial positions in gold futures and options. There are three sets of data on this chart. The first set of data is the gross long positions, the second is the gross short positions, and the third is the net position of these funds. One of the things that is most clear from the gold data is the enormous and steady increase in the gross and net long positions held by large investment entities in the gold contract since 2001. In part this reflects the migration to exchange traded contracts mentioned earlier, but it is also clear from other market evidence that the bulk of this increase to record levels represents a significant shift in investment funds' attitudes and postures toward gold during the period from 2001 to 2005.

Another interesting aspect of the market that shows up on this chart is the extreme volatility in investor positions during 2005. Prior to that time, investors would build up large positions and hold them for a few months

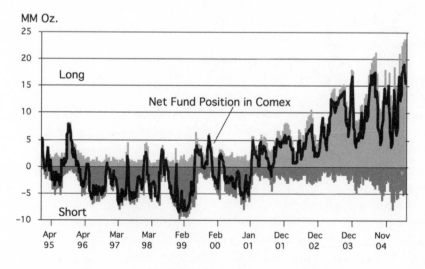

Figure 6.1 **Gold Noncommercial Comex Positions**

Billion lbs.

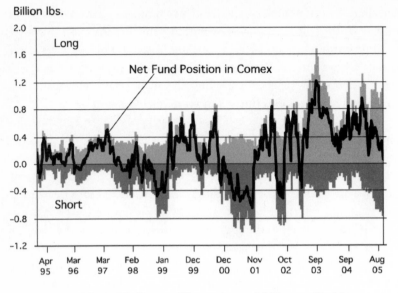

Figure 6.2 **Copper Noncommercial Comex Positions**

before taking profits or liquidating. As prices rose to what were seen as high levels in 2005, investor attitudes toward what constituted a low or high gold price fluctuated sharply. Investors would come to the collective view that gold prices were ready to rise and they would flood into gold futures and options. This would push prices sharply higher. Investors would quickly take profits and unwind their long positions, leading to an equally sharp and sudden decline in the long positions they held.

A final point to notice on the gold Commitment of Traders chart also appears on the copper chart (Figure 6.2), and perhaps was even more significant for copper than it was for gold in 2005. In both of these markets the gross short positions held by funds had dropped to extremely low levels in the early part of this decade. As gold and copper prices rose to high levels—record levels for copper—there was a large increase in short positions taken on in both of these metals' markets by institutional investors betting against further increases.

How one interprets this increase in short positions reflects more on one's personality and analysis of the underlying markets. Bulls looked at the increase in short positions at a time of still-rising prices and concluded that if prices could rise in the face of such shorting, there was a tremendous amount of underlying strength in other segments of these markets.

Fabrication demand, or investor demand for physical gold or copper on the London Metals Exchange, was overriding the negative effects of this short-selling on the Comex. Bears would look at the growth in the short positions as confirmation that the market (or at least large institutional investment fund managers) was concluding that the price increases in gold and copper had ridden their course and were due to reverse.

Putting This into Practice

Examining a set of hypothetical silver trades in recent years in greater detail will yield some insights into how to handle a series of investment decisions using value investing and hedging as parts of a key strategy.

Let us start with a decision to buy silver around $6.00 in late December 2003. That was already a very high price for silver, which had traded between $4.40 and $5.40 for most of the previous 10 years. Silver had a technical resistance level around $5.80, which it blew through in December 2003. At $6.00 one could choose to sell silver, on the expectation it would fall back into its long-held lower trading range, or one could go long with the view that prices were finally breaking out of that range and were likely to move into a higher range in the future. I had predicted for several years that such a breakout would occur at some point. By late 2003 market fundamentals were tightening, and it looked like the change might come. But having seen many false starts, I had a natural inclination to be suspicious about the sustainability of the rally starting in December 2003.

One solution would have been to purchase silver calls and puts, a strangle, at that time. Another would be to buy silver futures or forwards and to hedge the exposure to a drop in prices by purchasing a put. Let us assume that we bought a silver strangle—that is, we would buy March 2004 puts around $5.80 and March 2004 calls around $6.20. The calls were surprisingly cheap at the time, indicating that the market did not expect the rally to last, but rather to fizzle out as previous silver price rallies had. As 2004 progressed the price of silver continued to rise, surprising many in the market who felt that silver prices could not mount a sustained rally above $5.40 and were more likely to drop back to $4.40 or lower. There was so much bearishness toward silver that some silver market observers felt brave enough to say they thought silver would drop to $2.00 or lower, levels not seen since the 1970s.

Silver prices shot up to $6.75 by the middle of January. The March calls became extremely valuable. We could have sold them back to a dealer for a profit or exercised them early, but instead we held on to them and sold silver futures against them. This allowed us to lock in a profit if prices fell back. Prices indeed did fall back on profit taking, dropping back to $5.95 in the first week of February. At that point, around $6.00, we bought back the short futures position, locking in the profits on that. We still had some time left on the puts and calls that we had bought.

In making these trades we see a few things. First, we are investing primarily through options, and using futures to hedge the options position. Second, we are capitalizing profits as the market moves, keeping a core position in place while taking cash out of the position. In contrast to using stop-loss orders, trading in this way allows us to continue to have exposure to further beneficial price developments while capitalizing some of our gains and taking advantage of shorter-term price moves.

Within a week, during the second week of February, silver had recovered to trade between $6.25 and $6.50. The March options were expiring, so we exercised the calls at $6.20, converting them into March futures. The puts we had bought at $5.80 were virtually worthless, so we held on to them and let them expire a week later. We then rolled the March long futures position into July, to give ourselves more time.

This is when the market really gets exciting, moving in our favor far beyond what we would have expected. Silver prices skyrocket to $8.34 in early April. This is way off the charts, the highest silver price since early 1998, when Berkshire Hathaway was taking delivery of its silver position. The market has gone crazy. The silver bulls who have long predicted the end of the world, the collapse of a silver price conspiracy, and $50 silver, have upped their antes. They are predicting $100 silver and the failure of some of the largest banks in the world, because "there is not enough silver to meet delivery commitments." More sober market participants and observers are beginning to question whether silver in fact is moving into the new, higher trading range that some analysts have predicted for a long time. Meanwhile, the analyst who had predicted that silver would fall to $1.50 is silent in the market, but busy updating his resume.

We are now long silver futures around $6.20, and have roughly $2.00 per ounce profits locked into this. The price seems too high to be sustained, but by the same token we do not want to jump in front of a speeding train. So we sell our July silver futures, locking in the profits. We take a small portion of the profits, maybe 10 percent or less, and buy some out-of-the-money calls with strike prices around $9.00 or so. In this way, if prices do continue to rise, we still have some exposure to rising prices. Meanwhile, we also take some of the profits and buy some puts below the market, just in case the price does fall. We are lucky—the price falls. Even though we are silver bulls, we have profited from a decline in prices. Silver plunges all the way back to $6.00 within two weeks of its peak, and ultimately drops to $5.50 by early May. We do not wait that long. When the price gets back to $6.00, the level at which we started in December 2003, we sell back the puts for a hefty profit, and buy some calls above the market, around $6.40. In other words, we start the process all over again.

This is one example of how investors can use value investing techniques and instincts, combined with hedging strategies to simultaneously hold a longer-term core position while seeking to take profits out of the market based on shorter-term price moves. The one tenet left out of this rendition was diversification. We handled that by also trading silver mining shares during this time, and hedging them with options on the XAU gold and silver equity index traded in Philadelphia.

Principal Protected Accounts and Structured Products

Another approach I like to take toward investing is a longer-term stance, taking hedged positions and seeking to profit from multiyear price moves in commodities. While the previous example focused on how to profit from shorter-term price developments while preserving longer-term exposure to price trends, this strategy is focused more on the longer term. That said, by handling these positions as managed accounts, as opposed to structured notes or bonds, one can modify them to take advantage of shorter-term interim price moves as well.

The concept of principal guaranteed notes emerged in the 1980s as a response to mutual funds' desires to participate in commodity-linked investments. Mutual funds are considered long-term investment vehicles by the tax authorities in the United States and other countries, while commodities are viewed as short-term investments. A long-term investment fund that makes too large of a portion of its profits from short-term investments can lose its long-term tax status and find all of its profits taxed at higher short-term rates. As a result, most mutual funds traditionally have avoided investing in commodities—the risk was just too great.

In the middle of the 1980s, commodity-linked structured notes were conceived as a way around this. Mutual funds and other investment funds with long-term tax status could invest in corporate notes or bonds issued by money-center banks or brokers, with the returns of these notes indexed to a specific commodity or a basket of commodities. The first notes were very simple: If the price of the underlying commodity rose, the notes paid a yield commensurate to the increase. If the price of the underlying commodity fell, the notes would lose value for the investors. The funds were investing in corporate debt issued by an investment-grade company. There was no direct exposure to commodities prices, so even if the return on such investments rose sharply at a time when other assets in the fund's portfolio were deteriorating, the fund would maintain its long-term tax status.

The banks or brokerage companies that wrote these notes would protect themselves by purchasing puts or calls to cover their exposure to rising or falling commodity prices. Meanwhile, they borrowed money at extremely competitive rates.

As time passed the notes became more sophisticated. Some notes were written that would guarantee the investor would get its principal back if it held the note or bond to maturity, typically three to five years. The yield on the note might be zero or some small nominal return if the price of the underlying commodity was unchanged or flat at maturity, and it would rise in proportion to any increase in the commodity price above a reference price. These were called guaranteed principal notes. Figure 6.3 illustrates one such note.

Further nuances were added, and principal protected notes were structured. These might offer greater exposure to rising prices in return for the investor accepting the risk of some downside losses. An investor could choose to accept a maximum loss of 5 or 10 percent of its principal. The greater its risk tolerance, the greater could be its exposure to rising prices.

My company has been heavily involved in advising institutional investors about how to structure such notes, beginning in the middle of the 1980s and continuing to the present day. We developed a further nuance by imbedding both a put and a call into the hedge behind the note. In this way, the investor could have a guaranteed or protected principal and benefit from higher yields if the price of the underlying commodity, or index, rose or fell.

Figure 6.4 shows two such notes. Both are five-year notes, but one was written in December 2001 for December 2006, while the other was writ-

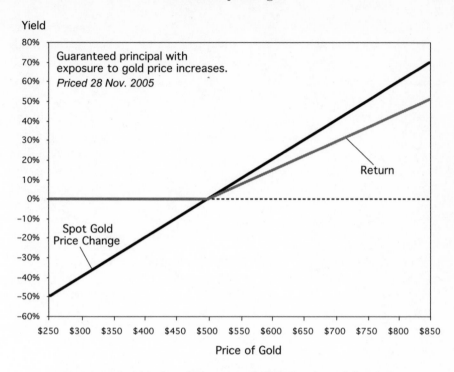

Figure 6.3 Gold-Indexed Five-Year Bullish Structured Account

ten in December 2005 for December 2010. I put them together to show how the increase in gold prices, investor interest in gold, and gold price volatility changes the risk-reward profile of such an investment during the intervening four years. A bull market makes quite a difference. In late 2001 an investor could buy a five-year gold note that had a guarantee of the principal at maturity, gave the investor 85 percent of any increase over a base reference price, and offered the investor a return of –85 percent of the difference between the reference price and prices if the price of gold fell. By December 2005 the investor would have to accept a 9 percent potential risk on its principal (only 91 percent of its principal is protected) in order to receive an 84 percent exposure to rising prices and a –41.8 percent correlation to declining prices.

These notes are a very interesting way to invest in commodities. Even better is the fact that if an investor is not a publicly offered fund with a long-term investment tax status, the investor can emulate the risk-reward profile of such structured notes and bonds by constructing managed accounts consisting of the components of such notes. In essence, the money

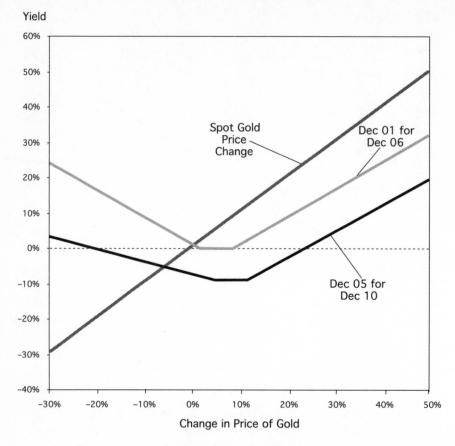

Figure 6.4 **Gold-Indexed Five-Year Structured Accounts**

invested in a note like the ones shown here is distributed as follows. Perhaps 15 percent of the principal is used to buy long-dated puts and calls.
These have to be done in the dealer market, as five-year options generally
are not available on an exchange. Another couple of percent goes to pay
various bank, broker, and advisory fees. The remainder goes into zero-
coupon notes. The principal on the notes earns interest over the five years
that brings the principal back up toward its original amount after five
years. Back when interest rates were higher and commodity prices were
less volatile, it was possible to structure these notes and accounts with
three-year maturities, and get back to 100 percent of the principal, or even
more. With interest rates rather low, even after 18 months of increases in
short-term rates, and commodity prices much more volatile, the accounts

that could be structured in late 2005 were less attractive to investors than they had been in the past. That does not mean they were unattractive. Compared to other ways to invest in commodities, such accounts offer interesting and attractive risk-reward ratios.

Ratio Trading

Some investors trade in ratios. There are intermarket ratios, such as the gold-oil ratio and the gold-silver ratio, and there are also spreads, such as the crack spread, between crude oil and distillates such as heating oil and gasoline.

For the most part, I am not interested in ratio trading. These ratios of the prices of different commodities generally mean very little to the markets. The average ratio has been around 16 barrels of oil per ounce of gold since 1968, meaning that on average over this time it would have taken the sale of 16 barrels of oil to generate revenues sufficient to purchase one ounce of gold. The range of ratios prior to 2004–2005 was between 10 barrels and 38 barrels of oil per ounce of gold, so the average ratio masks a very wide range of experiences. Prior to 1968 oil prices were largely determined by Aramco, and gold prices were fixed by central banks at $35 per ounce, so prices and the consequent ratio moved very little. Historical data prior to 1968 is meaningless.

People will take this ratio and say that it somehow represents what the relationship between gold and oil prices ought to be, as if, on average, the market was right in the past and whatever the relationship between gold and oil prices was back then should be maintained forever in the future. All of that is nonsense, of course. Others talk about reversion to the mean, which is just a way to pretend there is some intellectual weight behind the thought that whatever the price relationship in the past was ought to be maintained in the future. Intellectually, such a concept does not hold up to even cursory examination.

Now, a ratio such as the gold-oil ratio can tell you something about the relative strength of gold and oil prices. But it will tell you nothing about why that relationship is what it is at any time. Nor will it tell you anything about where the price relationship might reasonably be expected to go in the future.

The gold-oil ratio, shown in Figure 6.5, recently has been at historical lows, reflecting that oil prices have risen sharply against gold prices. This

Barrels/Oz.

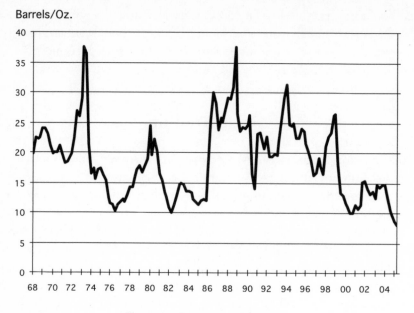

Figure 6.5 **The Gold–Oil Ratio**

reflects the fact that people are using oil at a faster pace than they have in the past, while oil supplies have been constrained by lagged production de- velopment due to the previous period of low oil prices and what appears to be some increase in oil prices due to international political conditions since 2003. Gold prices have risen, but not as rapidly or as far as oil prices. Will they continue to rise, or play catch-up with oil? Maybe, but maybe not.

There are real economic reasons why gold and oil prices should be expected to rise and fall in line with each other. Higher oil prices tend to be inflationary, hurt corporate profits and share prices, drive up interest rates, and weaken the U.S. dollar. All of these trends tend to stimulate in- vestment demand for gold. Therefore, as oil prices rise, they tend to trigger economic trends supportive of higher gold prices. Also, as oil prices rise there is an increased flow of U.S. dollars into oil-exporting countries, just as the dollar is coming under downward pressure. Oil exporters tend to seek ways to sterilize some of their suddenly increased inflow and expo- sure to the U.S. dollar, by selling dollars and moving the proceeds of such sales into alternative assets. Gold is one of the prime alternative assets, one toward which many oil exporters have a cultural proclivity. This also stim- ulates increased investment demand for gold, driving gold prices higher.

The same factors are true in reverse when oil prices fall. So there are real economic and fundamental reasons to expect gold and oil prices to move broadly in line with each other.

There is no reason, however, to assume their increases and declines ought to move at a fixed pace. Also, economic conditions change over time. The impact on gold of oil price changes shifts over time as other factors become more or less important. The growth of the world financial market, the rise of alternatives to gold for investors, the increased use of hedging programs in petroleum and U.S. dollars, and other trends have changed the relationship between gold and oil from what it was 30 years ago. So, while the ratio is interesting, it is not a good basis on which to rest commodities investment decisions.

The same is true of other ratios. Figure 6.6 shows the gold–silver ratio. This ratio has ranged from 16:1 to 100:1 over the past four decades. As with the gold–oil ratio, there are people who grab the average, around 33:1, and assume that the ratio must revert toward that someday. Others will lock in on the 16:1 ratio, used by Sir Isaac Newton in 1717 to establish the relationship between gold and silver in the British currency system, as the "natural" ratio between these two metals. Again, there is no reason—physical, geological, chemical, economic, or otherwise—why any given gold–silver price ratio ought to exist.

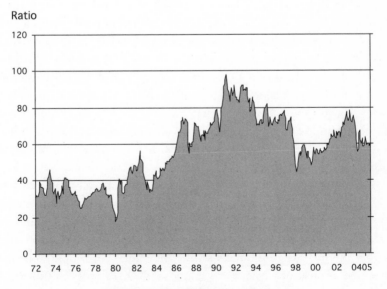

Figure 6.6 **The Gold–Silver Ratio**

Commodity Indexes

One of the consequences of the large stash of uninvested cash in investors' portfolios around the world in recent years has been a broad move into commodities as an asset class by a wide range of institutional and individual investors, searching for better returns than they expect in stocks and bonds at this time. Most of these investors are novices to commodities. Many of them have adopted a shotgun approach to investing in commodities. Rather than attempt to distinguish interesting commodities investments from a broad spectrum of potential choices, these investors have adopted an indexed approach toward commodities.

How much money has moved into commodities and commodity-oriented investment instruments is not clear, but it probably was in excess of $100 billion over the course of 2004 and 2005. From the beginning of 2004 into June 2005, in just 18 months, it is estimated that $23 billion was invested in commodity-indexed investment products. That clearly is only one small portion of the overall commodity investment market.

The concept of using commodity-indexed products to invest in commodities is based on the theory that an investor ought not try to study the markets for individual commodities and undertake any structured analysis. Instead, investors ought to use commodity-indexed investment funds and instruments to buy exposure to a range of commodities. Part of the basis for such a train of thought is the belief that commodities prices across a range of commodities are set to rise for the next 17, 20, or 60 years, as commodities prices are in the midst of a major upward price move. In Chapters 1 and 2 I laid out all the reasons why I do not share this opinion, and why investors should avoid the pitfall of buying into commodities indexes based on expectations of easy money. One look at the long-term commodity index charts in Chapter 2 should explain at a glance why this theory does not seem to be based on reality, and why such investment approaches ought to be avoided.

The most popular index is the Goldman Sachs Commodities Index (GSCI), but there are many others around. Literally billions of dollars of funds have poured into commodity-indexed investment products since 2003. These investments have been made indiscriminately, irrespective of whether the investors are bullish on the individual commodities in a given index. These positions have been taken solely because these futures contracts are part of the GSCI. The role of such passive investments in determining prices for these commodities must not be overlooked. Even a change in the composition of these indexes can have a price effect on the individual commodities.

For example, copper represents 2.3 percent of the GSCI, while gold is 1.7 percent and silver 0.2 percent. That means that for every $100 million invested in GSCI-indexed bonds or notes, $2.3 million is used to buy copper exposure, $1.7 million gold, and $200,000 silver. The figure for silver is not particularly large by silver market standards, but one can quickly comprehend the influx of investment dollars into copper and gold based on these purely mechanical investment systems. By the middle of 2005 there was $585 million invested in gold by investors using GSCI-related instruments, with no regard for gold's fundamental outlook or price considerations. This amount had increased from $384 million in December 2003. That is 1.4 million ounces of gold at $425 per ounce, the price in the market in the middle of 2005, up from 500,000 ounces just 18 months ago.

Similar influxes of investor money have poured into everything from coffee and cotton to cattle and wheat. The impact on prices has been evident. The size of the positions being taken by these investors relative to total open interest in the various exchanges is quite large. If and when these positions are liquidated, that action could contribute to a sudden sharp drop in prices, for no reason related to the underlying markets, the same way that the influx of this money has pushed commodities prices higher since 2003.

7

Precious Metals

I stated at the outset of this book that I am interested in commodities
much more than futures. In fact, most of the work I have done in the
commodities markets since the 1970s has been in the physical and
over-the-counter markets, and not in futures or exchange traded options.
While I have invested in some futures and exchange traded options for my
own account and for some clients, most of the advice I provide to producers, users, central banks, and institutional investors focuses on forwards,
physicals, and dealer options. For the purposes of this book, however, I am
focusing on commodities that are traded mostly on organized exchanges
in the United States.

There are dozens of commodities in which one can invest. Most of
them have some interest to me or to other investors. One has to invest the
time to understand the markets, however. I have mentioned it before but it
bears repeating: Otherwise sober investors often seem to throw logic, wisdom, and their best analytical processes to the wind when it comes to investing in commodities. Investors who follow extremely rigorous and
disciplined fundamental methodologies for investing in stocks seem to believe that when it comes to commodities there are easy earnings to be had.
They read an incredible report from an unknown person taken from the
Internet and throw money at the wildest concepts in commodities. If they

were to read a similar report about a stock, they would run for the hills, but when it comes to commodities logic goes out the window.

The next five chapters discuss 16 commodities. There are many more of interest, but time and space dictate that I limit myself here. For example, I discuss cocoa, coffee, and cotton among the tropical agricultural commodities. That does not mean that I do not like orange juice and sugar, both of which rose sharply in price during 2005 and offer interesting futures. If I had the space I would include them here, as well as the new ethanol contract trading on the New York Board of Trade. Ethanol is made from corn in the United States, but in Brazil it is made from sugar. The rise in oil prices has stimulated enormous demand for ethanol as a replacement fuel or supplement, and the diversion of Brazilian sugar from exports to ethanol production has had a role in the increase in sugar prices.

This chapter covers the four major precious metals: gold, silver, platinum, and palladium. Gold is perhaps the most important commodity market for investors. While oil, natural gas, copper, aluminum, cotton, corn, and possibly some other commodities have larger physical markets in terms of supply and demand, gold has an enormous paper market that nowadays is roughly 40 to 50 times the size of its physical market. That is down from its earlier size of 100 times larger. In terms of the overall dollar value of the paper commodities markets, gold is the largest market by far. For this reason, and because it is one of the commodities on which most of my career has been focused, I spend more time and space on gold here than I do on other commodities. I also spend more time on silver, platinum, and palladium than I do on more industrial commodities, reflecting their greater importance to investors.

Gold

Gold is the granddaddy of all commodities. It has been the single most intensely pursued commodity in the history of mankind, the stuff that dreams are made of. Gold is the commodity that has most fueled the worst aspects of mankind's vices, from greed to murder. I have been told that the only human culture that did not value and pursue gold was that of the native North Americans.

Gold has served three purposes in history. First, it has been a monetary asset, a key part of governments' monetary systems. Related, but importantly different, gold has been a financial asset, by which I mean that it has been held by individuals and governments as an investment and form of savings. The differences between gold's roles as a monetary asset and as a financial asset are critical to understanding the gold market today. Gold was demonetized for the most part by governments in the early 1970s, when the formal link between gold and the international currency exchange rate regime was severed. Central banks have continued to hold gold as a reserve asset in the ensuing three decades, but this largely has been as a residual. Few central banks have added to their gold reserves during this time, and gold has had a greatly diminished relationship to money on an official basis. However, gold's importance as a financial asset has remained strong during this time and has probably even increased.

The third function of gold is as a commodity, used primarily in jewelry but also in a host of industrial applications, from electronic components to coating for reflectors used in industrial ovens to bake paint onto metal. Still, most gold goes into jewelry. In 2005 jewelry manufacturers used around 71.4 million ounces of gold, excluding the amounts used in China that are impossible to get a good measure on. This represented 65 percent of the 110 million ounces of gold that entered the international market last year from mines, scrap refining, and central bank sales. This share of the market for jewelry actually was historically low, reflecting the gold rush underway in 2005 on the part of investors. Over the past 25 years, jewelry has accounted for 78 percent of total new gold supply, or 1.6 billion ounces of the 2.1 billion ounces sold into the physical gold market from 1981 through 2005. That is typical in the long run. During periods of intense investor interest in gold, such as has been seen from 2001 through 2005, investors bid up the price of gold, buy more, discourage jewelry demand, and take a larger share of the gold market.

Investor buying, which reflects gold's role as a financial asset and is central to whether gold prices rise or fall, is a smaller portion of physical demand for gold. Markets are made at the margin, and it is the levels of marginal buying by investors that determines gold prices.

Unlike many commodities, gold has a long and illustrious history. Gold has been with mankind for at least 5,000 years. In fact, some of the gold that circulates today almost certainly has been making the rounds of commerce for several millennia. People tend not to lose gold. Less than 10 percent of all of the gold mined since the beginning of time is estimated to have been lost. Most of that loss has occurred in the past few decades, with the use of gold in electronic components, medical implants, and other products that have not been recycled.

That said, most of the gold around today is relatively young. Around 170 million ounces of gold were estimated to have been mined from antiquity through 1869. Since then, another 4,330 million ounces have been mined—25 times as much as was produced in the previous four millennia. Of the 4,500 million ounces estimated to have been mined through 2004, 96 percent of it was mined in the past 135 years, and more than a third of it since 1980, when gold prices jumped to $850 per ounce and the gold market changed forever. With the exception of only a few metals, no other commodity has had such a long involvement with mankind. Of these, only gold and silver have been hoarded and preserved so diligently through the ages.

Defining the Gold Market

Gold represents less than 2 percent of the dollar value of all commodities produced worldwide in a given year. It is given a weighting of 1.67 percent in the Goldman Sachs Commodity Index, as of 2005, but that index does not include all commodities by a wide margin. While gold is a small part of the physical commodities market overall, gold accounts for a larger portion of commodities trading. Gold accounts for more than 30 percent of worldwide commodities derivative trading—paper trades that include futures, forwards, options, and other commodities-linked financial instruments. That is down from more than 50 percent in the 1990s.

Around 170 million ounces of gold were estimated to have been mined from antiquity through 1869. Since then, another 4,330 million ounces have been mined—25 times as much as was produced in the previous four millennia.

Given this, it should not be a surprise to anyone that gold does not really trade so much as a commodity as it does as a financial asset. If you compare the way gold is bought and sold around the world, it looks more like a financial asset than like a commodity.

Figure 7.1 compares the volumes of gold that are produced and consumed on a physical basis each year to the amount of gold that trades across the world's major gold futures and options exchanges (in New York, Tokyo and Chicago) and the amount of gold that clears through the London interbank gold market. This latter market, the London interbank market, is the largest volume gold trading facility in the world. It is not an exchange, but rather a network of banks, dealers, brokerage companies, and other financial institutions that have agreed to a set of terms and condi-

Million Ounces

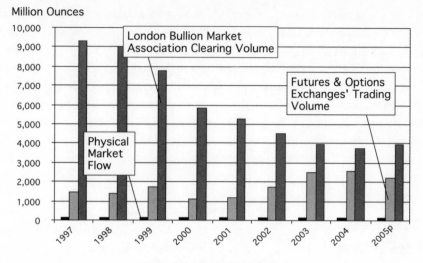

Figure 7.1 **The Gold Market**

tions under which they will trade gold and silver among themselves, both for their own accounts and for their clients. As opposed to a formal exchange with a physical facility, these traders are connected by telephones, e-mail, and electronic telecommunications systems.

The chart shows that during the first half of 2005, gold trading in the London market was running at an annual pace of nearly four billion ounces. Trading on the New York Comex, the Tokyo Commodities Exchange, and the Chicago Mercantile Exchanges meanwhile was running at an annual pace of more than two billion ounces. This contrasts to around 110 million ounces of gold being mined and refined from scrap each year, and being sold as jewelry, investment products, or in manufactured goods. The ratio of these derivatives to the underlying physical gold market is around 60:1. That is down sharply from a ratio of 100:1 in the late 1990s. This decline represents the fact that from the late 1990s until recently many bullion banks,[1] broker companies, and dealers pulled back sharply on the amount of proprietary trading—trading for their own accounts—in the gold and silver markets. But even with the massive decline in trading

---

[1]The various types of financial institutions that trade gold often are referred to as *bullion banks* as a market shorthand, even though many of them are not legally and formally organized as banks. This term will be used here to refer to the full range of such trading operations collectively.

by the banks, the amount of paper gold trading relative to the physical market far outstrips similar trading patterns in all other commodities, with the exception of silver.

Statistics are not available to verify it, but market estimates are that in almost all other commodities the ratio of derivatives to the underlying physical markets is around 5:1 to 10:1. Heavily traded commodities like oil may have ratios around 20:1 or somewhat higher, but other commodities have much less paper trading relative to their underlying physical markets. Gold and silver have much deeper and broader forward markets, derivative forwards, futures, and options, based on the supposition that there is some physical commodity deliverable if need be.

> *Gold and silver have much deeper and broader forward markets, derivative forwards, futures, and options, based on the supposition that there is some physical commodity deliverable if need be.*

This begs the question of why gold and silver's ratios are so different from those of other commodities. Gold conspiracy theorists point to these ratios as evidence that there is something unusual going on in gold and silver. In fact, the explanation is much less sinister. The fact is that gold and silver trade like financial assets, and not like commodities. One finds similar ratios of derivatives to physicals in currency trading and interest rate markets, like the U.S. Treasury bills and bonds markets.

The Price of Gold

The price of gold has been fixed by governments for much of history, to an extent. Governments have used gold as the basis for monetary systems. They set the price of gold and keep it fixed against a currency. Inevitably, the relationship between the value of gold and the value of the currency gets out of line, and the gold standard collapses. As mentioned earlier, this has happened repeatedly throughout history, from the Roman Empire to the early 1970s.

Given this, much of the history of gold prices represents long periods of time in which gold prices are restrained by government decree, followed by sharp upward corrections when the decrees fall apart. This was the case most recently in the late 1960s and early 1970s. Gold prices were fixed at $35 per ounce from 1933 until 1968, with the exception of a period of time during World War II when gold prices on the international market fluctuated. By the late 1960s, the dollar-gold international currency regime created at the end of World War II had built up unsupportable disequilibrium, and the U.S. government was forced by market forces to abandon its efforts to keep gold priced at $35 per ounce. The price was floated in the private market in 1968, and then in the intergovernmental market used by central banks in 1971.

Gold prices rose sharply after that, as shown in Figure 7.2. Partly this was catch-up after decades of prices fixed by government decree. Partly it reflected the economic and political messes of the 1970s. Gold prices rose to $183 in December 1974, on the eve of the lifting of the 1933 restrictions against American citizens owning gold. Prices fell back over the next two years, but then rose to $850 as economic, financial, and political conditions deteriorated sharply in 1978 through 1980. Prices declined again after that and spent most of the period from 1984 through 1997 between $320 and $500 per ounce. Prices slumped in late 1997, and entered a five-year period in which gold traded between $250 and $300 for most of the time. Prices began rising again in 2001, as economic, financial, and political conditions worsened once again.

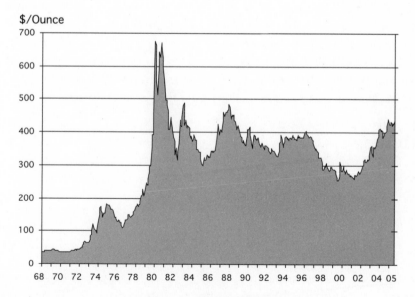

Figure 7.2 **The Price of Gold**

Investment Demand Drives Gold Prices

Comprehending the relative size of the gold derivatives market and the reasons why is is so large is critical to understanding the differences between gold and silver, on the one hand, and other commodities. The ratios are direct evidence that gold and silver are financial assets as well as commodities. In the years 1999 to 2002, many people felt the gold market was dead, that investors no longer would be interested in gold. We begged to differ. Gold still traded like a financial asset, even during the period of low prices. Its price was higher than it would have been had gold become "merely a commodity," as the gloomy crowd claimed. Even at its low, around $252 per ounce, gold prices were much higher than this metal's supply and demand fundamentals would have supported, had it not been for investors buying gold.

Gold prices are determined largely by investment buying patterns. Figure 7.3 tracks this relationship from 1966 to early 2005. When investors want to buy a lot of gold, they tend to drive the price higher. When they want less gold, the price tends to fall. Mine production trends, central bank sales, fabrication demand, and other factors also influence gold prices, but the most important factor by a wide margin is investment demand.

Investment demand on a global basis is almost always positive. That is, in all but three years since 1965 investors have been net buyers or accumulators of gold on a worldwide basis. It is very rare that investors are net sellers of gold in any given year. When investors are bearish on gold, they buy less gold. This reflects the fact that there are so many investors who buy gold, and that they have so many differing reasons for buying it.

We tend to say that investors buy gold for six basic reasons:

1. Inflation hedge
2. Currency hedge
3. Portfolio diversifier
4. Safe haven
5. Commodity
6. Form of savings

Different investors buy gold for different reasons. Also, they are spread out all over the world. Thus, there have been years, such as in the late 1990s, when most investors in most parts of the world did not want gold. Inflation was low; the dollar was rising and strong; stocks and bonds were attractive as investments; the world's financial markets had been lulled into a strong, albeit false, sense of stability and security; and gold's supply and demand were not particularly compelling, with steadily rising supply, heavy volumes of central bank sales, and modest growth in fabrication demand. Even so, there were some investors somewhere buying gold. If all else was letting gold down, there were still those investors in Asia and the Middle East who were buying gold as a form of savings, not comfortable with the idea of putting their money either in national banks or in their domestic stock markets.

At other times more than one of these factors is stimulating investor interest in gold. In the late 1980s there was a period when inflation was low but the dollar was falling. Investors who saw gold as an inflation hedge were not buying gold, while those who swore that gold traded against the dollar were buying gold. Prices rose at a relatively modest pace.

Sometimes all of the factors that trigger gold investment buying have been flashing red. This is what happened in 1979 through 1980, when inflation was running at 14 percent, interest rates were 21 percent, U.S. hostages were in Iran, Soviet troops were invading Afghanistan, the stock market stunk, the dollar had been weak for several years, oil prices had quadrupled for the second time in a decade, and the world was headed into its worst recession since the Great Depression. In this environment investors poured their money into gold, and the price rose from $200 to $850.

In 2003 through 2005 all of the factors that stimulate investor interest in gold were once again positive for gold investors. Things were not as bad as they had been in 1979 and 1980, but they were the worst they had been since that time. In this environment, investors poured into gold once more, pushing the price of gold from around $260 to $500.

Figure 7.3 shows that the difference between rising and falling gold prices tends to be the difference between years in which investors are buying more than 20 million ounces of gold and years when they buy less than that. Since gold prices were freed in 1968, there have been six periods in which the economic, financial, and political factors that flavor investor attitudes toward gold were stimulating keen interest in this metal. In the first five episodes, the period of strong investor demand, characterized as net annual investor demand for gold of more than 20 million ounces, lasted one or two years.

The sixth episode, the current one, turned five in 2005. Never in the history of mankind have so many investors put so much money into buying so much gold over such an extended period of time. Investors have

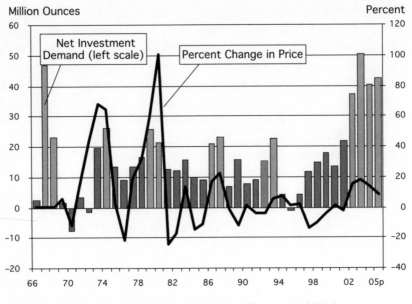

Figure 7.3 **Investment Demand's Effect on Gold Prices**

purchased roughly 200 million ounces of gold on a net basis and added this to their long-term physical gold holdings since 2000.

Democratization of Gold Ownership

One of the interesting developments in the gold market is that there has been a long-term shift in gold ownership away from governments toward individual investors. Around the end of 2005 it appears that the amount of gold owned by private investors exceeded the amount of gold owned by governments for the first time in the history of mankind. (See Figure 7.4.) Central banks have sold some of their gold over the past four decades, although the extent of these sales has been grossly misunderstood and exaggerated in the market, as I discuss later. Meanwhile, investors have bought roughly three times as much gold as central banks have sold since the middle of the 1960s. This shift reflects a much broader shift in ownership of a wide range of assets away from governments toward private individuals, corporations, and investment management companies.

Central banks used to own gold for several reasons. One was that it was a monetary asset. As the center of the international foreign exchange system, gold was used to settle trade balances among nations. If the United

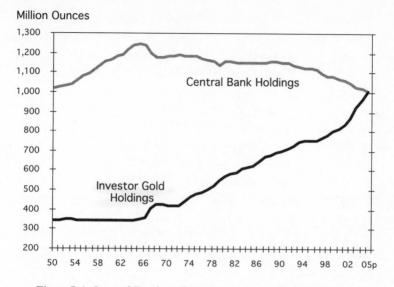

Figure 7.4 **Central Bank and Private Investor Gold Holdings**

States was importing more goods from Germany than it was shipping to Germany, for example, the Germans would deposit their dollars with their domestic banks, which would aggregate the dollars with the Bundesbank. The Bundesbank then would deliver the dollars to the U.S. Treasury, and take gold in exchange. This was one of gold's primary monetary roles, a job it has not fulfilled since 1971.

> *One of the interesting developments in the gold market is that there has been a long-term shift in gold ownership away from governments toward individual investors.*

Central bank gold peaked around 1.3 billion ounces in the early 1960s. Around 1964 private individuals—those few who could legally own gold back then—began turning in dollars for gold. There was a run on central bank gold, primarily the gold held by the U.S. Treasury. In April 1968 the U.S. government closed what was called the private gold window, through which individuals could exchange their dollars for gold. The Treasury continued to trade gold for dollars with other central banks, however, so the drain on U.S. gold reserves continued until Nixon closed the official gold window in August 1971. Since that time, central bank gold reserves have declined steadily. Central banks as a group have been net sellers in most of the years since the middle of the 1960s. The pace of sales quickened after 1989, as those European central banks that were opt-ing into the European Central Bank (ECB) system moved to sell the gold they wanted to sell before the ECB began operations in 1999. After 1999 the Bank of England and the Swiss National Bank, both of which had opted out of the ECB, sold some of their gold.

By 2005 it appeared that central banks had sold most of what they wanted to sell, and it was expected that sales would decline sharply, perhaps as early as 2006.

As I mentioned earlier, the extent of central bank gold sales has been overemphasized by many market participants. The decline in central bank sales, on the order of 235 million ounces since 1965, has been relatively small compared to total central bank holdings. Central banks still own around 81 percent of the gold they held during the dollar-gold interna-tional currency regime. The market has focused on central banks sales, but in fact central banks have not sold most of their gold and do not appear to want to sell it. Meanwhile, the value of their gold holdings has risen from $35 per ounce in 1965, when the selling started, to $500 in late 2005. The value of the banks' gold holdings far exceeds what it was at its peak in vol-ume 40 years earlier.

Much more dramatic and important is the fact that private investors have roughly tripled the amount of gold bullion they own, from around 347 million ounces in 1965 to around 998 million ounces of gold in 2005. Private investors have bought not only the equivalent of the gold sold by central banks during the past 40 years, but nearly three times as much gold as that, and have added it to their long-term holdings on a net basis.

Private sector holdings were relatively flat from 1950 until around 1965, reflecting the fact that during that period most people in the world were not legally allowed to own gold. Some did, but laws either prevented or discour-aged it. In the middle of the 1960s, gold market deregulation began, first in parts of Europe. It spread to the United States in 1975; then to Japan, where imports and exports were prohibited until the late 1970s; then to India, in the late 1980s and early 1990s; and to China around five years ago.

I wrote a speech in the early 1980s for a meeting of the New York chapter of the Society of Mining Engineers in which I discussed the "de-mocratization of the gold market." I was referring to the opening of gold markets to private investors around the world and the shift of gold owner-ship from governments to people. As of 2005, it seems the balance has tipped to the private sector.

George Milling-Stanley of the World Gold Council made a very poignant comment at the "Future of Gold II" roundtable we organized for the International Precious Metals Institute in June 2005. Mr. Milling-Stanley made the point that "in 1845 there were two central banks in the world, one in England and one in France, and they collectively owned something like 40 metric tons of gold (1.28 million ounces). A little over 100 years later, there were 120 central banks, and they owned 1,000 times that 40 metric tons." He went on to explain that he did not "regret the fact that some central banks are comfortable in selling some of their gold. I like to see gold go from hands that don't seem to want as much as they have to hands that seem to want a lot more than they have. If gold is going from governments that are starting to get a little shaky about owning gold into the private sector, which seems to be buying it with increasing confidence, whether for jewelry or as an investment, I am actually happy to see that kind of development. I think that is very important." ("The Future of Gold II" proceedings are available at the IPMI's web site, www.ipmi.org and at CPM Group's site, www.cpmgroup.com.)

Fact and Fiction in Gold

Unlike most other investments, including stocks, bonds, and commodities, gold is something that many people believe in. Some investors believe adamantly, if not violently, that gold is solely an inflation hedge and nothing more. Others feel that gold trades against the dollar, simply and purely. Never mind that both of these beliefs are quantitatively wrong, and that even the most cursory analysis will show this.

Perhaps the most bitterly ironic aspect of the beliefs that swirl around gold relates to a landmark book titled *The Golden Constant* (New York: John Wiley & Sons, 1977). The great statistical economist Roy Jastram produced this book, which reviewed the purchasing power of gold in England and the United States over several centuries. His quantitatively showed that gold in fact did not preserve purchasing powers, the way many people believe. Gold is good at protecting one's wealth against catastrophic inflation and major financial disruptions. Historically gold has not done well in protecting purchasing power against the slow drip of nagging inflation that corrodes purchasing power over time. This partly reflects the fact that gold prices historically have been set by governments for extended periods of time on a nominal basis, so that the real or inflation-adjusted value of gold has deteriorated slowly until such time as the system breaks. Regardless, the point of the book was that the concept of a "golden constant" in terms of gold's ability to preserve purchasing power and protect against inflation is a myth. Even so, many people know of the book but apparently have never read it, because gold market pundits and others often refer to Dr. Jastram's book reverentially, while misrepresenting its conclusions.

There are many other myths about gold's purchasing power. One has it that a Ford mustang could be bought for the same number of ounces of gold in the late 1960s as today. Another was that an ounce of gold could purchase a good meal for two at the River Room restaurant in London's Savoy Hotel in both 1917 and 1977. There are many more, using men's suits and all sorts of other numerators. I obtained a series of historical menus from the River Room. It is true that an ounce of gold could purchase a meal for two in 1917 and 1977. It is also true that in between those two dates the purchasing power of an ounce of gold in the River Room ranged from less than one meal to a banquet for 17. The proponents of the concept of a golden constant picked two points in time and drew a line between the two, ignoring the extreme volatility in between.

My friend David Nelson, who worked for Dean Witter and later Carr Futures, used to introduce me to people as the world's foremost authority on iridium. I asked him why. He said, "If I introduced you as the foremost authority on gold, people would constantly be picking fights with you. Everyone thinks they know all they need to about gold. Everyone is an authority on gold, even if everything they know is wrong."

That is true. There are too many myths and conspiracy theories related to gold to cover here—they would fill at least one book. Suffice it to say that I have never seen any concrete evidence of a conspiracy to manipulate gold prices, not on the part of governments, central banks, or bullion banks. Gold conspiracy theories go back at least to ancient Rome (when some of them proved to be true), and probably even further back.

Some people, it seems, need to believe that the world is stacked against them. Others have been long and wrong, and, unable to admit to themselves that they were wrong in their analysis, conclude that there must be a conspiracy, something they did not see, that caused them to be wrong. Others clearly have realized that there is a market for newsletters and organizations that cater to conspiracy theorists, and that it is much easier to make a living feeding off of these fears and suspicions than it is to

Gold conspiracy theories go back at least to ancient Rome (when some of them proved to be true), and probably even further back.

invest in commodities. One of the most infamous movements to prove a gold conspiracy indeed started off as a group of investors who had been long and wrong and decided to use the U.S. judicial system to fish for information about how bullion banks and others trade gold, in the hope of finding, through the legal discovery process, what they had missed. When they realized that investors and others would pay them to pursue this, their efforts became a business.

In the early 1990s the newsletter of one of the gold conspiracy theorists was circulating in South Africa, getting an undue amount of attention from gold mining industry executives. The letter had talked about the usual irrefutable if nonexistent evidence that the Federal Reserve Board was buying and selling gold to manipulate the price of gold. These mining executives are normally exceedingly sober and straightforward people. I asked one why he would think that the U.S. central bank would bother to undertake these measures, and he replied, "Our central bank does these sorts of things all the time. Why shouldn't yours?"

Another gold myth has it that the price of gold rose sharply in March 1993 after George Soros and Sir James Goldsmith held a press conference at which both said how bullish they were about gold and how they both had bought gold assets. There are gold bugs who swear this is the case, saying they remember the press conference. Such a press conference never occurred. What happened was as follows. Sir James had bought around 49 percent of Newmont Mining from Hanson Trust in the early 1990s. Hanson had taken over Consolidated Gold Fields (Consgold), which owned Newmont and several other companies. Interestingly, Lord Hanson was not interested in Consgold for its gold mining operations, but rather for its gravel operations, Amy Roadstones. Hanson Trust proceeded to dispose of most of the gold assets. Lord Hanson swapped Hanson's Newmont shares with Sir James in exchange for some Canadian timber resources. Sir James was bullish on gold at the time, and felt Newmont was a good way to invest in gold. Over the next couple of years he came to feel that he wanted a different form of exposure to rising gold prices.

Soros Funds, meanwhile, in late 1992 began to turn bullish on gold, building a position in futures and options, and possibly physical gold. In early 1993, after gold prices had started their upward move, Soros swapped some of its gold positions with Sir James in exchange for his Newmont shares. Because this included the change in ownership of 49 percent of a U.S. publicly traded company, the transaction had to be reported to the SEC. The proper forms were duly filed. A *Wall Street Journal* reporter whose task it was to review the daily SEC filings for interesting news ran across the filing, did some research, and wrote a report about the transaction. The parties confirmed the transaction but did not provide any additional information on the trade. Other business publications picked up on the story. That was the end of it. However, today you will find innumerable gold bugs who speak about the Soros-Goldsmith press conference that touched off the 1993 rally in gold prices as if it were a fact.

Official Transactions

I want to return to central bank sales because, looking into the future, one of the most important and potentially bullish factors facing the gold market is a fact I mentioned almost in passing earlier: Central banks have sold most of the gold they wish to sell. While central banks still own roughly one billion ounces of gold, most of what they wanted to sell has been sold, and most of what is left is gold that they would like to keep.

Figure 7.5 shows how central banks have been net sellers of gold for most of the years since 1965. There were some purchases in the late 1960s and early 1970s, as the dollar-gold system collapsed. There were also a few

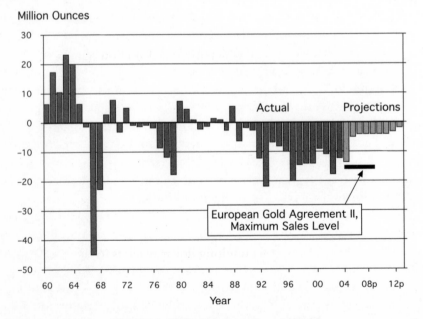

Figure 7.5 **Official Transactions of Gold**

purchases later, around the early 1980s, as oil exporting countries sterilized the massive inflows of U.S. dollars they were experiencing, converting some of their dollar receipts for the higher-priced oil into gold. In the late 1980s the Bank of China in Taiwan also bought a lot of gold, at a time when Taiwan was running massive trade surpluses with the United States, was facing political hostility in the United States because of this, and was watching the dollar fall. The dollar declined from first quarter 1985 through 1987. Toward the end of this period the Taiwanese central bank converted some of its dollars into gold. It proved to be at the top of the gold market and the bottom of the dollar's decline. This was a large political embarrassment. More important, it was an embarrassment witnessed by central bank managers around the world, especially in Asia. As a result of this, and of much more substantive research they have conducted into whether they should want to add gold to their monetary reserves, Asian central banks have shunned the idea of doing so, despite numerous rumors to the contrary in the North American and European gold markets.

Apart from these purchases, central banks have been primarily sellers of gold over the past 40 years. In fact, since the late 1980s the official sector has become a critically important source of physical gold for the market, supplying roughly 14 million ounces per year on average during this time. Most of this gold came from the central banks of Europe, which held large amounts of gold as a residual from the old gold standard days prior to 1971. Canada, Australia, and several other central banks have sold gold as well. The United States, which owns 261 million ounces of the remaining billion ounces in central bank coffers, has not sold any gold since the late 1970s.

Meanwhile, as previously explained, much of the gold held by central banks that they wanted to sell has now been sold. Many central banks, such as those of England and Switzerland, have sold half of the gold that they held at the end of the gold standards. Others, notably the central banks of Germany, Italy, and France, have not sold any, or have sold very little. The German central bank, the Bundesbank, has considered selling gold but has only sold small amounts to date. There is a dispute between the bankers and politicians. The politicians would like the Bundesbank to sell some gold and transfer the resulting dollar receipts to the government for use in reducing its budget deficits. The Bundesbank thinks any proceeds from its gold sales should remain in its foreign exchange reserves. The Banque de France meanwhile avowed it did not want to sell any gold for years, until 2004. In 2004 it announced that it would sell some gold in order to provide some liquidity to the gold market. It has been selling gold since September 2004.

Even taking into account the sales plans of the Banque de France and others, it seems likely that in the future, central bank gold sales will decline from the 14 million ounces per year of the past 16 years or so, possibly to around 5 to 7 million ounces per year. The market largely expects gold sales to be roughly in line with the maximum level of sales set by the European central banks in their 2004 agreement for the years from 2005 through 2009, which is 16.1 million ounces per year. Actual sales may fall quite a bit short of that, however.

This is important for the gold market, since the flow of gold from central banks has been a major source of physical metal for jewelers and investors over the past two decades. The potential decline in central bank gold sales is one of the most bullish fundamental factors for gold prices over the next few years. Other sectors of the physical gold market, reviewed in the following sections, are less bullish for prices.

Supply

Gold supply consists of mine production and secondary supply—metal recovered from scrap. We include a third line item in our gold balance sheet: Net exports from the so-called "transitional economies." This is the net amount of gold coming into the international market from China, Russia, the other former Soviet republics, and other nonmarket states. We do this because the amount of gold being used in fabricated products and bought by investors in these countries cannot accurately be estimated, and to include mine production for these countries but not scrap refining, fabrication demand, and investment demand would skew the world statistical portrait of supply and demand. So we keep them segregated for now. Another form of supply is net sales from central banks. We separate this from other supply as well, since this represents sales of gold from inventories, as opposed to relatively recently mined or refined metal. It is a stock flow, as opposed to the result of a manufacturing process.

Total supply of physical gold, as so defined, was around 108.4 million ounces in 2005. This was down from a peak of 111.4 million ounces in 2003, before the years of low gold prices started decaying world mine output sharply. This contrasts with annual total supply on the order of 50 million ounces per year in the late 1970s and early 1980s. In other words, the gold market is double the size it was a quarter century ago, when gold prices rose sharply to $850.

That is important to note, since it explains in part why investors today could be buying so much more gold compared to what they purchased in the past, yet the price has risen only to $500. Investor buying of less than half as much gold a quarter-century ago as in the past five years caused gold prices to rise roughly fourfold. Much greater levels of demand for physical metal since 2001 have caused prices to double.

Of this total supply, around 62.3 to 63.0 million ounces of gold came from newly mined output in 2005. This was up between 0.5 percent and 1.5 percent from the year before. Many gold market observers had assumed that mine production was falling in 2005, continuing a trend that had begun in 2000. In fact, mine production already was rising. Production was down sharply in South Africa, still the world's largest producer, while it also fell in the United States and Canada. Since most of the largest gold mining companies in the world are headquartered in these countries, a great deal of attention is paid to output in these nations.

> *Investor buying of less than half as much gold a quarter-century ago as in the past five years caused gold prices to rise roughly fourfold. Much greater levels of demand for physical metal since 2001 have caused prices to double.*

However, production was rising, sharply in some cases, in other countries in 2005. Production rose nearly 10 percent in Peru, which nowadays produces more gold than Canada. Output was also rising in Australia, which was producing at a higher annual rate than the United States in 2004 and 2005. Production was expanding in numerous countries, from Tanzania, Mali, Burkina Faso, and Ghana to Indonesia and other Asian nations. In many cases the production that is coming online in these countries is at lower-cost mining operations than the mines that are cutting back or closing in the older mining centers of North America and South Africa.

Previously, mine production had been falling. It dropped from 68.7 million ounces in 1999 to 62.1 million ounces in 2004. This was the direct result of the fact that gold prices had traded in a very low range of $250 to $300 for most of the time from late 1997 through 2002. At such low prices mining companies had difficulty justifying continuing production at a number of higher-cost mines, much less spending a lot of money on exploration and development of new mines. Some new mines were brought into production during this time, but mostly these were mines with very low operating costs.

As gold prices began rising after 2002, mining companies began reviving their operations. Their market capitalization rose, allowing them to raise funds through both equity and debt issues. They more than tripled their exploration expenditures between 2002 and 2005, and dusted off a number of expansion plans and new mine development programs that had been put on hold during the period of lower prices. As a result, by 2004 and 2005, several dozen new mines or expansions were under development, which collectively were slated to boost world gold mining capacity by roughly 20 to 25 percent from 2004 to 2010.

One ironic sideline to this was that even as all of this was occurring, the gold bulls kept saying that gold production would continue to fall sharply, because gold prices, even at $500, were too low to justify new gold mine developments. The mining companies meanwhile were trumpeting their plans. These are good things that mining companies want to broadcast to the world of investors, to show them how well they are being managed and to encourage investing in their shares. However, you could attend a gold mining conference throughout 2004 and 2005 and listen to a steady stream of gold mining executives all preaching the same gospel: Gold mine production on a global basis would have to continue to fall, because there is not enough money going into exploration and development . . . except at *our* mines. You could hear eight mining companies all deliver the same message. A few analysts in the audience would add up the expansions each one said it was undertaking, and they would see the potential for another 15 to 20 million ounces of annual mining capacity to come online over the next few years. Yet a surprisingly large portion of the audience would come away believing that gold mine production would fall sharply.

Over the next few years there are in fact many million ounces of gold mining capacity slated to come online. This does not necessarily mean that gold prices will fall sharply, but the increased supply should be expected to restrain gold prices to some extent. Partly because of the expected sharp decline in central bank sales, the increases in mine production may be more of an offset to the reduction in gold coming into the market from government disposals.

Another 20 million ounces or so of gold comes into the international market from mine and scrap production in China, Russia, Uzbekistan, Kazakhstan, and other countries listed as transitional economies. On top of that, around 20 million ounces more comes into the market each year from scrap—primarily old jewelry but also obsolete electronics, dental alloys, and other gold-bearing scrap. Scrap recovery, especially from jewelry, is extremely price sensitive and rose sharply from 2003 through 2005, reflecting people selling their gold jewelry for the gold content. This is a particularly common practice throughout Asia, including China and India, and in the Middle East, where jewelry is a form of savings and has a low price markup relative to its gold content.

Figure 7.6 shows that total supply has been moving in a volatile sideways pattern over the past few years, after rising sharply for the past two decades. This reflects the fact that while mine production was declining, the drop was offset by high central bank sales, rising secondary recovery of gold from scrap, and rising output and exports from China, Russia, and various central Asian republics.

Fabrication Demand

Figure 7.6 also shows that gold fabrication demand, most of which goes into jewelry, has been declining sharply since 2000. This reflects the effects of higher gold prices. Jewelry demand is highly price elastic. When gold prices rise, jewelers start using less gold per piece of jewelry. In markets

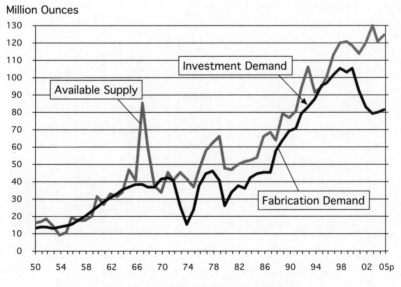

Figure 7.6 **Gold Supply and Demand**

where gold jewelry is sold at close to its gold price, consumers pull back from purchasing gold. In these same markets, consumers also step up sales of old gold jewelry for its gold content, some of which is directly reused by jewelers, reducing their purchases in the market of newly refined gold.

For all of these reasons, jewelry demand has fallen sharply since 2000. This is in contrast to the rosy statements made by some gold promotional agencies. Nevertheless, it is true. Again, it is basic economic laws of supply, demand, and price in action. In addition to the effect of the higher prices in restraining demand, there also was some reduction in jewelry demand in the early 2000s due to the recessionary economic conditions that hit large parts of the world.

While we are on the topic of gold use in jewelry, let me show you another chart that puts to rest another misconception about gold (see Figure 7.7). It was said in 2005 that gold jewelry no longer is an important source of demand for gold, and that gold use in jewelry had fallen to such low levels that the U.S. government even stopped collecting data on the subject in the middle of the 1990s.

That is not true. Gold jewelry use totaled around 71 million ounces in 2005. It represents the lion's share of gold use every year and provides the

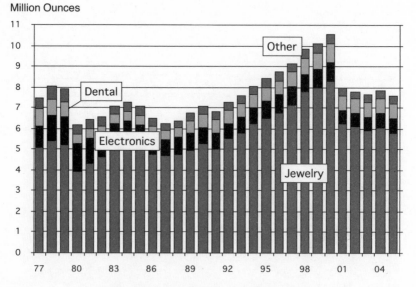

Figure 7.7 **Annual U.S. Gold Demand**

stable floor of gold demand on top of which investment demand dances in a more volatile fashion.

Gold jewelry demand meanwhile continues to rise. As is evident in Figure 7.7, although gold use in jewelry manufacturing declined sharply in 2001, gold use in jewelry still absorbs nearly six million ounces of gold in this country. Much more gold jewelry is manufactured abroad and sold in the United States. Jewelry use of gold actually rose at a steady and sharp pace from the late 1980s through 2000, even though U.S. manufacturing was losing market share to imported jewelry. Overall, American consumers have continued to spend more money on gold jewelry, and to use more metal.

What happened in the middle of the 1990s had nothing to do with actual demand trends in the United States. When the first Clinton administration took office in 1993, Vice President Al Gore was put in charge of a task to find at least one federal bureau that could be liquidated, to show that the Clinton Administration was determined to restrain the inexorable growth of the government bureaucracy. The Bureau of Mines, part of the Department of the Interior, was tipped to be the sacrificial bureau. The Bureau of Mines had run a program of voluntary surveys of metals consumption with U.S. manufacturers for decades. The program was not great, but it did provide a lot of valuable data and information. When the Interior Department liquidated the Bureau of Mines, parts of its operations were shifted to the U.S. Geological Survey and other parts of Interior. The voluntary surveys of demand were ended.

> *Overall, American consumers have continued to spend more money on gold jewelry, and to use more metal.*

The ending of the U.S. government's statistical series on the use of gold and other metals had nothing to do with trends in these markets, but merely reflected this political hatchet work on the Bureau of Mines. However, it stands as a very good example of how bad analysis of a development can lead to basic market fundamentals being entirely misrepresented.

How to Invest

As previously mentioned, gold is a relatively small part of the overall physical commodities market but the largest part of the commodities investment pool. This means that there are a lot more ways to invest in gold than

there are in other commodities, and a lot greater liquidity in gold investments than in comparable commodities-oriented investment sectors.

Gold is purchased in the forms of gold bullion coins, numismatic coins,
bars, ingots, and other bullion forms. It is purchased in futures, options,
over-the-counter forwards, and other derivatives. The recently created gold
exchange traded funds also provide interesting ways to invest in gold.

Many investors never purchase gold per se, but invest in gold mining
equities or mutual funds that specialize in gold, precious metals, or natural
resources. The average gold mining stock has a beta to gold prices of
around 3.0, meaning that the average mining share rises or falls about three
times as much as gold prices do. As a result, some investors prefer gold
shares, as they give greater leverage to gold price changes than do bullion,
coins, and exchange traded funds.

Silver

Silver, like gold, is both a commodity and a financial asset. It shares many
characteristics with gold. Like its wealthier cousin, silver was used as a
form of money for much of the past five millennia. Silver behaves more
like a financial asset than it does a commodity. A tremendous amount of
silver trades every day, far in excess of what one would expect based on
fundamentals of supply and demand. Silver trading in the London interbank market totals around 25 to 30 billion ounces per year, or 50 to 150
million ounces per day. Another 30 billion ounces of silver trades across the
New York Comex silver futures and options contracts each year. These
volumes compare to annual new supply and fabrication demand of less
than one billion ounces per year. These numbers, as astounding as they are,
are way off from the late 1990s. When the London Bullion Market Association began publishing its clearing volumes in late 1996 and early 1997,
more than 74 billion ounces per year were clearing through London
banks. Such volumes are characteristic of a financial asset, not a simple
commodity.

Silver's price is extremely volatile (see Figure 7.8). Some people call
silver the poor person's gold. I disagree. Others more accurately see silver
as a "high octane" gold, in that silver's price tends to outpace gold in percentage terms. That said, the two metals prices move only partially in tan-
dem with each other. People talk about the gold–silver ratio and base
their trades on it, which is a formula for losing money. The ratio has

$/Ounce

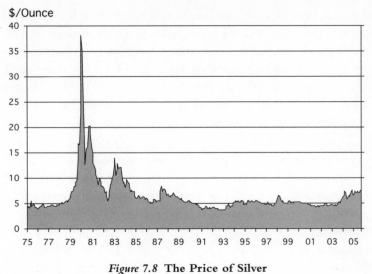

Figure 7.8 **The Price of Silver**

ranged from 16:1 to 100:1 over the past three decades. It is an excellent barometer of the relative value of each metal, one against the other, but there is no law of physics, chemistry, nature, or man that says the ratio ought to be anything in particular. Some people look at the average price ratio of these two metals and assume that sooner or later the ratio must revert toward its long-term average. That is not the case—there is no reason that should happen.

Silver prices rise when supply and demand would send the price of a more typical commodity lower, and fall when market observers think it ought to be rising. The man who amassed the largest stockpile of silver not held by a government—not anyone you would think—once said

Some people call silver the poor person's gold. I disagree.

that silver makes a fool out of everyone who touches it, bull or bear. Whatever you think you know about silver, you do not know enough to accurately call this metal's price patterns on a consistent basis over the long run. Thomas Mohide, one of the premier minerals economists, felt he met his match when he tried to pull together a compendium of silver market information and make sense of it. His tome, *The International Silver Trade* (Cambridge, England: Woodhead Publishing Limited, 1992), remains one of the best sources for basic information and historical background on silver.

Like gold, silver has a lot of true believers who think they understand this market, ascribe all sorts of unattainable attributes to silver, and then say there must be a conspiracy to control silver prices when silver does not live up to their outrageous and irrational expectations. Yes, there are silver market conspiracy theories. At one point I learned that I was considered simultaneously a member of one conspiracy to drive silver prices lower and another conspiracy seeking to drive silver prices higher. Perhaps unfortunately for my bottom line, I was oblivious to both conspiracies.

There are billions of ounces of silver existing in the world which have been mined through history, and a large amount of it is still around. In this way also, silver is like gold. Mine production of silver since the dawn of man may have brought around 42 billion ounces of silver out of the ground. The vast majority of this has been mined in the past century. About 6 billion of it has been mined in the past 15 years alone.

Of this total, perhaps 21 billion ounces can be identified. Around half a billion ounces is in bullion bar form, including the market standard 1,000-ounce bars and the smaller 100-ounce bars preferred by smaller investors. Another half billion ounces exists in coin form. Around 20 billion are in the form of jewelry, silverware, sterling objects, religious objects, and art. The remaining 21 billion ounces have been used in products from which it has not been reclaimed, or is otherwise lost. Since silver traditionally is less valuable than gold, there is a lower degree of recycling of silver than there is of gold. Even though there are regulations against discharging silver-bearing spent photographic developing solutions in many parts of the world, for example, it is obvious that enormous volumes of these solutions are simply flushed into wastewater systems.

The silver market has been susceptible to large investors making significant price impacts. (See Figure 7.9.) This reflects the relatively small size of the silver market. The dollar value of the silver market is much smaller than that of the gold market, and is utterly dwarfed by the size of overall financial markets. In the middle of the 1990s Berkshire Hathaway studied the silver market and concluded it would be a good place in which to invest. Berkshire Hathaway is an equity- and bond-oriented company and does not typically invest in commodities. At the time, from 1996 to 1997, it had around $35 billion under management, so a silver position, to be significant enough to its portfolio, would have needed to be around $750 million. That was larger than the market capitalization of all silver mining companies then in existence in the world. In other words, for Berkshire Hathaway to have been able to build a silver equity

$/Ounce

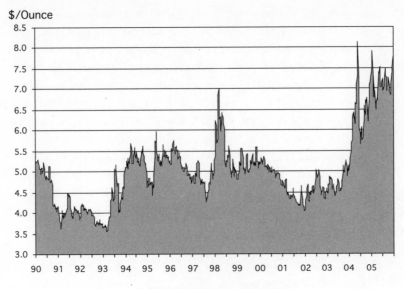

Figure 7.9 **Weekly Average Silver Prices**

position large enough to matter to it, it would have had to buy every share of every silver mining company, obviously an untenable approach. Intrigued by silver, the company decided to buy silver bullion. It further decided to buy the silver, take delivery of it, and hold it away from the major market participants.

Berkshire Hathaway is only the most recent and one of the most prominent silver investors. The silver market also saw the Hunt brothers invest in silver in the late 1970s. Others were involved in other periods as well. Several prominent investors have built sizable silver market positions at time, including the person to whom I referred above, whom I am not at liberty to identify.

One of the myths that has been accepted as biblical truth in the silver market is that the Hunt brothers, Nelson and Herbert, tried to corner the silver market in the 1970s. I had some contact with them at that time, and was plugged into other parts of the silver market. I never saw the Hunts try to corner the silver market, and I am willing to bet that is not what they were trying to do. What I saw was the Hunts buying a lot of silver. They seemed to think that the silver market was ready to see a sharp increase in prices, and they wanted to ride that wave. At some point, they had a really nice position established. They started telling everyone, from wealthy Arab sheiks and Brazilian magnates to brokers that dealt with smaller investors, what a great investment silver was. Silver prices were destined to rise, they told everyone. "We have loaded up on silver, and so should you." The basic story they had about silver, that supply and demand imbalances were likely to drive prices sharply higher, was based on reality; it was true, real, and honest. I am convinced, from what they said at the time and from everything that I saw, that the Hunts intended to establish a large silver position and then ride a wave. They may have helped create the wave, but they believed it was coming regardless of anything they would do or say.

A study conducted by an economist after the fact concluded that the Hunt's silver buying activity added very little to the price of silver, suggesting that the increase in silver prices from around $5 to $50 in late 1979 and early 1980 was due to other factors, coming as it did at the same time oil prices quadrupled, gold rose from $200 to $850, and platinum went from $340 to $1,040. This econometric study concluded that the Hunts had not done much to the price of silver.

This actually makes intuitive sense. Prices of a wide range of commodities were rising at the time, and not just the ones I mentioned in the previous paragraph. It was a dreadful time, as I described earlier, with 14 percent inflation, 21 percent interest rates, U.S. hostages in Iran, Soviet troops in Afghanistan, and Iranian and Soviet assets frozen worldwide. There was a wide range of equally ugly economic, financial market, and political problems. There were no easy ways for most investors around the world to hedge their exposure to stocks, bonds, and currencies. There were no currency options at the time, and no stock index options or futures. The only two readily available ways to protect oneself financially from all of this was to buy gold or silver.

Supply

Silver is mined in dozens of countries worldwide. Much of the silver mined in the world is produced in polymetallic mines, along with lead, zinc, copper, gold, and sometimes all sorts of other metals from bismuth and cadmium to tellurium and selenium. Around four-fifths of the silver mined in the world comes from mines at which silver is not the primary product.

Mexico traditionally has been the largest silver mining country. It has been producing close to 100 million ounces of silver per year since 2001.

Peru was an important producer, but as recently as the late 1990s was producing around 60 million ounces per year. Peruvian output has risen sharply since then, however, and now may be slightly larger than Mexican production. Other large silver mining countries include the United States, Canada, and Australia.

In total around 530 million ounces of silver is produced annually at mines in the market economy nations at present. China, Kazakhstan, and other countries also produce silver, but getting accurate counts of production has been slower to occur. It is occurring now, and better data are forthcoming.

China has become a major refiner of silver, both from domestic ores and from mining concentrates imported for their lead, zinc, and copper content. As China has developed economically over the past decade, it has taken a major role in the world as a refiner of these base metals. Much of the base metal concentrates that China imports from Indonesia, Peru, Mexico, Canada, and other countries has by-product gold and silver in it. Since China has more gold and silver than its domestic fabricators and investors want, the gold and silver has been exported and sold in Zurich, London, Saudi Arabia, India, and other countries. Additional amounts of silver have come from scrap, including old silver jewelry and foreign silver coins that were used as currency prior to the Communist revolution in 1949. Some people have misidentified these silver exports as coming from government stocks. Others have double-counted the metal, measuring silver content in mine production in various countries, and then adding silver exports from China onto these totals to come up with estimates of how much silver is coming into the market.

In addition to the 530 million ounces being refined from mine production, another 230 million ounces or so are refined from scrapped fabricated products each year. Some of this is jewelry and silverware, especially in India, Pakistan, and other Asian nations. The largest portion, however, is from spent photographic materials. I mentioned earlier that a lot of spent photographic developer solutions are believed to be illegally flushed into sewer systems. Even so, a tremendous amount of silver is recovered from photographic papers, films, and solutions. As much as 80 percent of the 230 million ounces of silver that is refined from scrap each year may come from photographic materials. There also are several million ounces of silver recovered from old electronics each year. A lot of other silver products do not get recycled, or get reprocessed in closed loops by the consuming companies. For example, silver is used as a catalyst in the manufacture of ethylene oxide, a basic plastic feedstock. These catalysts get recycled every so often, but the ownership of the silver does not change hands.

Demand

Around 800 million ounces of silver is used in fabricated products each year at present. Silver use in photographic papers and films formerly was the largest single end use, but silver use in photography has declined steadily since 1999 as digital imaging has made inroads into picture taking.

Silver use in jewelry and silverware has supplanted photography as the major end use. In reality, both photography and jewelry represent very broad ranges of uses. Silver use in jewelry and silverware includes higher-markup silver jewelry and sterlingware purchased in Europe, North America, and South Korea as luxury items. It also includes silver given as presents in India, where giving someone a small silver object has been a very common practice for many decades. It also includes silver jewelry with a low mark-up used as a form of savings and a silver investment vehicle in South Asia and the Middle East. Silver use in all of these forms of jewelry and silverware combined came to about 246 million ounces of silver in 2005. This was down from 294 million ounces in 1997, but the pace of decline in silver use in these products has not been as drastic as it has been in photography.

Silver also is used in a wide range of manufactured products. Most people know that silver is used as backing in mirrors. Some know that silver is used in batteries for hearing aids, cameras, calculators, and other small electronic products. It is also used in larger batteries used in torpedoes and other military applications. It is used in brazing alloys and solders, in electronics, in biocides, and in ethylene oxide and other chemical process catalysts.

Silver use appears to be growing as a sheathing in superconductive wire, although good estimates of how much silver is being used in this field are not available. The industry is being very close-mouthed about its silver requirements. Silver use also is growing in biocides, being used on everything from bandages and socks to industrial coatings on ships and seaside buildings. There has been talk about silver chemicals replacing chromated copper arsenate as a wood preservative, but this does not appear likely to happen. There are more efficient and lower-priced copper-based chemicals that do a better job in replacing this chemical, which environmental authorities in various countries around the world are trying to phase out for health reasons.

Market Balance and Outlook

One of the intriguing aspects of the silver market over the past 15 years has been the extended period of market deficits. The silver market's supply and demand tend to shift slowly, as shown in Figure 7.10. Partly this reflects low price sensitivity on both the supply and demand sides of the market. Much of silver supply comes as a by-product of other metals, or from scrap with very low operating costs. As a result, silver supply does not respond quickly or forcefully to changes in silver prices.

On the demand side of the market, much of silver's fabricated usage is highly price insensitive. A one-dollar increase in silver prices raises the price of taking a photograph about one cent. Few people will take fewer pictures because of price

Much of silver supply comes as a by-product of other metals, or from scrap with very low operating costs. As a result, silver supply does not respond quickly or forcefully to changes in silver prices.

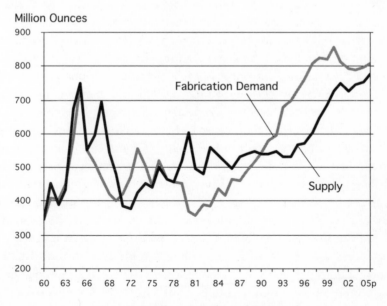

Figure 7.10 **Silver Supply and Demand**

increases in silver. The same is true in many other industrial applications, from silver use in batteries, electronic components and connectors, brazing alloys, and soldiers to silver use in bearings, ethylene oxide catalysts, and mirrors. The one place where price sensitivity is readily visible in the fabrication demand is in silver jewelry and silverware, especially in countries in South Asia and the Middle East where these products sometimes are forms of silver investments and savings.

The other factor that comes into play in the silver price's slow response to market balances is the fact of those 5,000 years of silver inventories. When the silver market moved into a deficit in 1990, I estimate that at least 2.4 billion ounces of silver were lying around in bullion bar form. Several hundred million ounces of silver was around in coin form, and some of the billions of ounces of silver held in jewelry and silverware form also were available to the market should prices start to rise.

As a result of these large inventories, the silver market was able to sustain a current account deficit of newly refined metal entering the market relative to fabrication demand for a long period of time without there being a price response so dramatic as to be noticeable to many in the market. You see this effect of large inventories in other markets, but the period of time is shorter because the inventory levels are smaller. People tend not to hoard copper, lead, coffee, or cocoa the way they do gold and silver. You do not have centuries worth of copper or coffee stacked up in bank vaults and private safes. With silver and gold, you do. So the market was able to move into a deficit in 1990, and the price took nearly 14 years to show any major response. That is an oversimplification, and there were indications as early as 1994 that these inventories were being drawn down. Prices bottomed out at $3.51 in 1991 and $3.52 in 1993, and then rose into a range roughly of $4.40 to $5.80 for many years while stocks were absorbed. The stocks were disappearing. Banks that had run vaulting business started getting out of that business by the late 1990s, because the silver inventories had dwindled to the point where the vaulting operations were no longer profitable. The forward carry in silver contracted sharply during this time, and the market saw a few spikes in prices when suddenly someone needed or wanted physical silver and adequate supplies were not there. So there were indications that the market indeed was operating in a current account deficit, and that stocks were falling steadily. It took until late 2003 for these bullion inventories to drop to levels low enough that prices started to more fully respond to tight silver supplies.

In the late 1980s I did a large amount of consulting work for Sunshine

Mining, which was one of the three largest silver mining companies in the United States at the time. Michael Boswell was the president of Sunshine then, having been appointed a decade earlier. He had worked for the Hunt family's sugar companies prior to getting involved in silver. As I mentioned earlier, at the time there were more than two billion ounces of silver lying around in bullion and coin form. Boswell asked me one day where all the metal came from. Precious metals do not rust or deteriorate—that is one of the things that makes them precious, I explained. Perhaps thinking about sugar, he asked if any of the really old silver might have gone bad. Not a chance, I said. That is another thing that makes them precious.

Later the Indian coast guard intercepted a smugglers' ship headed from Dubai to Mumbai loaded with silver. At that time, in the late 1980s and early 1990s, silver and gold imports and exports were illegal in India, and smuggling silver and gold into India was big business. The smugglers dumped several thousand ounces of silver overboard before being arrested. Boswell joked to me that at least that made a little dent in the enormous stash of silver hanging over the market. A few months later the Indian newspapers reported that coast guard divers had retrieved the silver and added it to the government's stock of seized silver. Some of that seized metal was beginning to be sold by the government of India in 2005. That is another sign that silver is precious.

How to Invest

Silver is a major investment product, like gold. There are physical silver investment products, including 1,000-ounce bars and 100-ounce bars. Some refiners also produce 1-ounce and 10-ounce silver bars and medallions for investors. There are silver bullion coins minted by the U.S. Mint (the Silver Eagle) and the Royal Canadian Mint (the Maple Leaf).

Silver futures and options are traded on the New York Comex. They are also traded, to a lesser extent, on the Tokyo Commodities Exchange and the Chicago Board of Trade.

Silver equities are a common way for investors to buy exposure to silver prices. The major silver producing companies include Hecla Mining, Coeur d'Alenes Mines, and Pan American Silver. Some companies are developing silver mines, including Apex Silver and Silver Standard. There are exploration companies and companies in the predevelopment phase, such as IMA Exploration, MacMin Silver, and Mines Management. There are larger Mexican producers, including Industrias Penoles.

There has been discussion about creating a silver exchange traded fund, similar to the gold ETFs that have been launched since 2003. Barclays Global Investors had submitted a proposal to the U.S. Securities Exchange Commission, which was approved in March 2006. There was some speculation in the silver market that the SEC might be hesitant to approve a silver ETF that called for physical silver to be purchased as backing for the shares, as the silver market was seen as illiquid compared to that of gold. Whereas gold bullion inventories have been increasing over the past two decades, silver inventories have been declining and are believed by market experts to have reached low levels.

> *The price of silver, meanwhile, has witnessed periodic spikes due to the buying patterns of one or two investors at various times, which could lead the SEC to be more cautious about silver than gold.*

The price of silver, meanwhile, has witnessed periodic spikes due to the buying patterns of one or two investors at various times, which could have made the SEC more cautious about silver than gold.

Platinum

Platinum is the senior of six metals known as the platinum group of metals (PGMs). The others include palladium, rhodium, ruthenium, iridium, and osmium. These metals are clustered together in the periodic table of elements. They share many physical, chemical, and electrical properties. They also demonstrate useful powers as catalysts—materials that aid in the performance of chemical processes without entering into the chemical reactions themselves. PGMs tend to be found together in nature. Typically ore is found to have all of these metals. In some instances the amounts of the minor PGMs—iridium, osmium, and ruthenium—are so low that refiners do not pay the mining companies for the metal content, so the metals are not always recovered from the ore during processing. Sometimes the metals are found apart from their sister metals. Osmiridium and other alloys of osmium and iridium are sometimes found in nature. Iridium also is found in many meteorites. Scientists have noted a layer of iridium widely distributed in the earth's crust, leading some to point to this as evidence of a prehistoric collision of a giant meteor into our planet, causing a catastrophe that led to the extinction of dinosaurs.

Platinum and its allied metals are relatively recent discoveries. Platinum first was misidentified as a form of silver in colonial Colombia. It has been mined from placer deposits in rivers there ever since. It really began to come into its own in the nineteenth century, when placer mining operations in Russia's Ural Mountains opened up and increased supply. The Czarist government issued some platinum coins at the time, while Faberge used it in some of his famous eggs and other forms of jewelry. By the early twentieth century platinum was being mined in South Africa, and several industrial uses were emerging.

Prices

Platinum spent most of the period from 1990 through 1999 at between $350 and $400 per ounce. Prices began rising toward the end of 1999 and rose sharply in 2000. (See Figure 7.11.) Platinum had averaged $373 in 1999. In 2000 it averaged $535, an increase of 43.5 percent. This reflected several shifts in supply and demand. Supply had been rising sharply up to 1997, as mine production increased around the world, secondary recovery from spent auto catalysts increased, and Russian exports rose sharply. Russian exports had risen sharply in the immediate aftermath of the Soviet Union's collapse, as central control over Russian exports of platinum and other precious commodities fell away and the authorities responsible for

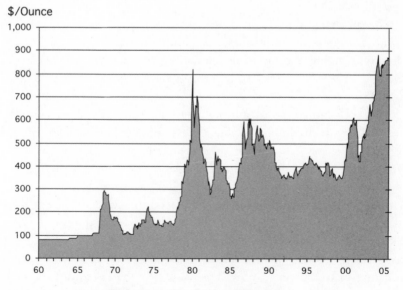

Figure 7.11 **The Price of Platinum**

selling these commodities ramped up exports sharply. At the end of 1996 the Russian Ministry of Finance reasserted control over Russian exports of platinum, palladium, rhodium, diamonds, and other precious commodities. As it tried to decide what to do, it stopped exporting these commodities for a time. This caused the markets for each of them to tighten sharply, and prices began to rise.

Initially the price increase in platinum was relatively mild, because supplies were rising from other sources and there was a great deal of metal lying around in inventories relatively available to the market. Even though the market moved into a steep deficit of newly refined metal entering the market relative to fabrication demand in 1996 and 1997, the availability of inventories kept prices from rising for a while.

By late 1999 inventories had declined, the growth in other supplies was slowing for a time, and investors were becoming aware of what had happened with the Russian exports. Investors began buying platinum, and prices began rising.

Platinum prices remained around 2000 levels for the next two years, trading largely between $410 and $610. This was a period of renewed increases in South African and other mine output, weak demand from electronics manufacturers and Japanese jewelers, and overall recessionary economic conditions. The latter discouraged investors from many commodities at this time, regardless of the individual commodities' fundamental positions.

This all changed in 2003, when investors began buying large volumes of platinum once more and the auto industry's use of platinum recovered in line with tightening emission standards and recovering auto sales. Platinum rose to $687 in 2003, to $843 in early 2004, and then to $1,036 in late 2005.

After platinum rose to around $840 in April 2004, prices dropped about $100 in 10 trading days. This reflected the thinness of this market at that time. The price had been pushed that high by investment demand from only a handful of institutional investment firms, including a few hedge funds, coupled with tight supplies available to deliver against Nymex platinum futures positions. Some of the fund managers became concerned that the price was high due to their buying, and not for any of the reasons being offered at the time by platinum promoters. So the funds took their profits. After prices stabilized around $750, these fund managers went long platinum once more. The view was that platinum might have one more run up in prices before this trend ended. By 2005 the fund managers' attitudes had changed noticeably. More funds were buying into platinum, including several new hedge funds created by people who had left the fund management companies that had been buyers in 2003 and 2004. As these new funds were being created and building up platinum positions, their presence in the market increased the breadth of platinum market liquidity. They became more comfortable with the idea that they could be long platinum at these high prices, since there were more new buyers to whom they could sell when the time came to liquidate their positions. As a result of this change of attitudes, there was a noticeable increase in fund long position taking, and stronger prices during the second half of 2005 than otherwise would have been seen.

Supply

Total platinum supply to the world market is around 7.3 million ounces per year at present. The two main sources of platinum are South Africa and Russia. South African platinum mine production totals around 5.2 million ounces and has been expanding rapidly for much of the past two decades. Russia produces roughly a million ounces more and exports most of it.

By 2005 the fund managers' attitudes had changed noticeably. More funds were buying into platinum, including several new hedge funds created by people who had left the fund management companies that had been buyers in 2003 and 2004.

Mine production has been rising in South Africa and other countries as demand for most platinum group metals, and platinum individually, has been rising steadily for much of the past two decades. In South Africa there are three large platinum mining companies and a number of smaller emerging companies. In the United States the Stillwater Mining Company began producing platinum and palladium at a mine in Montana in the 1980s, the only primary platinum mine in this country. Canadian mines produce around 250,000 ounces of platinum per year. Some of this is recovered as by-product at nickel and copper mines, while a small amount comes from a palladium mine that started production in the late 1990s.

In addition to mine production, platinum is recovered from old manufactured products containing this metal. Most of the platinum refined from scrap comes from spent auto catalytic converters—devices on the exhaust systems of automobiles that convert harmful emissions into benign water, carbon dioxide, oxygen, nitrogen, and hydrogen. Around 800,000 ounces of platinum is recovered from scrap each year. Of this about 600,000 ounces or more comes from old auto catalysts. The remainder comes from old electronic equipment, jewelry scrap, and chemical and petroleum refining catalysts that contain platinum.

Fabrication Demand

Platinum is used in a wide range of applications. It has been estimated that one in five manufactured products involves platinum in its production. That probably is true, since platinum is used in such varied areas as the manufacture of glass, petroleum refining, and the manufacture of several key chemical feedstocks. In many cases the platinum is not used in the products directly, but in the equipment used to manufacture the products.

Platinum's major use at present is in auto catalysts. It is also used as a catalyst in the refining of crude oil into its constituent products, in boosting gasoline's octane without the use of lead, and in the manufacture of some basic chemical feedstocks used in the manufacture of plastics, nitrogen-based fertilizers, explosives, and other applications. Platinum is used in jewelry, especially popular in Japan. There has been a lot of talk in the market since around 1998 about Chinese use of platinum in jewelry, but we think that the estimates of how much is actually being used in jewelry in China are too high.

Platinum is used in electronic applications, especially in semiconductors and other high-end components where its electrical conductivity and tarnish resistance lead to a high level of reliability. Platinum is used in spark plugs for jet engines, and some premium automotive spark plugs. Platinum-iridium alloys are said to be among the strongest metals devised. A range of platinum chemicals also are used in chemotherapy to fight various cancers.

It is used, with its allied metal rhodium, as an alloy in equipment used to manufacture glass. Because the PGMs do not interact with many chemicals, platinum rhodium alloys are used for all sorts of equipment that comes in contact with the molten glass; the use of platinum rhodium equipments keeps the glass from picking up impurities from the equipment. This is particularly important for glass used in the manufacture of fiber-glass for fiber optical wiring, but it is also valuable for other products manufactured out of glass.

In total, platinum use is running around 6.5 million ounces per year at present. This estimated demand level is less than supply, and the difference has been taken up by investors in recent years.

Market Balance

It is the opinion of our company that the platinum market is running in rather large surpluses at present, after a few years of deficits from 1996 through 2002. (See Figure 7.12.)

The view that the platinum market is in a sizable surplus is in contrast to the figures put out by some of the largest platinum sellers in the world. A couple of major differences between our statistics and theirs help explain the differences of opinion. Our figures for supply include all platinum recovered from scrap products that comes into the market; their scrap estimates only account for the platinum being recovered from automotive catalysts. On the demand side, we exclude investment demand from our fabrication demand figures, as is customary in commodities analyses. Finally, we have much lower figures for the use of platinum in jewelry in China in recent years. There was an aggressive move to try to stimulate a platinum jewelry market in China, beginning in the late 1990s after the platinum market had faced a decade full of enormous surpluses. Platinum was offered to Chinese jewelry manufacturers with incentives. The jewelers took a great deal of platinum, but unidentified platinum began appearing in Tokyo, Los Angeles, and Hong Kong. It looked to us, and others in the platinum market, as though the Chinese jewelers were taking

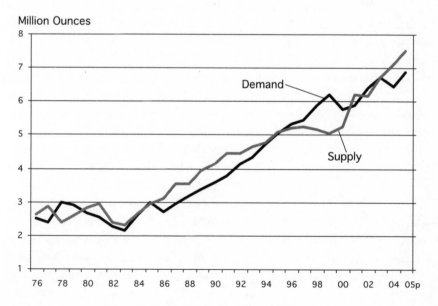

Figure 7.12 **Platinum Supply and Demand**

the platinum on the favorable marketing terms, melting it down into un-marked bars, and then selling it in various markets. This inflated estimates of the amount of platinum going into the Chinese jewelry market, and also contributed to some double-counting of this metal, as it was being measured as metal being sold to Chinese jewelers and then again as metal being sold in these other markets.

Outlook

We have thought that the price of platinum was too high for a couple of years now, and that prices should be expected to drop back toward $600 to $700 at some point. That has not happened. Some market observers say that the high platinum price reflects tight market supplies and booming demand. We do not agree with this. While our industrial clients have com-plained about paying the high prices for this metal, none of them have said a word for years about having difficulty finding sufficient metal. In fact, there appears to be plenty of platinum around to meet industrial needs and investment demand at present.

When a commodity is in a deficit market situation—when its fabrica-tion demand levels are greater than the amount of metal coming into the market through new sales from mines, scrap, and other sources—it gener-ally is positive for prices. If there are large inventories around, as in copper in the middle of the 1980s or silver from 1990 through 2003, the price might not rise even in the face of annual supply deficits until those stocks have been used up or drawn down. When a commodity is in a surplus, and the price is rising because of investor buying, it can be bullish for the price of that commodity, but that commodity's price increases are dependent on the whims of investors. That is a much more precarious position than a market with a supply deficit relative to fabrication demand. Investors do not have to be involved in any given asset's market. They can leave on a moment's no-tice, selling what they had bought.

This is how we see platinum at the start of 2006. Its price appears to us to have been pushed to historically high levels and kept there by investor demand. That seems dan-gerous to us. We would never advise anyone

When a commodity is in a deficit market situation—when its fabrication demand levels are greater than the amount of metal coming into the market through new sales from mines, scrap, and other sources—it generally is positive for prices.

to jump in front of a stampede, but if you see the price of a commodity pushed to record levels by a herd of bullish fund managers, you might want to stand prepared to jump in on the short side of the market when they decide to sell. The platinum market is a rather illiquid market. Buyers and sellers can disappear quickly, and when the herd decides to leave the palace, the doorway can seem way too small.

How to Invest

There are several approaches available to investors wishing to be long platinum. You can buy physical platinum in 1-ounce, 10-ounce, and 50-ounce bars. The bars purchased should always be refined and stamped by recognized companies in the market.

Investors can also buy 1-ounce and fractional Platinum Eagle coins minted by the U.S. Mint, and various other smaller mintage platinum coins. Included in the list are Canadian Maple Leaf and Australian Koala platinum coins. Investors sometimes buy these coins because they cost slightly less than Platinum Eagles. That may not be a wise move, however, since the discount investors receive when it is time to sell the coin can be much larger for these coins than for the U.S. Platinum Eagle. For example, one day in November 2005 a Platinum Eagle cost $1 more to buy than a Platinum Maple Leaf, and $2 more than a Platinum Koala. However, the resale price for both the Maple Leaf and Koala was $10.24 less than the resale price for a Platinum Eagle.

Platinum futures are traded on the Nymex in New York. There is also a mini contract traded in Chicago, and a platinum futures contract in Tokyo. The Nymex platinum market is the largest platinum futures market for U.S. investors. Nymex also has a platinum options contract, but it is extremely illiquid and many professionals avoid it.

Platinum physicals, forwards, and over-the-counter options are traded by major bullion dealers on a wholesale level.

Investors also invest in platinum through mining equities. The largest South African platinum group metals mining companies are Anglo Platinum, Impala Platinum, Lonplats, and Aquarius Platinum. The Stillwater Mining Company mentioned earlier is the only U.S. platinum mining company. North American Palladium is a palladium company with only modest platinum by-product production. There are a number of platinum group metals exploration companies, including Anooraq, Trend Mining, Pacific Northwest Capital, Mustang Minerals, and others. Most are listed in Canada, but some, such as Trend, are U.S. bulletin board companies. I should mention that virtually all of these companies are clients of mine, and I am on the board of directors of Trend.

Palladium

Palladium often is called the second platinum group metal, after platinum. I try to avoid calling it that, but it is in many ways an apt description of this metal. Palladium bears many similarities to its richer sister, but also has several notable differences. It has some of the same metallurgical, electronic, catalytic, and thermal properties as platinum. It tends to be mined in conjunction with platinum, although the relative amount of each metal that occurs in ore varies greatly from deposit to deposit. Whereas South Africa is the largest miner of platinum, Russia is the largest palladium mining company. In South Africa platinum is the primary product of the mines from which it comes, with palladium, gold, nickel, other platinum group metals, and copper as by-products. In Russia the primary product is nickel, and palladium is a by-product.

Palladium is used in many applications along with platinum, including the auto catalyst sector that is so hugely important to both metals. It may also be substituted for platinum in some products. Both may be used in electronic connectors and semiconductors, for example. Both may be used in some catalysts, in auto emission catalysts as well as some petroleum refining and chemical process catalysts.

However, the two metals are not entirely interchangeable. This may surprise some investors, who sometimes seem to believe that platinum and palladium may be substituted one for the other in virtually every application. The previous section discussed platinum's use in glass-making equipment. Palladium has never found a use in that industry. In many chemical processes, in chemotherapy drugs, and in other fields the two metals are not substitutable.

In many ways palladium has been the stepsister to platinum. I often find myself liking palladium more than platinum. That may be partly my personality, which runs toward the underdogs. More important is the fact that palladium has a lot going for it as a metal and an investment. It is not produced as a major product at most of the mines that produce it. Stillwater Mining in Montana is roughly equally a platinum and a palladium mine, in terms of the value of its output. North American Palladium's Lac des Isles mine in Ontario, Canada, is the only truly primary palladium mine in the world. This means that supply is much less price sensitive. Few companies would increase production at their nickel mines in Russia or platinum mines in South Africa to get at more palladium.

My fascination with palladium has paid off, although sometimes it is like trout fishing, in that you wait for years for the market to strike. In the middle part of the 1990s palladium was trading around $180 to $200 per ounce, near the upper end of the price range in which it has traded for most of the past several decades. I started projecting that palladium prices could rise as high as $500 per ounce. South African producers, bankers, mining analysts, and others thought I was crazy. The price rose to $1,082 within four years. Then they started saying I was way too bearish on palladium. The price dropped back to $140, and then $85. Let me get back to those price moves later.

Palladium prices rose sharply in the middle of the 1980s, for a time, and then receded. They rose again in the late 1990s, after the Russian Ministry of Finance asserted control over Russian palladium exports. They rose sharply during that time, and then fell even further from 2002 into early 2005. They were rising again as of late 2005 and early 2006.

All precious metals markets are secretive and shrouded in poor information flows, misinformation, disinformation, and vast uncertainties about what is going on. Palladium is even more obscured than the others. Often a large participant will appear in the market as a buyer or seller. Regardless of who it is, almost always Norilsk Nickel, the Russian nickel producer that is the largest palladium miner in the world, gets blamed for whatever it is that someone else does.

Palladium came to the public's attention in the late 1980s, when two physicists working in Utah announced that they had observed room-temperature nuclear fusion, or cold fusion, using palladium electrodes. The prospects of cold fusion in terms of cheap energy captured the world's imagination, and investors raced to buy palladium for a time. The tests proved hard to reproduce, and there appeared to be some sloppiness in the lab work, so the

> *All precious metals markets are secretive and shrouded in poor information flows, misinformation, disinformation, and vast uncertainties about what is going on. Palladium is even more obscured than the others.*

concept quickly became discredited. Interestingly, in the ensuing two decades hundreds of physicists have continued to study the cold fusion phenomenon, convinced that something unexplained was there. As of 2005 cold fusion research was regaining some respectability in more orthodox circles of research physicists. A number of interesting aspects of cold fusion were being observed and documented by scientists at various research laboratories around the world, although the prospects of cheap and limitless energy from the process still seemed extremely remote.

Prices

Palladium prices spent much of the period from the late 1970s until 1997 trading between about $60 to $80 on the low end and $180 on the high end. It was almost easy to make money trading palladium for much of this time. You would buy when prices were down around $80 or $110, depending on market conditions, and sell when palladium got to $160. Sometimes you would short the market at the top of the range, and make the same money on the way back down. This pattern was slightly complicated by shorter-term trading patterns in which dealers would go long palladium in advance of the actively traded palladium contract months on the Nymex (March, June, September, and December), and then sell off their positions once the shorts had paid a premium to roll their nearby active short positions into forward short positions. One trader was particularly notorious for this trade, and when he retired in the early 1990s some of the palladium traders in the New York market joked that they would no longer know how to make money in the palladium pit without his coattails to ride. See Figure 7.13 for a chart of this time line.

As described in the previous section on platinum, after the collapse of the Soviet Union there was a period in which the flow of palladium and other precious metals and diamonds out of Russia rose sharply. This period ended at the start of 1997, when the Ministry of Finance took over directing exports. The Ministry stopped shipments in January 1997 while it assessed the situation. At first, the market did not seem to catch on to what was happening. There were enormous inventories of palladium backed up in the international market, so no one seemed concerned that Russian exports had been halted temporarily. There seemed to be plenty of metal to go around, and everyone assumed the interruption in Russian sales would be limited in time. By April or May 1997, however, the market became concerned about this situation, and various consumers, semifabricators, dealers, investors, and proprietary traders began stocking up on palladium. At first prices rose to $180, their traditional peak. Then they rose to $220. At this point a lot of

$/Ounce

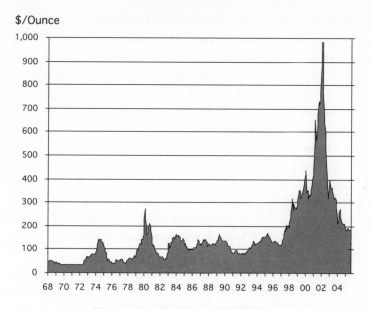

Figure 7.13 **The Price of Palladium**

longs decided to take their profits, having bought in around $120 or so, and prices subsided. A lot of others decided to stay in the market, and maybe even add to their long positions. This was a new situation.

Russian exports became very erratic for several years, however, and the supply disruptions exerted a great deal of upward pressure on prices. During this time, the years 1998 to 2001, the technology boom was in full swing, and people were buying electronic gear with palladium-bearing semiconductors hand over fist. Demand was rising sharply. Prices rose to $398 in 1998, and then $455 in 1999. As the price rose, and supplies tightened further, buying for inventories increased. Ultimately, the price of palladium rose to $1,082, in the first quarter of 2001. At this point, the bubble burst, and palladium prices started to fall. They hit $315 by late 2001.

A bit of history has to be told here to understand what happened next. In the late period of the Soviet Union and the first decade of post-Soviet Russia, the government had used palladium as collateral against international loans. As much as 3.2 million ounces of palladium may have been shipped to bonded warehouses in Switzerland to be held against loans made to the government. The amount of palladium was a secret. The figure here is our estimate of what was involved, based on various pieces of information we gathered over time.

When palladium prices rose to $1,082, and then started to fall, the Russian government decided to unwind these loans and pay them off with the palladium. The Russian government is estimated by us to have unwound these loans and sold the palladium when prices were between $600 and $700 per ounce, in the first half of 2001. The bank that had done the loan with the Russian government decided to hang on to the metal. The price of palladium had been $1,000 just a few months earlier. As prices continued to slide, the bank decided to sell. It began selling its palladium, perhaps more than three million ounces, around October 2002, when the price of palladium was around $320 per ounce. It sold this metal steadily throughout the next seven months, as prices sagged under the weight of nearly six months' worth of additional supply coming onto the market. Anyone who wanted palladium knew whom to call to get as much as he wanted, at the market price, no haggling involved. Prices fell to $140 in April 2003. The day after the bank had sold its last ounce prices began rising once more.

Palladium prices rose from $140 in April 2003 to $200 within five weeks. Prices came off a bit, but held above $175. In early 2004 prices rose to $337 briefly, before falling back to around $220 later in that year. Prices broke below $210 in December 2004, under the weight of heavy short-selling. Prices dropped to around $80 in early 2005, before recovering. By December 2005 prices had risen back to $300 briefly once again, and then dropped off to around $260.

The bank sold its metal to whoever wanted it. Some went to industrial users. A large amount of it appears to have been sold to hedge funds and other institutional investors. Some of these investors appear to have continued to hold the palladium as of late 2005, while others had sold some of the metal. New hedge funds that opened in 2004 and 2005, some of them run by people who had worked at the hedge funds that had bought the metal in 2002 and 2003, were buying palladium even as their former employers were selling, helping to keep palladium prices higher than they would have been had this metal been sold into a market in which such institutional investors were disinterested in this metal.

Supply

Total palladium supplies reached nearly 7.3 million ounces in 2005. This was up around 8.4 percent from 2004 levels, and more than double the annual amount of palladium that was coming into the market from newly refined sources in the early 1980s. Palladium supplies have increased sharply over the past 15 years, as industrial demand for palladium, platinum, and the other platinum group metals stimulated higher prices, which in turn led mining companies to boost output.

The largest source of palladium is Norilsk Nickel. As of this writing, how much palladium this company produces annually remains unreported, as Russian laws still consider domestic production of PGMs state secrets, a holdover from a law Joseph Stalin passed in the early 1930s. Reports that this law was changing have circulated since the 1990s, but the actual implementation of any relaxation of this regulation has yet to be realized. Norilsk is

> *Palladium supplies have increased sharply over the past 15 years, as industrial demand for palladium, platinum, and the other platinum group metals stimulated higher prices, which in turn led mining companies to boost output.*

estimated to produce anywhere from 2.4 million to 3.4 million ounces of palladium per year. It appears to be selling around 2.0 to 2.2 million ounces annually. This suggests to me that production may be around that lower level, since Norilsk's modern management would seem unlikely to hold large inventories of unsold metal.

The Soviet government had been willing to hold metal in inventories, seeing the palladium and other platinum group metals as part of the national patrimony, and being unwilling to glut the international market. That former government was willing to hold enormous stocks of metal for extended periods of time as strategic reserves of critical metals—as did the western governments at the time. Those times have passed, and Norilsk today is run as a private corporation focused on profitability, so it probably sells what it produces. Whether the Russian government is buying some of this metal to replenish government stockpiles depleted in the period 1991 to 1996, in the immediate aftermath of the Soviet Union, is unclear, but this also seems unlikely. The Russian government is believed to have added metal to its inventories from 1997 into the early part of this decade, but it appears to have ended that program, sold off metal it had used as collateral for loans, and it appears to have sold additional metal since 2003 from its government inventories. It is believed to hold several million ounces of palladium, but this figure also is considered a state secret, and thus is the subject of great speculation. Market estimates of how much palladium the Russian government holds range from a few million ounces to tens of millions of ounces. Our estimate is that the Russian government may hold around 9 or 10 million ounces.

Let me inject an anecdote here. I always say that the highest compliment an authoritarian regime can give an analyst is to investigate his sources. When I published what was probably the first platinum group metals report in May 1981, internal investigations were launched to see who was slipping me information, not only by the Soviet government but by management at the two largest platinum mining companies in South Africa at the time, Rustenburg Platinum Mines (the predecessor of today's Anglo Platinum) and Impala Platinum Mines. (Platinum mine production, let alone production costs, were corporate secrets in South Africa until the late 1990s.) I was glad they did this, as it was the only indication that my guesses and estimates were accurate. They would not have investigated whether I had inside sources if my estimates had been wide of the mark.

In addition to the metal that comes into the market from Norilsk Nickel's production and any Russian government sales, palladium comes from mines around the world and from scrap refining, also known as secondary recovery.

Total mine production is around 3.9 million ounces outside of Russia. (Some palladium is also being produced in China, but there are no good estimates yet as to how much metal is being recovered from domestic ores in that country.) South African mining companies are producing around 2.6 million ounces per year now. The eight mines run by Anglo Platinum produce about half of that. Palladium also is produced by Impala Platinum, Northam, Aquarius, and some smaller operations. North American Palladium produces palladium as its primary product at a mine in Ontario, Canada; and Stillwater Mining produces palladium at a platinum-palladium mine in Montana. A few PGM mines have been opened in Zimbabwe over the past decade. Other palladium is produced in Colombia, at placer mining operations, and as a by-product of nickel or copper mining in Canada, the United States, Finland, Australia, and the Philippines. All totaled, production in all of these countries other than Russia and South Africa comes up to around 1.3 million ounces.

Another 1.4 million ounces of palladium comes from secondary recovery from scrap each year. Much of this is electronic scrap. A growing portion of this is coming from old, spent auto catalysts, which contain platinum and rhodium as well as palladium. Traditionally, however, a large amount of palladium comes from electronic scrap. Palladium was used in the old electromechanical telephone switching gears that fill all of those windowless buildings owned by telephone companies around the world. Starting in the late 1960s in the United States and continuing elsewhere in the world today, these old switching systems are being replaced by solid-state electronic switches. The newer switches may use some palladium, but a large portion of these connectors is gold plated. The old palladium switching gear has been recycled with its metals recovered. A little-known fact is that the old AT&T used to be the largest refiner and supplier of palladium to the world market for much of the 1970s and 1980s, when it operated a refinery in New York that recovered this metal.

Today electronics recycling represents a major source of palladium on an ongoing basis. An international network of companies collect old electronics, deconstruct them, and recycle the metals and other recoverable materials from them. They have done this since at least the 1970s. Some of the companies in this network, most of which are smaller privately owned companies, have been extremely profitable. This industry, which has thrived for decades, has its own industry associations, annual meetings, and directories. It is not hiding in any way. Even so, many people treat it as nonexistent. A few years ago someone wrote a report about how electronics scrap would become an important source of palladium, gold, silver, and platinum in the years ahead, as if the industry did not already exist. Others ignore electronic scrap from their palladium and platinum supply and demand estimates. Governments meanwhile speak about the

> *Electronics recycling represents a major source of palladium.*

need to establish recycling networks to handle the flood of electronic scrap—again, seemingly oblivious to the existence of this industry. It is one of the more interesting examples of denial in the precious metals markets.

Fabrication Demand

Palladium use in fabricated products is around 6.3 million ounces per year at present. This is up sharply. The patterns of palladium usage have shifted dramatically over the past decade. Today auto catalysts represent the lion's share of palladium use, accounting for perhaps 55 percent of annual use. Electronics is the second largest use, taking about 15 percent of the market, while dental alloys represent another 15 percent. A wide range of other uses—from jewelry to chemical catalysts used in everything from petroleum refining to making acetaminophen—account for around 15 percent of the market combined.

As recently as 1994 electronics was the largest use of palladium by a wide margin, followed by dental alloys, while auto catalysts were a distant third. This was at a time when auto companies were just beginning to use more palladium-intense loadings in their catalytic converters. Palladium prices had been relatively stable and low, trading between $80 and $180 for most of the previous two decades.

In the ensuing decade the auto industry more than quadrupled its palladium use. Prices shot higher, while supplies became very erratic from 1997 until around 2001. These conditions led dental alloy manufacturers to shift away from palladium. For a while this use looked doomed, but dental use of palladium has staged a renaissance in the early 2000s.

Electronics use meanwhile fell sharply at the start of this decade. As recently as 1996 to 1998, 85 percent of all semiconductors used palladium. The high price and erratic supply of palladium caused chip manufacturers to consider shifting away from it. By 2000 perhaps half of this market had shifted to other metals, from nickel and tantalum to platinum and gold, and palladium was being used in only 45 percent of all semiconductors. Also at that time the electronics industry entered a steep recession, following the blow-out of the tech bubble. Semiconductor output fell on the order of 95 percent. Many manufacturers had built up inventories of palladium when prices were high, and they did not need metal—no one was buying their products, so there was no reason for them to buy palladium. Electronics demand for palladium fell 74 percent from 2.6 million ounces in 2000 to 675,000 ounces in 2001. Demand fell further in 2002, and has since begun a steady recovery. By 2005 perhaps one million ounces of palladium was being used in electronics once more. While this was up sharply from 2001 and 2002 levels, it was roughly one-third of what it had been in the late 1990s. Further growth is expected in the future. The electronics industry seems to believe that the substitution period is behind it.

There was a lot of talk in the palladium market in 2004 and 2005 about burgeoning demand for palladium in jewelry in China. Just as CPM Group believes that much of the hype about platinum use in Chinese jewelry from 1998 to the present is inaccurate, we have a lot of questions about palladium jewelry in China as well. From what we can tell, a group tried to market palladium jewelry in China in 2004, shipping in perhaps 500,000 ounces. It was our impression that the jewelry did not sell well. In the middle of 2005 there was persistent selling of palladium from China. We assumed that this was palladium that had been manufactured into jewelry which went unsold, having been remelted and cast into refined palladium for sale. As 2005 was ending, however, there were reports that not only had the half-million ounces of palladium jewelry sold in 2004, but another million or more ounces of palladium jewelry had been sold into China during 2005. These figures did not agree with what seemed to be going on in the palladium market at that time. Prices were very low for palladium for most of 2005. There were reports of ample supplies and persistent sales in east Asia. It did not seem that there was a strong growth in jewelry demand for palladium in China; rather, there seemed to be a strong disinterest. It was only after some fund managers in the United States heard reports of heavy Chinese jewelry demand for palladium that they started buying, and palladium prices started rising, repeating a pattern that has been seen repeatedly from gold to nickel to cotton.

Market Balance and Outlook

In fact, the palladium market has been heavily supplied over the past few years, a trend that continued in 2005 (see Figure 7.14). The surpluses of newly refined palladium entering the market in excess of fabrication demand reached 1.6 million ounces in 2003, excluding the older Russian metal estimated to have been being sold in the first four months of that year by the

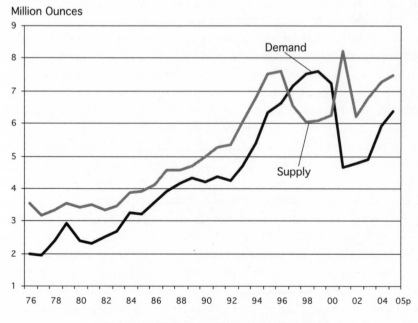

Figure 7.14 **Palladium Supply and Demand**

European bank I mentioned earlier. That sale may have totaled 3.2 million
ounces between October 2002 and April 2003, adding around 1.6 million
ounces to the 2003 surplus. By 2004 that metal had been absorbed by industrial users and fund managers. The annual current account surplus meanwhile
declined to a still large 1.1 million ounces, but the tidal wave of palladium entering the market was slowing. In 2005 the surplus continued to shrink, and
may have been around 900,000 ounces. A further contraction was projected
for 2006 and beyond, as fabrication demand continues to expand.

Fund managers are focusing on this rapid contraction of the annual
surpluses of palladium. They are well aware that palladium is an extremely
versatile metal used in a number of high-tech applications, emerging technologies, and important, widespread industrial applications. The view is
that industrial demand for palladium will rise at a rapid rate in the long
run. At times the market will become too tight and prices will rise sharply.
Fabricators will back off then. Miners and scrap refiners will step up production and sales. The price of palladium will fall, perhaps sharply as it did
from 2000 into 2005. Then the cycle will repeat itself. Given palladium's
many uses and the growth projected in these applications, from electronics
and dental alloys to auto catalysts, chemical process catalysts, and petroleum refining catalysts, the long-term growth prospects for palladium use
appear positive to these investors. If there also is growing jewelry demand
in China, that is icing on the cake, in their view. If there is not, and it is just
marketing hype that stimulates investor buying and pushes the price
higher from time to time, these fund managers find that acceptable as well.

Our view is similar. There is a tremendous amount of palladium lying
around in inventories in the hands of investors, some banks, and maybe
even the Russian government. Such inventories do not necessarily depress
the price of palladium, however, as long as the inventory owners are willing to continue to hold this metal. They may do that because they expect
prices to rise, or for other reasons. As long as they hold their metal, the
metal is neutral to the price of palladium. The risk to investors in palladium is that those inventory holders' attitudes may change. An announce-
ment of a new substitute for palladium in some application, or sharp future
increases in mine production, could prompt such a change in attitudes. For
now, however, investors seem interested in continuing to hold palladium,
and more new investors seem to be joining the ranks, willing to buy any
metal that older investors seek to sell. This, combined with stronger palladium fundamentals, could support palladium prices and lead them to move
higher in the years ahead.

How to Invest

Palladium is less of an investment metal than are gold, silver, and platinum. Palladium is traded worldwide in 100-ounce bars, although most of its industrial buyers do not purchase bars but rather a powdered metal, called sponge by the industrial sector. Investors tend to buy 100-ounce bars of palladium. There are some smaller, 1-ounce bars around.

In addition to physical palladium, palladium futures are traded on the New York Mercantile Exchange and the Tokyo Commodities Exchange.

There are no futures options offered on palladium. Sometimes dealers will quote options, especially to industrial customers such as mining companies and users. These over-the-counter options are not readily tradable, and the palladium option business is highly illiquid. Generally speaking we have warned investors not to buy dealer options, as there can be great illiquidity and price differentials that are not attractive when it comes time to sell the options back to the dealer.

> *There is a tremendous amount of palladium lying around in inventories in the hands of investors, some banks, and maybe even the Russian government. Such inventories do not necessarily depress the price of palladium, however, as long as the inventory owners are willing to continue to hold this metal.*

Similarly, there are no palladium coins in circulation, and those one-ounce palladium medallions and bars produced by private enterprises tend to carry a high premium over the market price. From time to time a politician from Montana, where Stillwater Mining operates, will suggest that the U.S. government start minting a palladium coin, but more sensible voices have prevailed to date.

As mentioned earlier, North American Palladium is a relatively small Canadian company that produces palladium as its primary product. Its shares trade on the American Stock Exchange and the Toronto Stock Exchange. Stillwater Mining is another equity that some investors buy and sell as a surrogate for palladium. Others trade Norilsk Nickel as a palladium share, although it really is a nickel company.

8

Energy Commodities

This chapter focuses on the following energy commodities: petroleum, natural gas, and uranium. Uranium is the only commodity included in this book that is not traded on a futures exchange. I chose it because it has been of particular interest to investors over the past two years and is likely to continue to be interesting. The reason for including oil and gas is obvious. Oil is currently the single most important commodity in the world. The dollar value of gold derivatives trading (futures, forwards, options, and swaps) is larger than the volume of oil trading, but the dollar value of physical oil dwarfs gold, by a factor of about 20. Furthermore, oil fuels the world, from transportation to electricity generation. It is central to economic activity, and paramount these days in international and domestic politics.

Petroleum

Petroleum prices have risen sharply, from a cyclical low around $10 per barrel in 1999 to more than $70 in late August 2005. Prices backed off from there, but as of early 2006 oil still was trading around $60. (See Figure 8.1.) The outlook for petroleum prices probably was less ascertainable than ever before as of late 2005 and early 2006. Predictions as to future prices

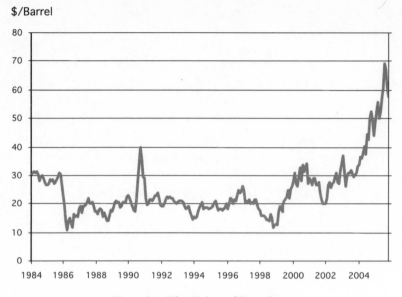

$/Barrel

Figure 8.1 **The Price of Petroleum**

from respectable sources ranged from $25 to $100, and that is excluding the fringe crazies.

I expect oil prices to remain strong. That does not mean they will continue to rise at the pace seen since 2003. It does not mean that prices will rise to $100 and stay there. It means that prices could rise to $100 in a spike. It also means that I doubt that oil prices will fall back to the $10 to $22 range seen from 1986 into late 1999. Prices may find a new base around $35 or $40, or maybe even higher.

One point I would make about oil is this: Economics still apply. The rise in prices currently under way will increase supplies sharply in the years ahead, at least for a time. Five years ago there were thousands of idle drill rigs available for rent or sale around the world. Today you are lucky to get your name on a long waiting list. Everyone who can is drilling for oil right now, and they will find it. This, coupled with a modest slowing in the rate of increase of demand, will help prices come lower.

Why the Higher Prices?

Figure 8.1 tracks the price of oil from 1984 to the present. There are three main reasons for the current increase in oil prices. First and foremost, prices have risen because the world's use of oil is rising sharply. The second factor is that oil prices had been low for many years. Oil prices traded between $10 and $22 for most of the time from 1986 through 1999. This had the effect of discouraging exploration for and development of new oil fields, which

The rise in prices currently under way will increase supplies sharply in the years ahead, at least for a time.

was reflected in lower production more recently. It also led to the closing of some older fields that required higher oil prices to justify continued production. The third reason is international politics.

Other developments have factored into the rise in prices, but they have been less important. Some are short-term events. Interruptions in oil production, refining, and transportation in the U.S. Gulf Coast due to Hurricane Katrina at the end of August 2005 contributed to the spike in prices to $70, although longer-term factors had taken prices to around $60 already. Speculative buying of petroleum futures by investors has also been a major factor. Some of this investment buying has been based on analyses of the fundamental trends that have been pushing oil prices higher. Additional buying came from commodity-index investments, from investors who bought into the commodities supercycle theory, and other investors who have listened to and believed market commentary suggesting that the world is running out of oil.

The single most important factor has been the growth in petroleum consumption. Oil demand was growing at an annual rate close to 1.5 percent for many years, from the early 1980s through the early 1990s. Demand growth rates accelerated to 1.7 percent per annum after 1995, and then accelerated further to rates around 2.1 to 2.5 percent per year in 2003 through 2005. This seemingly marginal increase in oil consumption actually translated into the world needing several million barrels per day more oil than it did the year before, every year.

Superficial analyses have focused on the rise of Chinese economic activities contributing to this increase. Chinese demand has been a major factor, but the reality is that oil use is rising more rapidly around the world. U.S. demand has been rising rapidly at rates above the historical trend, as consumers in the United States have shown an extremely high tolerance for paying for petroleum as long as they can get it. Demand also is rising in other industrialized economies, although not as rapidly as in the United States. Almost as important as the growth in Chinese demand for oil has been, and continues to be, the growth in demand in other developing countries, from Russia and India to Brazil and Peru and everywhere in between. More people are using more oil each year now, and the rate of growth is accelerating.

The second factor is that oil output has not quite kept up with the rate of growth in demand. This is partly due to the fact that oil prices were relatively low for much of the period from 1986 until 2000. Oil prices were restrained by several factors during this time. The major reason was that oil production rose sharply following the two sharp increases in oil prices in the 1970s. Those price increases, from around $1 per barrel at the start of the 1970s to $40 for a time in the early 1980s, led to a sharp drop in oil consumption, the tail end of which can be seen on the supply and demand chart in Figure 8.2, later in this section. They also led to enormous increases in production, which later contributed mightily to the price weakness.

Some people like to look for conspiracies and collusion. The major forces behind the low growth rates in production were natural economic forces like low prices. Interestingly, in the middle of the 1980s, the then Minister of Petroleum in Saudi Arabia, Sheik Yamani, outlined a strategy for the Organization of Petroleum Exporting Countries (OPEC) to regain pricing power by producing sufficient oil to discourage production and new developments of oil fields in non-OPEC countries. His view was that if OPEC produced sufficient oil to keep prices below $25 for an extended period of time it would lead to the deterioration of non-OPEC capacity, allowing OPEC to reassert itself later. He lost his job and OPEC officially did not adopt such a policy. It did not have to do so, as it turned out, since the laws of economics successfully effected these developments without OPEC having to appear to be a heavy in the market.

The third major factor behind the recent rise in oil prices is international politics. After the invasion of Iraq in early 2003, the U.S. government lost almost all of the goodwill and respect it had in the international arena. This was true in Europe and Japan as well as in the Arab and Muslim world, including many oil producing nations. The consensus view was that the United States was attacking Iraq as part of a long-term colonialist oil grab. The Bush administration's use of the word *crusade* to describe its plans to impose democracy in Arab oil producing countries did not help any counter-arguments. Arab oil exporting governments have been careful not to directly oppose the U.S. government out of fear of reprisals, but the sharp rise in oil prices starting immediately after the U.S. invasion of Iraq represents a form of indirect opposition.

Anyone who does not think that the U.S. invasion of Iraq has had an effect on the price of petroleum only needs to draw a line where the U.S. invasion started on the petroleum price chart in Figure 8.1. Prices had risen from around $10 to around $30 prior to the war. Since then prices have more than doubled again. In the current period, since 2001, the move from $10 to $40 can be attributed to the petroleum market fundamentals of rising demand and price-induced lower production. Much of the increase in oil prices above $40 may be attributed to the deterioration of international cooperation, and the lower U.S. dollar, since the start of the war in 2003.

Supply

Oil supplies totaled around 84 million barrels per day as of 2005 (see Figure 8.2). This was up from 77 million barrels a day just four years earlier and around 49 million barrels a day in the early 1970s. About 51 million barrels of this oil comes from non-OPEC sources, including the United States, Canada, Mexico, Norway, the United Kingdom, Russia, and other countries. OPEC nations produce the rest. The share of world oil production coming from OPEC countries has been increasing again in the past couple of years.

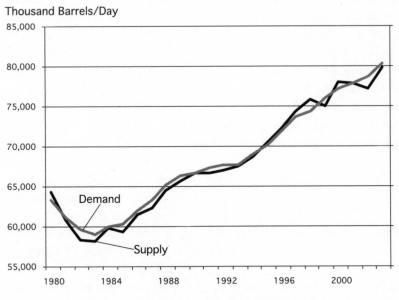

Figure 8.2 **Petroleum Supply and Demand**

Much of the increase in oil prices above $40 may be attributed to the deterioration of international cooperation, and the lower U.S. dollar, since the start of the war in 2003.

Oil production is set to rise sharply in the years ahead. Saudi Arabia and numerous other OPEC nations have announced enormous expansion programs, seeking to boost oil production 75 percent over the next quarter century. Production also is coming on stream in Russia and other countries that were republics of the former Soviet Union, as well as Canada, the United States, and China. Vast tracts of China have not been explored thoroughly for oil as yet.

One of the factors that has fueled investor interest in oil in recent years has been a revival of a debate as to whether the world is running out of oil. A series of studies conducted by oil geologists have suggested that the rate of discovery of new oil deposits will peak soon and that world oil production will begin to decrease within the next few decades. Other petroleum economists have examined the work behind these conclusions and pointed out various erroneous suppositions that call the conclusions into question.

The International Energy Agency estimates that over the past 100-plus years in which humans have used oil and natural gas we have consumed oil and gas equivalent to around 1.5 trillion barrels of oil. It further estimates that the world will use about that much oil and gas again over the next 25 years. It estimates that there are at least 20 trillion barrels of oil-equivalent in oil and gas reserves and resources. Of this, between 5 and 10 trillion barrels are technically recoverable. They may not be recoverable at today's oil and gas prices, but they are technically able to be recovered. Currently around 35 to 40 percent of the reserves and resources in a given oil field are recovered. If the technology can be developed to increase the recovery rates at existing, former, and known oil fields, it could boost recoverable reserves by an amount greater than Saudi Arabia's presently known reserves.

There clearly are some very real geological issues here related to the fact that there has been a tremendous amount of petroleum discovered and extracted over the past century. At some point, oil in the ground is a finite matter. Reserves really are dependent on geology, and the world may well run out of oil someday. However, reserve estimates are not based only on the amount of resources geologically identified and inferred to be in the ground. The amount of oil reserves that are economically recoverable is a function not only of the geological realities of the earth's crust, but also economics and politics. The amount of oil economically recoverable increases with the price of oil. The amount of exploration and discovery also increases with the price of oil. There are geological constraints to this, but they have not yet been found.

The Club of Rome expounded the view that the world was running out of oil 35 years ago. Like the current proponents of this view, they saw oil reserves as a purely geological function: Either they are physically there or they are not. In 1973 the world was using around 48 million barrels of oil per day, and expectations were that we would run out of oil by the mid to late 1970s. Since then daily petroleum consumption has risen 75 percent to more than 84 million barrels per day, and we have more reserves today than we did back then. The reasons for this include the higher oil price, advances in petroleum exploration and production technology, and massive discoveries of previously undiscovered oil fields, in part due to the higher prices and better exploration technology. We are much better at finding and extracting oil today than we were back then.

Other constraints that have been felt are of a political nature. There are vast tracts of land that have not been explored in a systematic fashion using modern technology, which leads to the conclusion that one ought not put much credence in statements that most of the oil that is in the earth's crust has already been discovered. Until 2003 there was a move toward liberalization and opening up much of the unexplored portions of the globe to exploration and development. In the past few years resistance to this movement has grown, but these restrictions may prove temporary. However, "temporary" in this case may be measured in decades.

Much of the world remains unexplored. Statements that all of the oil to be discovered in the world has been identified are overlooking the fact that 90 percent of Libya, one of the world's largest sources of oil, has never been explored for oil, and the 10 percent that was surveyed was studied using 1970s technology. The same is true in many other existing oil producing regions, as well as for vast tracts of China, the republics of what used to be the Soviet Union, large expanses of Africa, and many other regions.

Demand

The world is consuming around 84 million barrels per day at present. Supply and demand thus are rather closely matched. As already mentioned, world oil consumption has been rising at an accelerating pace over the past two decades. Demand was around 48 million barrels a day in the early

1970s. The sharp price increases in 1973 and 1974 and then again in 1978 through 1980 reduced oil consumption for a while. Consumption fell in the early 1980s, a consequence of both conservation efforts due to high prices and tight supplies, and the reduction in demand due to the most severe recession since the Great Depression, from 1980 into late 1982. By the end of 1982 the world was coming out of that recession and demand was showing signs of bottoming out. Even so, the price fell sharply in the first quarter of 1983, as oil producers bowed to the downward pressures of the extended period of reduced oil demand. Annual use of oil has risen every year since 1983, as shown in Figure 8.2.

It is worth noting that China was producing around 3.5 million barrels per day in 2005, up from 3.3 million barrels per day in 2001. Its oil consumption meanwhile has risen from 4.7 million barrels per day in 2001 to 6.9 million barrels per day. The gap has gone from 1.4 million barrels per day in 2001 to 3.4 million barrels per day in 2005, which explains the focus on China as a source of rising demand.

Compare this to the rest of Asia, however. Other Asian nations were producing 2.4 million barrels per day in 2001, while consuming 7.6 million barrels per day, for a gap of 5.2 million barrels per day that needed to be made up with imports. By 2005 demand in these countries had risen to 8.8 million barrels per day, while their domestic supply was at 2.7 million barrels per day, leaving a gap of 6.1 million barrels per day. Obviously, China is not the only large and growing consumer and importer of oil.

Nevertheless, the United States remains the largest consumer and importer of oil by far. U.S. production was running at 7.8 million barrels per day by 2005, while consumption was at 20.8 million barrels per day, according to the International Energy Agency.

Outlook

The longer-term outlook for petroleum prices naturally depends on the extensions of the three primary trends that have brought the price to where it is in 2006. Insofar as the world's use of oil is expected to remain along a rapid growth trajectory, prices will remain strong and could move higher. The move toward alternative energy sources, including the natural gas and uranium for nuclear power generation described in the rest of this chapter, could limit the growth in demand for oil, but such efforts and their impact on oil demand and price should not be expected to show up for many years. In the meantime, there will be pressures for higher prices.

These pressures also will be offset by rising world oil production. Production will be increasing sharply over the next several years. This could cap prices and move them lower, toward the lows previously mentioned.

The wild card remains international politics. If the world becomes a more cooperative place, the political risk premium would come off of the oil price. There are at least three components to this. One is political stability in the Middle East. The second is the U.S. government's ability to repair the strains and broken trust around the world. The third is the damage that these strains on U.S. relations have had, and will continue to exert, on the value of the U.S. dollar. If one believes that these three political issues are likely to improve in the future, one would expect prices to subside, albeit not to the levels seen from 1986 through 1999. If one believes that these issues will remain a problem in the future, and could worsen, then one may be inclined to expect oil prices to move higher, and possibly spike even higher at times in the years ahead when political problems arise in the Middle East, in other oil producing countries such as Venezuela, or between the United States government and some of its major trading counterparts, from China to oil exporting nations.

> *If the world becomes a more cooperative place, the political risk premium would come off of the oil price.*

How to Invest

Investors can invest in petroleum through a number of vehicles. Oil is traded primarily on the New York Mercantile Exchange, or Nymex. Oil is traded to a lesser extent on the International Petroleum Exchange (IPE) based in London. There is an active dealer market for professional market participants, which includes a number of larger institutional investors. Options are offered on the Nymex and in the dealer market.

There are numerous oil and gas producing companies, as well as an even greater number of exploration and development companies. There are petroleum and natural gas trusts and a wide range of other equity-oriented vehicles. There also are energy-oriented mutual funds.

Natural Gas

Natural gas represents a significant source of energy worldwide. This fuel appears to have a bright future. For one thing, natural gas reserves are enormous worldwide. Also, natural gas tends to be a cleaner-burning fossil fuel than is petroleum. Natural gas is a mixture of combustible gases, the primary one being methane.

Natural gas has been something of a stepsister to petroleum for many years. It often occurs with petroleum in underground reservoirs, and many oil producers flare or burn off the natural gas. There are enormous amounts of gas that are considered stranded, in that they are too far away from user markets. Efforts to liquefy this gas and move it to market have progressed, although in some countries, such as the United States, local and state resistance to having liquefied natural gas ports and storage facilities has slowed the spread of natural gas use.

Interestingly, natural gas is called "natural" because it replaced manufactured gas. In the early days of gas being used as a fuel, in the so-called gaslight era, the gas was made from coal and was called coal gas. Natural gas was known to exist, and ultimately it came to replace coal gas as a cheaper source. Thus, the appellation *natural* was attached to it. This may be one of the few instances in which a natural product replaced a manufactured good. Usually it is the other way around.

Another anecdote speaks volumes about the attractiveness of natural gas as a fuel for electricity generation. In New York City, where I live, there was a push to build and operate a number of small natural gas electricity generators placed around the city. The effort took years to get through permitting and past neighborhood opposition. Ultimately state-of-the-art plants were built. One was built not too far from my home in Brooklyn. A couple of years after it was installed and started, a neighbor of mine was attending a local community board meeting. Our city council representative at that time stated at the meeting that even though the state power authorities had succeeded in building the power plant in our neighborhood over the opposition of him and others, he would fight tooth and nail to keep it from operating. After a pause someone pointed out to him that it had been operating nearly continuously for two years. The plant was so clean and quiet, he and others had not even realized it was running.

Natural gas use has doubled in the past quarter century and is expected to rise further in the future. The price meanwhile has broken out of a multiyear range between $1.25 and $2.80 per million British thermal units (Btus). (See Figure 8.3.) Prices shot up to around $9.00 in 2000, came back off sharply, and then rose back to record levels in 2005.

$/MMBtu

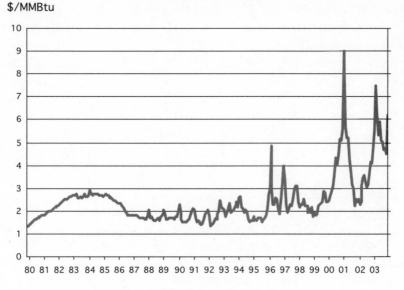

Figure 8.3 **The Price of Natural Gas**

Supply and Demand

Natural gas exists both alone and in conjunction with petroleum, around the world. Total world production is around 100 quadrillion Btus per year at present. The largest producer is Russia, followed by the United States. These two countries represent the lion's share of current natural gas production. Other producers include Canada, the United Kingdom, Mexico, and The Netherlands.

Demand roughly matches supply, although supply has been rising at a slightly faster pace than demand over the past few years. (See Figure 8.4.) Demand has been growing at a 2.7 percent compounded rate since 1980. The rate was slightly more rapid in the 1980s, around 3.4 percent per annum, representing a strong push to move away from petroleum to natural gas. The shift paused in the early 1990s, in part because of low oil prices at the time, which reduced the incentives to substitute natural gas for oil. The pace of growth has begun to accelerate once more over the past few years. Not only does natural gas have certain economic advantages over petroleum in many applications, but it also is seen as a cleaner fuel, in that its emissions are less than those of petroleum.

In recent years natural gas is accounting for around 21 percent of world energy production, up from around 16 percent in the early 1970s.

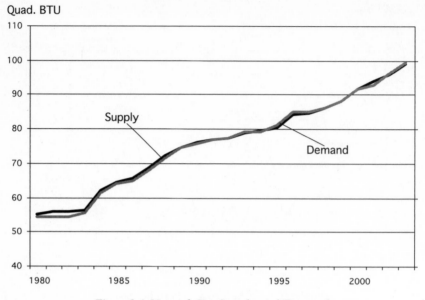

Quad. BTU

Figure 8.4 **Natural Gas Supply and Demand**

Outlook

I believe the outlook for natural gas is very good. Gas has advantages over petroleum. It also is extremely plentiful and available in the United States, and it is becoming more widely accepted. There are interesting plans for developing far-offshore liquefied natural gas terminals, which may be able to placate both local "not in my backyard" opposition and national security concerns. This would help make natural gas more readily available than it is today.

There are other interesting applications for natural gas. At least two companies, Syntroleum Corporation in the United States and South Africa's Sasol, have developed catalytic technologies that allow them to convert natural gas into ultra-clean diesel fuel. Diesel fuel is seen as potentially commanding a greater share of the automotive fuel market over the next few decades. It already is taking larger stakes in Europe and other parts of the world. In the United States diesel passenger cars have met consumer resistance in the past, but some automakers think they will be able to overcome this. Diesel fuel today has a high sulfur content and still has particulate emission problems. The latter can be solved, and there are U.S. regulations slated to come into effect over the next few years that will mandate sharply lowering the sulfur content of diesel fuel. Synthetic diesel fuel made from natural gas by the Syntroleum process is sulfur free, so it far exceeds the future U.S. regulations for sulfur content in diesel fuel. This and other applications suggest to me that natural gas may have an even brighter future than many others expect for it.

How to Invest

Natural gas is traded on the Nymex, in both futures and options. The IPE also trades gas in London. As with petroleum, there are many natural gas companies to invest in, ranging from large energy producers to exploration and development companies.

Uranium

I include uranium in this book for a variety of reasons. It is the only commodity I am spotlighting that is not traded on a formal futures or options exchange. However, it is an important commodity, and one on which a great deal of investor interest has focused since 2003.

The uranium market seemed to be all but dead for much of the past two decades. Supplies from government inventories and low prices devastated the mining sector for this hybrid commodity, which is both a metal and an energy source. Few power plants were being built in most parts of the world. Public sentiment was negative on nuclear power, which is the prime use for uranium, and the public perception was that both nuclear power and uranium mining were dead.

In fact, demand has more than tripled since 1980 and far exceeds the amount of uranium being mined each year, as is shown later in Figure 8.6. A revolution was occurring in nuclear power generation during this time, and the stage was being set for a dramatic recovery in both nuclear power and uranium. Since 2001 prices have exploded. Prices more than doubled from $6.40 in early 2001 to $14.40 by December 2003. Since then prices have more than doubled again, touching $33.00 in September 2005. (See Figure 8.5.)

Upward pressure on uranium prices began building as early as 2003, along with investor interest. In 2004, the rate at which prices were increasing accelerated significantly. That trend continued through 2005. As a result of the increase in prices, existing uranium mines and leach extraction

$/lb

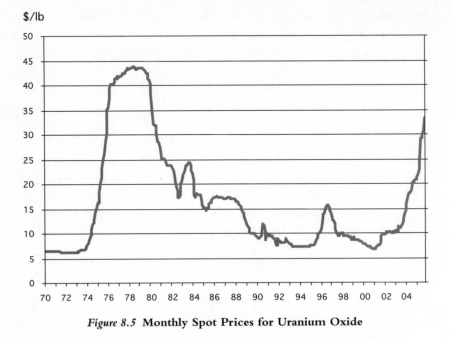

Figure 8.5 **Monthly Spot Prices for Uranium Oxide**

operations are being expanded, new projects are proliferating, and exploration is booming.

Accompanying these events has been a wave of frenetic publicity in the investment and mining communities. Articles about uranium in high-profile business publications and on Internet news sites are becoming commonplace. Politicians in many countries, energy industry experts, and even many environmentalists are calling for the world to take a fresh look at nuclear power as a source of electricity. The nuclear power industry, a pariah since the late 1970s, is being touted as the savior from fossil fuels and greenhouse gas emissions.

As a result of the increase in prices, existing uranium mines and leach extraction operations are being expanded, new projects are proliferating, and exploration is booming.

Much of this actually is true. Certain provisos are required to understand what is happening, and, as in most markets, the supply and demand dynamics are not as straightforward as proponents and opponents, bulls and bears, would like us to believe. However, the fact is that nuclear power is experiencing a revival around the world as the need for electricity accelerates, just at a time when the secondary, or nonmining, supply of uranium appears to be turning downward. (See Figure 8.6.)

Uranium supplies seem likely to remain tight and grow even tighter in the near future than they have been over the past two years. This suggests that uranium prices may remain strong, and could rise much further than they already have. Some industry experts suggest that uranium prices around $60 to $70 per pound are needed to justify the mine production expansions and developments that will be needed to meet projected uranium demand. While this may be the case, much of the restraint on mines development now is not price related, but rather related to politics, Native land issues in Australia and the United States, and other noneconomic factors. In these cases, the price of uranium matters little. This is true of all mining, but it becomes all the more important when you are speaking of radioactive uranium. Further complicating matters is the fact that a lot of the minable deposits are on Native lands in Australia and the United States.

All of this has come as a surprise to many people, who just assumed that the nuclear power industry and the uranium market had died as a result of public opposition, compounded by the disastrous after-effects of

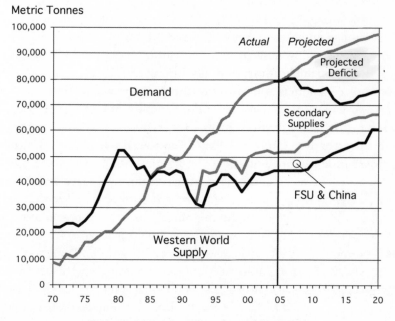

Figure 8.6 **Uranium Supply and Demand**

the Three Mile Island and Chernobyl problems in the late 1970s and 1986, respectively.

The nuclear power industry and uranium market have not gone away. They are more important today than they were prior to Three Mile Island. Today the market has been transformed. Nuclear power plants now generate nearly 17 percent of the world's electrical power, up from about 10 percent in 1985 and roughly 1 percent in 1970. In the three largest economies—the United States, Japan, and Germany—nuclear energy supplies approximately 20 to 30 percent of electrical power. In France, nearly 80 percent of all electrical power is generated at nuclear power plants. Between 1970 and 2000 nuclear power's share of global electricity generation grew at an annual average rate of 17.5 percent. There was similar growth in nuclear power's share of the U.S. energy market as well, even though there was not a single power plant commissioned for decades. The increase in power output from nuclear plants reflected modernization and more efficient operations. Power plants are being run today in radically different ways and are said to be far safer than the ones running three decades ago, even though they are the same power plants.

The price increase is coming from a confluence of factors. Demand is rising, as power plants run at high rates of operation. New plants are coming online around the world, except in the United States so far. The construction boom is greatest in India, and also China, but power plant construction is under way all over. Even Iran, a major oil producer, says it is pursuing nuclear power plant development. The present U.S. administration refuses to believe that Iran might be pursuing nuclear power for the purpose of generating electricity, but the fact is that virtually every other country and government in the world, including the U.S. government, is doing just that, and it may just be that Iran is, too.

Just as demand continues to rise, mine supply has reached at least a temporary plateau, as will the flow of uranium from other sources, primarily inventories being reprocessed from decommissioned nuclear warheads. These conversions have been under way for more than a decade, and the stockpile of military grade uranium available to be reprocessed into lower grade power plant material is diminishing. Stocks held by power plants and other commercial entities also are declining.

All of this is occurring in an economic environment characterized by rising prices for oil and natural gas, stimulating interest in alternative energy sources. Concern about the production of greenhouse gases by burning fossil fuels is also stimulating interest in nuclear power as an alternative to these fuels, while there has been a strong rate of increase in demand for electricity around the world. The prospect of future energy shortages in most parts of the world, flavored by sporadic problems already cropping up, adds to this interest in nuclear power, while the realization that nuclear power plants are more efficient and have improved safety features has lessened public opposition to nuclear power.

These trends and developments have combined to push uranium prices higher. Investors then entered the picture, attracted by all of these factors and by the fact that uranium prices already are rising. Investors like to buy into rising markets.

One of the key differences between uranium and many other commodities is that it is both a fuel and a highly strategic material, and thus has been repeatedly influenced by a unique set of political circumstances. Uranium has continuing military applications, and it is used in small research reactors, but the vast majority of supply is used to fuel nuclear power plants for electricity generation. Most uranium is recovered from underground, open-pit, or in-situ leach (ISL) mining operations. The first mining boom occurred in the 1950s, when the U.S. government initiated its "Atoms for Peace" program and began formulating the regulatory foundation for a civilian nuclear power industry. Another uranium boom occurred when the oil shocks of the 1970s resulted in a rush to alternate sources of power.

The end of the Cold War had the effect of diverting large quantities of reprocessed weapons-grade uranium to the commercial power market. Mine cutbacks and closures became commonplace throughout the 1990s. Prices stagnated for the most part. A relatively brief upturn in prices in 1996 had more to do with aberrations in trading and deliveries than with solid market fundamentals. A major news magazine recently described the uranium industry for most of the period since 1990 as being "all but dead."

Supply

Total uranium supplies in 2005 were estimated to have been around 78,600 metric tonnes. Of this, 44,000 metric tonnes came from uranium mines outside of the transitional economies of China and the former Soviet Union. Another 7,300 metric tonnes came from Russian metal reprocessing, and perhaps 27,700 metric tonnes came from a range of other secondary sources of supply.

Mine Production

The uranium mining industry and the number of producing mines is greatly reduced from previous decades. In 1958, approximately 850 underground mines and 200 open-pit mines were producing uranium worldwide. Today, there are fewer than 100 mines operating globally.

Uranium presently is produced in 23 countries. The predominant producing regions include Canada, Australia, central Asia, and Africa. On the surface it would seem that production is widely diversified. In fact, more than half of total mine supply (about 51 percent in 2004) was produced by fewer than half a dozen mines in Canada and Australia.

U.S. and South African production is negligible. U.S. production, for example, declined from nearly 20,000 metric tonnes of uranium oxide in 1980 to 4,000 in 1990. By 2003, U.S. production had shrunk to just 900 metric tonnes. South African output has shrunk from a peak of 7,257 metric tonnes in 1980 to 1,030 in the early part of this decade, some of it byproduct at gold mines.

The uranium market from 1980 until 2003 was characterized by lengthy periods of low prices and huge government and consumer stockpiles. The mining industry during this period experienced significant contraction and consolidation. Mine production fell each year between 1988 and 1994. Production then increased from 1995 to 1997, before declining again through 2000. Annual uranium oxide production declined nearly 19 percent in the course of a decade, from more than 44,150 metric tonnes in 1989 to around 35,900 in 1999. Production increased in 2000, declined slightly in each of the next three years, and finally moved decisively upward in 2004 to 44,000 metric tonnes, the highest level in 15 years.

Existing mine supply is far below the levels needed to meet current reactor requirements when secondary sources of uranium dry up or reactor fuel requirements increase. It will take time for new mine supply to reach the market—at least three to five years for greenfield mine projects.

Secondary Supply

The flow of uranium from all secondary sources, including Russian and U.S. government inventories, reprocessed spent fuel, and industry inventories, peaked in 1999 at an estimated 37,289 metric tonnes. Since then the supply of uranium from these sources has dropped to 27,600 metric tonnes in 2004. The largest decline was from sales from commercial inventories.

The U.S. and Russian governments reached an agreement in 1993 whereby Russia would convert 500 metric tonnes of weapons grade, highly enriched uranium (HEU) to low enriched uranium over 20 years. Russian HEU has been supplying approximately 15 percent of world reactor requirements. Russian stockpile supplies are allowed to enter the market at a fixed rate and have remained more or less constant at around 8,000 metric tonnes of uranium oxide equivalent annually for more than a decade.

> *Existing mine supply is far below the levels needed to meet current reactor requirements when secondary sources of uranium dry up or reactor fuel requirements increase.*

Demand

Today 441 nuclear power plants in 33 countries consume about 79,000 metric tonnes of uranium oxide per year to generate a combined 367,000 megawatts of electrical power. Worldwide, nuclear plant generating output grew by about 4 percent in 2004 to 2,696 billion kilowatt hours.

The United States has the largest share, with 103 operating reactors in 32 states that together account for about 31 percent of the world's nuclear generating capacity. As a U.S. fuel source, uranium is second only to coal and meets about 20 percent of the nation's electricity needs, up from roughly 5 percent 30 years ago. Worldwide, at least 26 nuclear power plants are currently under construction, and scores more are in the active planning stage or are being considered.

Market Balance

World mine production in 2004 only met about 59 percent of reactor demand. The last time mine production met 100 percent of demand was in the middle of the 1980s. Throughout the 1990s, nonmine sources of supply met 40 percent or more of total demand. As stated previously, the supply-demand gap has been filled largely from two sources: consumer stocks and military stockpiles of recycled weapons-grade uranium. Both of these sources have dwindled.

Industry

The uranium industry is consolidating at a rapid rate. This is as true of power providers as it is of mining companies. Between July 1999 and

October 2003, a dozen U.S. nuclear plants were purchased by utilities that had made the decision to grow in that direction.

Spot prices for uranium oxide (U_3O_8), the feedstock purchased by nuclear power plants, have more than doubled since early 2003 to their highest levels in more than two decades. The emergence of commodity fund activity began to make itself felt in the market in late 2004 and is believed to have helped drive prices higher in 2005. Spot prices for uranium oxide in September 2005 reached $33 per pound, with long-term contract prices even higher.

Outlook

Global electricity demand is projected to double between 2001 and 2025 to around 24,000 billion kilowatt hours, according to the Energy Information Agency of the U.S. Department of Energy (DOE). Most of this demand will be in the developing world, particularly in eastern and southern Asia. Both India and China have large programs to build numerous nuclear power plants over the next several decades. They are not alone, with many other countries elsewhere in Asia and around the world also planning to rely more on nuclear power for electricity generation in the future. During the same period, U.S. electricity needs are projected to increase by about 50 percent to approximately 5,800 billion kilowatt hours. Nuclear plants (which emit minimal or no greenhouse gases) are viewed in many quarters as an increasingly attractive power generation option.

Global electricity demand is projected to double between 2001 and 2025 to around 24,000 billion kilowatt hours.

Overall, even the most conservative estimates project an increase of roughly 10 percent in nuclear power generating capacity over the next 15 years. This implies that an additional 30 or 35 nuclear plants, not including those already under construction, would need to be built by 2020. Demand for uranium is projected to increase from around 79,400 metric tonnes in 2005 to around 97,000 metric tonnes per year in 2020.

Mining Production Outlook

Meanwhile, there is not a significant amount of dormant mine capacity waiting in the wings, but there are a few plans to reopen long-shuttered mines. Expansions of existing mines show more promise and are either under way or being planned at two large mines: Cameco's MacArthur River mine in Canada, and Western Mining Corporation's Olympic Dam mine in Australia.

There are also constraints on the capacity to convert uranium into the forms usable at power plants. Uranium conversion prices doubled between late 2003 and the middle of 2005, and have approximately quadrupled in less than five years. Prices rose to $12 per kilogram of uranium hexafluoride (UF$_6$) by early May 2005, an all-time high. Conversion capacity has been adequate with the reduced mine output levels of recent years, but that may not continue to be the case.

How to Invest

There may be a rare window of investment opportunity related to uranium over the next several years, possibly longer. Consumer stocks already are low, particularly in the United States, where just-in-time inventory control has been practiced by power plant operators for many years. Government stockpiles, however large they once were and still are, are finite and will run out. Exactly when that will happen is uncertain. The Russian government has indicated that it will ship less uranium from its weapons grade stocks after 2008. Russia may continue to honor its agreement with the U.S. government and supply significant amounts of world demand through 2013, but those amounts will apparently be smaller going forward.

A new factor has emerged in the uranium market since the second half of 2004, which has compounded the recent price increase. This is the appearance of investors willing to purchase and hold uranium inventories. Traditionally investors have sought to participate in rising metals prices by investing in the equities of mining companies. However, there are only a small number of pure-play uranium mining companies or uranium enrichment providers. Additionally, investing in uranium exploration companies offers a broader choice of companies and potentially higher returns, albeit with far greater risk. This continues to be the preferred investment approach of most natural resource–oriented investors. Others, however, are showing increasing propensity to purchase the commodity directly.

Given the absence of any futures or forward uranium markets, such investors are purchasing physical uranium and arranging for it to be stored for them. At least three funds have been organized outside of the United States to buy and hold uranium. To date they appear to have purchased only relatively small amounts of uranium, and their purchases probably have not had a dramatic direct impact on uranium prices.

Other investment options include purchasing the equities of nuclear power plant builders, equipment providers, utilities, and/or service providers involved in the uranium and nuclear power industries. There are two power plant builders currently active in the U.S. market, for example: General Electric (GE) and Westinghouse, a subsidiary of British Nuclear Fuels (BNFL). For both of these companies, nuclear power represents a relatively small portion of their revenue, so an investment in these companies would not be expected to track conditions in the uranium market very well. There is currently only one uranium enrichment company operating in the United States: USEC Inc., a privatized government entity formerly known as the U.S. Enrichment Corp. USEC's share price on the New York Stock Exchange more than doubled in the first four months of 2005, but came right back down to its January levels by October.

The duration of uranium's window of opportunity depends on how soon new power plants enter service, how quickly new mine production can be ramped up, how much Russian and U.S. government inventories are converted to the low enriched uranium used in power plants and sold into the market in the future, and how well key sectors of the global economy perform over the remainder of the decade.

9

Tropical Agriculturals

This chapter focuses on three of the tropical agriculturals: cocoa, coffee, and cotton. Sugar is another important tropical agricultural commodity, as are palm oil, orange juice, and other crops. While my company does sugar research now, I avoided it for many years. As far as I could tell, there was not a sugar market per se, but around 125 of them. It seemed that each country's government messed around with sugar. The U.S. government does the most damage, thanks to presidential politics and the money that fuels it. U.S. consumers pay more than twice what they could pay if the U.S. government did not support domestic sugar growers. The international sugar price has traded below 10 cents per pound for many years, rising above it only in 2005 and early 2006. U.S. sugar prices meanwhile are above 20 cents. I have omitted a discussion of sugar from this book, although it is a very interesting market. Cocoa, coffee, and cotton also present interesting opportunities for investors. Each of these markets has a set of dynamics that is moving the price of that crop in its own direction and its own pace.

Cocoa

Everyone knows cocoa as the basic ingredient in chocolate, and that is its major use. Cocoa also appears in some industrial products such as soaps and cosmetics in the form of cocoa butter. Most cocoa comes from West Africa, although the plant is not native to that region, having originated in the Americas.

Most cocoa ultimately is used in the manufacture of chocolate. In recent years various studies have indicated medicinal values to cocoa consumption, especially in the form of the dark chocolate that is more popular outside of the United States, where milk chocolate is preferred. A common misconception is that cocoa contains caffeine. It actually contains theobromine, a chemical that is closely related to caffeine and has similar stimulative effects.

Cocoa prices were trading around $1,500 per metric tonnes at the end of 2005. This price level is roughly in the middle of recent highs and lows. (See Figure 9.1.) Cocoa prices had risen sharply in the 1970s, after having spent most of the time from the end of World War II until the early 1970s trading between $500 and $1,000. Prices shot up to $5,500 in the middle of the 1970s, and then fell back to around $1,600 toward the end of the decade. Prices traded between that low and $2,500 for much of the early 1980s, with another spike up to $3,000 during that period. Increased production pushed prices down to around $1,200 to $1,500 in the late 1980s. Prices recovered in the 1990s, after the expansion, some of which occurred in newer growing areas in Asia, leveled off. Even so, prices remained

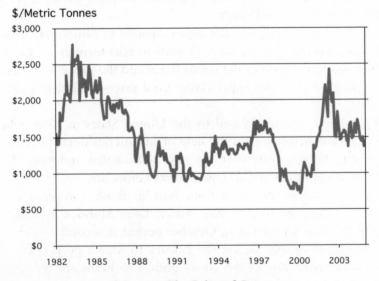

Figure 9.1 **The Price of Cocoa**

around $1,500 to $1,700. Prices dropped once again, to around $1,000, in the late 1990s, after production rebounded to newer highs. The outbreak of civil war in 2002 in Côte d'Ivoire, which accounts for more than 40 percent of world cocoa production, pushed prices to $2,500 briefly. Since then prices have traded around $1,400 to $1,700, with periodic spasms of unrest in the simmering civil war contributing to spikes upward in prices.

History

Cultivation of cocoa dates back to 1500 B.C., when the Olemac Indians grew cocoa trees as a domestic crop. More history is known about the Mayans, who consumed a bitter drink made from unsweetened ground cocoa beans. When the Mayans migrated to Central America in 600 A.D. they instituted the first cocoa plantations in Yucatán.

During the fourteenth century the cocoa drink became popular among the Aztec elites, who acquired the drink from the Mayans and started imposing taxes on the beans. The prepared mixture of ground cocoa beans crossed the ocean to Europe in 1544, when the Mayans brought the drink as a gift for Prince Phillip of Spain. In Spain the drink was prepared with sugar and other flavorings to make a hot, sweet cocoa beverage, used for both aphrodisiac and medicinal purposes. Official trading of cocoa beans began in 1585, when shipments came to Seville from Veracruz, Mexico. Over the next century Spain and Portugal shared their found treasure with the rest of Europe.

In 1657, the first chocolate house opened in London. Cocoa bean processing evolved over the next 17 years to take form as a solid chocolate. However, the price of the cocoa beans and the processing costs limited consumption to the upper classes until prices declined significantly in 1730.

Cocoa was first introduced to the United States in 1765, when an Irish chocolate maker sought the help of an America doctor to refine the production. Fifteen years later the two collaborated and built the first chocolate mill in the United States, Baker's Chocolate.

The production of cocoa from start to finish comprises multiple steps. Harvesting the fruit in West Africa, Latin America, and Asia takes place during the September to October period. A secondary harvest occurs in some countries during the January to March period. The cocoa beans are scooped out of the cocoa pods. The beans are fermented or cured, and left to dry in the sun. Beans then are cleaned and roasted to re-

veal the distinctive chocolate flavor. Following the roasting, the beans are
ground to make either cocoa butter or cocoa powder. About two-thirds of
the product is made into cocoa butter for use in chocolate and other products, with the other third being sold as cocoa powder. However, a trend has
emerged to process the bean for cocoa powder as opposed to cocoa butter
in an effort to compete with cheaper substitutes in the manufacture of
chocolate.

Supply

In the year 2003 to 2004, world cocoa bean production reached a record
output of 3,517,000 metric tonnes (see Figure 9.2). Four countries in West
Africa produce more than 70 percent of the world's cocoa supply. Of these
countries, Côte d'Ivoire is the largest grower, solely producing roughly 40
percent of the world supply, or 1,405,000 metric tonnes in the 2004 crop
year. The second largest producer is Ghana, which accounts for more than
20 percent of world supply. Production in Ghana rose sharply, roughly 48
percent in the 2004 crop year, as higher prices followed the outbreak of

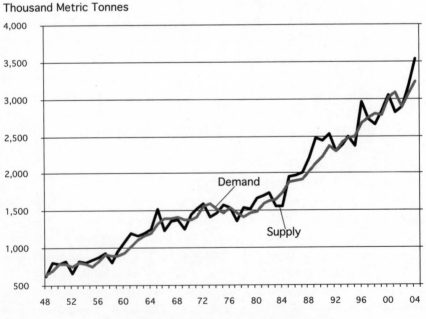

Figure 9.2 Cocoa Supply and Demand

civil war in Côte d'Ivoire, and government-backed spraying programs dramatically increased the yield. Additionally, there were rumors that cocoa was being smuggled across the border from Côte d'Ivoire and sold in Ghana, boosting reported Ghanaian production. Two other African countries, Nigeria and Cameroon, account for approximately 5 percent and 4 percent, respectively, of current world cocoa production.

Indonesia and Malaysia sought to build cocoa plantations and compete with the West African producers. For a while they experienced some success, but Indonesia's crop has decreased roughly 9 percent over the past few years. Nonetheless, Indonesia remains the third largest producer, after Côte d'Ivoire and Ghana, producing around 11 percent of the world's supply. The growth of Brazil's production was stunted by disease and drought in recent years, but has shown signs of recovering lately. Cocoa is also produced in Colombia, Ecuador, and numerous other countries.

Demand

World cocoa demand has been rising almost continually over most of the past few decades. During this time the rate of increase in annual cocoa consumption has slowed markedly, however. During the 1980s annual growth in demand was running 4.1 percent. In the 1990s it slowed to 2.7 percent per year, reflecting a move away from chocolate consumption during this time. Consumption fell in 2001, but since then it has recovered and risen to record levels. Factoring in the 2001 decline, it would seem that the rate of growth in cocoa consumption has slowed further in the first half of this decade compared to the rate in the 1990s and the 1980s. The slowdown was concentrated in 2001, which saw major interruptions in the important chocolate-consuming year-end holidays. Taking 2001 out as an anomaly, demand was very strong in 2002 and 2003 and was modestly strong in 2004 and 2005.

Demand for cocoa beans is measured in terms of the amount of cocoa beans ground into cocoa powder or butter. In the 2003 to 2004 crop year, world grindings reached a record high of 3,206,000 metric tonnes. The Netherlands has been the world consumer since 2000/01, when operations exceeded those of the United States. In 2003/04 the Netherlands and the United States accounted for roughly 14 percent and 13 percent of the world's total cocoa grinding operations, respectively. Côte d'Ivoire is the third largest processor, grinding nearly 10 percent of the world's cocoa.

Industry

The International Cocoa Organization (ICCO) was established in 1973 under stipulations of the International Cocoa Agreement of 1972. The ICCO is supported by the United Nations with a mission to foster a "sustainable cocoa economy." This objective encompasses all areas of the industry, including market participants, farming practices, stability, and crop prices.

Demand for cocoa beans is measured in terms of the amount of cocoa beans ground into cocoa powder or butter. In the 2003 to 2004 crop year, world grindings reached a record high of 3,206,000 metric tonnes.

The leading cocoa pressing company is Archer Daniels Midland, grinding 470,000 metric tonnes, 15 percent of the world market share. Following are Cargill and Barry Callebaut with grinding volumes of 14 percent and 13 percent of world market share, respectively. Blommer, Petra Foods, and Nestlé each account for roughly 5 percent of the world grinding output. Other companies with roughly 2 to 3 percent of market share each are Cadbury, Cantalou/Cemoi, Hershey, Ferrero, Schwarteuer Werke (KVB), Philip Morris/KJS, Schokinag, and Mars. Smaller companies grind the remaining 27 percent of the market share.

Outlook

The price of cocoa is neither high nor low at present. If conditions worsened in Côte d'Ivoire, prices could rise sharply. As of the end of 2005, ongoing efforts to broker a truce among the warring factions by the governments of South Africa, France, and the United Nations appears to be bearing some fruit, with a coalition government being announced. In the face of peace in Côte d'Ivoire prices might subside toward $1,200. However, prices may not fall back to their low levels seen in the late 1990s. Demand is rising, and there is increased interest in cocoa for its cancer-fighting attributes. But in 2005 researchers announced development of synthetic compounds that mimic the anti-cancer agents in cocoa, which could limit interest in cocoa for these purposes in the future. Nevertheless, the taste of chocolate will keep interest in cocoa alive on the part of consumers worldwide. Additionally, as of 2005 there were efforts to begin creating chains of cocoa and hot chocolate stores, in an attempt to do for cocoa what Starbucks and its followers have done for coffee.

The International Cocoa Organization estimated that world production was dropping roughly 9.2 percent to 3,194,000 metric tonnes in the 2004/05 crop year, while world consumption, measured in terms of the grinding of cocoa beans into powder and liquor, was projected to increase 1.9 percent to 3,268,000 metric tonnes. World end-of-season stocks were expected to drop 7.2 percent. Such a shortfall of current supply relative to demand was expected to provide support to cocoa prices. Inventories of cocoa were around 1.1 million metric tonnes, equivalent to roughly four months of consumption. This was down from levels of 1.5 to 1.6 million metric tonnes in the late 1990s, but was seen as being adequate to buffer the market in the event of political unrest in Côte d'Ivoire or other producing nations. However, the quality of some of these stocks was questioned by some in the market.

Future prices will depend to some extent on the outcome of the peace efforts in Côte d'Ivoire. While successes were being registered in late 2005, regional unrest in other countries around Côte d'Ivoire suggested that political instability could remain a question facing the cocoa market for many years.

How to Invest

Cocoa futures and options are traded on the New York Board of Trade (NYBOT) and on the London International Financial Futures and Options Exchange (LIFFE). There are no real cocoa producing companies in which U.S. citizens can easily invest. Some investors will trade chocolate manufacturers' stocks as a surrogate for cocoa, but many of these companies today are diversified food processing companies, and their financial performance is not clearly tied to cocoa prices. Furthermore, one is never certain whether they are beneficiaries or victims of rising prices.

Coffee

Coffee is a major crop and commodities market. The dollar value of the world's coffee crop makes it one of the largest physical commodities markets in terms of the value of material traded. Coffee is produced in dozens of countries in tropical regions. In many of these countries the coffee industry is a major portion of national income, a major source of taxes for the government, and a major source of foreign exchange earnings for the country. The range of coffee operations extends from many small farmers who earn so little money from their farming that they cannot afford to buy a cup of coffee, to enormous plantations owned by wealthy individuals or, in the case of Vietnam, the government.

There are two basic types of coffee, arabica and robusta. Arabica is grown at higher altitudes and is the most common product, comprising roughly 70 percent of the world's total crop. Many consumers prefer arabica's flavor, but people in the coffee business quickly develop a diplomatic way of indicating that they like both arabica and robusta. Robusta grows at lower altitudes and tends to have a higher caffeine content than arabica. Often it is roasted to a darker degree and used in espresso. Arabica is traded on the NYBOT while robusta is traded on the LIFFE. Coffee is also traded on exchanges in Brazil and Tokyo.

Arabica coffee prices rose sharply in the early 1970s, and traded between $1.20 and $3.30 per pound in the period from 1976 through 1985. Prices weakened in the late 1980s, dropping as low as 40 cents per pound in 1991 and 1992. (The prices on the charts here are monthly average prices, which mask the interday highs and lows to some extent.) Prices then recovered. There were two spikes in prices to higher levels during the late 1990s, briefly taking prices to levels above $2.00 and $2.50, respectively. (See Figure 9.3.) This round of higher prices was accompanied by large plantations of coffee

***Figure 9.3* Arabica Coffee Prices**

trees being established which, after a lag for the maturation of the trees, led to a large oversupply of coffee on world markets. Prices fell again, to levels around 40 to 60 cents, in 2001. Since then prices have begun to recover, and rose to around $1.30 during the year 2005. (Robusta prices move roughly in line with Arabica, as there is some substitution potential between the two types of coffee. I tend to focus on the arabica coffee traded on the NYBOT, although some people will trade an arbitrage between the arabica traded in New York and the robusta traded in London.)

History

Coffee plants originally were cultivated in the Horn of Africa, most likely in Yemen. Legend has it that goat herders began using coffee beans after they noticed that goats seemed more active than usual after they had dined on the red coffee cherries. Originally coffee beans were used to make wine. Later, around 1000 A.D., brewed coffee emerged in the Arabian Peninsula. The drink was said to have a mystical quality and was utilized by priests and doctors in ceremonies, and as a medicinal product.

During the fifteenth century the cultivation of coffee surfaced in the Yemen province of Arabia, which would soon be the primary source of coffee for the world. The Yemen port was heavily guarded to try to keep the plants within the kingdom, but this did not prevent fertilized coffee plants from crossing its many borders. During many of the Muslim migrations to Mecca, coffee was smuggled back to migrants' homelands, helping to spread cultivation of the plants.

Popularity of the crop began to sweep over to Europe in 1615, as trading grew with Venetians and Arabic merchants along the Spice Route. By 1616, the Dutch had won the race to grow coffee beans in greenhouses in Holland. By the middle of the seventeenth century the Dutch had cornered the coffee market. They cultivated coffee in Indonesia; the plant took root in Sumatra, Java, Sulawesi, and Bali. Indonesia today is the fourth largest exporter of coffee.

The plant made its way to Latin America in the eighteenth century. French colonists were the first to bring coffee to the New World, sowing a lone tree in Martinique. It was the Dutch who continued to cultivate the plant throughout their new lands, and growth in South and Central America spread. During this time, a plant disease spread through the coffee fields in Southeast Asia, killing much of the crop it infected. Many decades later Brazil began to emerge as the dominant coffee producer.

Supply

World coffee supply for the 2003/04 year was approximately 120 million 60-kilogram bags. This amount does not take into account coffee stocks or inventories. World coffee stocks at the start of the 2004/05 agricultural year were estimated to be at 29 million 60-kilo bags. World production of coffee has been increasing over the past decades, in line with rising consumption.

Roughly 50 countries produce coffee today. Brazil contributes close to 30 percent of the world's coffee production. Vietnam is the world's second largest supplier of coffee, contributing around 11 percent of total world coffee output. Colombia is the third largest producer of coffee, contributing close to 9 percent of total production. These three countries account for about half of total world coffee production. Many other countries produce smaller amounts of coffee, including Costa Rica, El Salvador, Ethiopia, Guatemala, Honduras, Indonesia, India, Côte d'Ivoire, Mexico, Peru, and Uganda. World production is expected to decrease 5.6 percent to 113 million 60-kilo bags in the 2005/06 year.

Coffee crops are greatly affected by the climate. Cold weather can have a significant impact on the yield of the coffee crop for a given season and can damage a coffee tree's ability to produce in subsequent years. Brazil's coffee-growing regions suffer from cold frosts during the winter months, typically between June and September. Brazil's harvest, because it represents 30 percent of coffee supplies, can significantly affect world supplies and therefore world prices. As a result, the weather in these regions during Brazil's winter months is closely watched by the world coffee trade. Signs of cold spells can drive prices higher, while the absence of damaging frosts can depress coffee prices.

Coffee production increased during the 1990s as Vietnam, Mexico, and other countries developed large plantations. The coffee price had risen sharply in two spurts during the 1990s, which stimulated the creation of new plantations and led to a dramatic increase in coffee output. There is a seven-year delay between the planting of new coffee trees and the first harvest, so there is a similar lag between increases in price and the resulting rise in output. Production is also affected by fertilization and tending of plantations. During the period of low prices from 1999 into 2004, many plantation managers cut back on tending their trees. This led to a reduction in the yield per tree, which was reflected in a decline in overall coffee production that helped restore the market to balance and increase prices. (See Figure 9.4.)

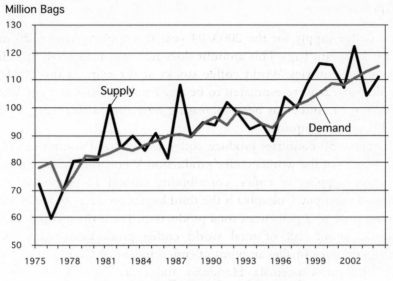

Million Bags

Figure 9.4 **Coffee Supply and Demand**

Coffee supply cannot react to immediate increases in demand. For farmers to increase supply, prices must stay high in order to lure new entrants to the market or entice existing farmers to return to growing coffee trees. There is a three- to five-year lag after an increase in demand and price before the supply side can respond to the change. Fertilization and protection are expensive. Subsequent years' crops suffer from reduced upkeep. When prices are low, production will fall in following years. Then prices are driven back up by a decrease in supply. Supply is currently high and prices have been low recent years—thus crop preservation is in jeopardy.

> *Coffee supply cannot react to immediate increases in demand.*

Demand

Worldwide consumption was expected to amount to 115 million 60-kilo bags in the 2004/05 crop year. Since 1975 coffee demand worldwide has been expanding at a rate of 1.4 percent per annum. World supply meanwhile has had an annual growth rate of 1.8 percent since 1975.

The United States is the largest consumer of coffee, consuming approximately 20 to 25 percent of the world's total production. Most of the coffee consumed in the United States is imported from the major producers, including Brazil, Colombia, and Vietnam. In 2004, the United States consumed 20.7 million 60-kilo bags. Brazil is the second largest consumer, accounting for 13 percent of world consumption. The third largest consumer of coffee is Germany, although this is at the processing level—coffee roasted and ground in Germany is exported to many other countries. Germany processes approximately 10 million 60-kilo bags per year, which makes up close to 9 percent of world demand. Japan also is a major consumer, representing roughly 5 percent of world demand. These four countries represent about 50 percent of world demand. The whole of Europe, including Germany, accounts for between 35 and 38 percent of world demand. Other major consuming countries are France, Italy, Spain, the United Kingdom, and Indonesia. Coffee demand is expected to rise due to increased demand at both ends of the coffee scale—specialty coffees classified as higher-quality blends and instant coffees classified as lower-quality blends.

Outlook

Overall demand for coffee has been rising steadily over the past decade. Coffee has become increasingly popular in some Asian and European markets where tea formerly predominated, aided by the spread of coffee shops and cafes. Demand also is rising in some producing countries. Supply meanwhile has been much more volatile, rising sharply for much of the 1990s before declining during the first part of this decade.

The market moved from a large persistent surplus of new production to a market balance in which new supply was less than demand over the previous two years. This has allowed for some reductions in inventories of coffee beans, and has allowed prices to rise once more.

Some plantations have been uprooted and replaced with other cash crops during the period of low prices, while others have been abandoned. More often the plantations have been neglected but could be rehabilitated if higher coffee prices make such efforts financially worthwhile over the next few years. In 2005 some coffee growing areas were severely damaged by a series of severe hurricanes. The combination of these events may extend the period in which coffee consumption exceeds new supply. This could move coffee prices even higher over the next few years. If this proves to be the case, a spike back to $2.00 or higher cannot be ruled out.

The USDA forecasts the world coffee production will drop 6 percent to slightly more than 113 million bags in the 2005/06 crop year. This decrease would reflect a 14 percent decline in Brazil's production. Consumption meanwhile is anticipated to increase 2 percent in this period.

How to Invest

Arabica coffee futures and options are traded on the NYBOT; robusta futures and options are traded on the LIFFE. Coffee also is traded at the Bolsa de Mercadorias y Futuros (BM&F) in Brazil, and the Tokyo Grain Exchange (TGE), although generally speaking U.S. investors do not get involved in these markets.

There are few coffee producing companies that trade publicly. Many of the coffee roasters are parts of diversified food processing companies, and their share prices do not reflect changes in coffee prices very closely. Additionally, these are coffee buyers, for whom increases in coffee prices increase their raw material costs. One of the most well-known of these is Starbucks.

Cotton

Globally, cotton is the primary fiber used in clothing. The origination of cotton is hard to pinpoint. When searching through caves in Mexico scientists discovered bits of cotton bolls and fragments of cotton fiber dating back approximately 7,000 years. Cotton has been cultivated in India and Egypt for almost 5,000 years now.

Cotton grows best in temperate climatic conditions with evenly distributed rainfall. The crop requires dry weather during harvest, which is when cotton bolls are most sensitive to wind and rain. The fiber can be broadly classified into two types based on length—long staple and short staple. Long staple cotton is approximately 1.2 inches in length and its cultivation is largely concentrated in the United States, Egypt, Peru, and Sudan. This variety is used mainly for sewing thread, lace yarn, and high-quality fabrics. Short staple fabric is usually much harder to use. In addition to textiles, cotton is also used for cordage, automobile tires, and plastic reinforcing.

When cotton was first introduced to Europe, Europeans were familiar with only animal fibers such as wool. This gave birth to a fable, "The Vegetable Lamb of Tartary." This legend claims that early Europeans thought cotton came from a sort of animal plant. As they were unfamiliar with the concept of cloth being made from plant fiber as opposed to animal fibers, they assumed that cotton was a form of wool. They imagined that cotton bolls were tiny sheep attached to the plant by their navels.

Cotton bolls contain the lint, from which thread and cloth are spun, and seeds. The seeds can be difficult to separate out, but the invention of cotton gins in the seventeenth century speeded the process of separating the lint from the seeds and led to the advent of mass production of cotton cloth in England. Cotton fiber was exported to England from India at the time.

Supply

Twelve of the world's largest producers contribute approximately 86.5 percent of the total world cotton production. The countries in this list include China, the United States, India, Pakistan, Uzbekistan, Brazil, Turkey, Egypt, Sudan, Argentina, Iran, and Mexico. There are approximately 39 cotton-producing countries.

Of these, the top three producers are China, the United States, and India. These three countries in aggregate produce approximately 60 percent of the total world production. China has been leading the pack, consistently surpassing the cotton production in the United States since 1982/83. China overtook India's production in 1952/53, falling behind only between 1961 and 1963. There are indications that Chinese cotton production may not rise further in the future, and actually could drop. As Chinese economic development progresses, farmers in that country may be shifting to higher-value cash crops and relying more on cotton imports to meet domestic requirements. Nevertheless, reports suggested China would continue to head the pack with an estimated 5.4 to 5.5 million tons output for 2005/06.

In addition to these major producers, cotton is produced in a number of other countries, including many developing countries, such as Mali, Burkina Faso, Uganda, Kenya, Tanzania, and Zimbabwe. Some of these countries have complained that U.S. government subsidies to U.S. cotton growers have depressed world cotton prices, and they have been trying to get the United States to end its subsidies program for years. Brazil sued the U.S. government in the World Trade Organization over a smaller por-

There are indications that Chinese cotton production may not rise further in the future, and actually could drop.

tion of its subsidies program, which paid U.S. cotton farmers fees to compensate for their lack of competitive advantage in European export markets. Brazil won the court case, and the U.S. government agreed to end that subsidy in 2006. The larger subsidies will continue indefinitely.

The broad trend in cotton production has been positive. Production in 2004/05 saw a significant jump, with world production at 120.4 million bales as reported by the United States Department of Agriculture (USDA). This is an increase of 26.6 percent from the previous year. Of this, China contributed 29.0 million bales, approximately a quarter of total world production. The United States followed with production at 23.2 million bales.

Improved farming technologies coupled with better pest management in major cotton growing nations is helping cut production costs. This has assisted farmers to sustain production in the current low price environment.

The longer-term decline in prices since the 1990s has been discouraging to farmers, however, and production in 2005/06 is expected to fall 7.5 percent. Part of this decline could also be attributed to poor weather conditions in major cotton growing regions. The single largest decline in production will be experienced in China, where production is projected to back off in 2005/06 closer to levels seen earlier in this decade.

Demand

The largest consumers of cotton are China, India, Pakistan, and the United States. These countries collectively have accounted for approximately half of total world consumption. It is interesting to note that the largest producers of cotton are also the largest consumers of the fiber.

In recent years Pakistan's consumption has exceeded that of the United States. Consumption in the United States has been steadily declining since 1998/99, while that of Pakistan has been increasing consistently over the same period and has grown 54.0 percent.

Cotton consumption in China has been growing at a steady rate since 1998/99 and has roughly doubled in this time. China's consumption in 2004/05 stood at 38.5 million bales. This was an increase of 20.3 percent from the previous year. Also, China accounted for 35.4 percent of world consumption in 2004/05. The expiration of global quotas for textiles on January 1, 2005, was a significant contributing factor to this increase. The abolishment of the quotas for a time in early 2005 could have reduced

Thousand 480 lb. Bales

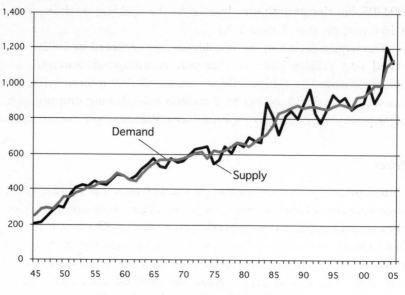

Figure 9.5 **Cotton Supply and Demand**

consumption in other labor-intensive countries, like India, Bangladesh, Pakistan, Sri Lanka, and Cambodia. The import quotas in Europe and the United States were reimposed but then renegotiated. Quotas on Chinese cotton products will be phased out in Europe and the United States over the next several years.

Consumption has grown 11.0 percent in India between 2003/04 and 2004/05. Consumption grew 11.9 percent in Pakistan, and 7.8 percent in Bangladesh over the same period.

Market Balance

The cotton market has been closely balanced over the past decade. The occurrences of annual shortfalls or surpluses of new cotton production relative to demand have been equally distributed during this time. Because cotton is an annual crop, as opposed to a crop such as cocoa or coffee that grows on perennial bushes or trees, cotton growers can scale back or increase their plantings from year to year to more closely match consumption. The largest surplus over the past decade was recorded in 2004/05, totaling 11.6 million bales. The excellent crop yields in the 2004/05 season were responsible for this outcome. Demand grew 10.7 percent in 2004/05, but this growth was dwarfed by the sizable growth in production of 26.6 percent. (See Figure 9.5.)

The largest deficit in the last decade was recorded in 2002/03, which totaled 10.1 million bales. In that year consumption amounted to 98.3 million bales, led by China, which consumed 29.9 million bales. Production was lagging and totaled 88.2 million bales, having dropped in all the major producing countries—China, India, Pakistan, and the United States.

Prices

Cotton prices spent most of the period between 1984 and 2005 in the range between 40 and 80 cents per pound. Many economists say that U.S. cotton subsidies put a cap on world prices around 83 cents. Prices peaked above the $1.00 mark briefly in early 1995, but quickly fell back to levels around 70 to 80 cents. Cotton prices saw their worst years in late 2001 and early 2002. The lowest price cotton has touched since May 1984 was a monthly average of 29.90 cents in September 2001. Prices have risen since then, peaking at a monthly average of 76.73 cents in September 2003. The average price since September 2003 has been approximately 55 cents. (See Figure 9.6.)

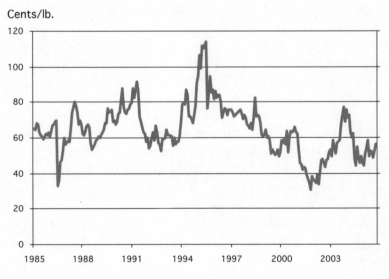

Figure 9.6 **The Price of Cotton**

Industry

The United States subsidizes its cotton farmers extensively. The government makes approximately $3.0 billion in transfer payments annually to its 35,000 cotton farmers. The European Union provides similar subsidies to its farmers.

The United States exports approximately 40 percent of its total output. This is a significant amount considering that it is the world's second largest producer. The large proportion of exports exacerbates the effects these subsidies have on world trade and prices.

> *The government makes approximately $3.0 billion in transfer payments annually to its 35,000 cotton farmers.*

Subsidies provided by the United States are said by many to have given its farmers an unfair advantage over other producing nations. The United States was able to increase production even in times of declining prices. Such practices have had a distorting effect on world trade and prices. Those affected most are farmers in less-developed countries in Africa.

While the U.S. and EU governments have floated suggestions that they might phase out their subsidies programs in the future, many observers believe that these proposals either will not be converted into concrete actions, or will be designed to continue to compensate U.S. and European cotton growers in ways that continue to distort world cotton markets.

If the U.S. government were to seriously remove these subsidies, it would be extremely bullish for cotton prices. U.S. cotton farmers take issue with such statements, but it is true. Prices would rise sharply if U.S. subsidies really were abandoned.

China has become a dominant player in the textile market. Completion of the phaseout of the Multifiber Agreement (MFA) on January 1, 2005, opened doors for China's textile exports, which increased 64 percent in the first eight months of 2005 to $15.4 billion. This exponential growth triggered several restrictions from the United States and the European Union, whose domestic industries were suffering. China was successful in reaching new agreements with both of these entities to allow the restrictions on Chinese cotton manufactured clothing to be phased out in the years ahead.

Outlook

Projections made by the USDA indicate a decrease in world cotton production in the 2005/06 year. The USDA also forecasts a marginal increase in consumption. Total production for 2005/06 is forecast at 111.4 million bales, down from 120.4 million bales in 2004/05. Meanwhile consumption is forecast at 112.9 million bales, up from 108.7 million bales. Ending stocks are projected to remain approximately constant at 50.9 million bales. Imports from China are expected to increase dramatically in 2005/06. They stood at 6.3 million bales in 2004/05, but are forecasted by the USDA to increase to 15.5 million bales in 2005/06, an increase of 142.7 percent. This jump could be attributed largely to a 15.5 percent decline in China's production, from 29.0 million bales in 2004/05 to 24.5 million bales in 2005/06.

How to Invest

Investment can be made in cotton by investing directly in futures and options at the New York Board of Trade. Cotton is also traded in Liverpool on the LIFFE.

10

Grains and Oilseeds

This chapter covers corn, soybeans, and wheat—two grains and a legume grown for its oil, meal, and beans. All three are among the largest agricultural commodities markets in the world. Each is an annual crop, planted new each year. As such, these crops differ in an important way from some of the tropical agricultural crops discussed in the previous chapter. The fact that these crops, like cotton, are newly planted every year means that farmers have much greater flexibility in responding to changes in demand and price. Farmers are able to switch crops from year to year in response to shifts in demand, anticipated changes in demand, and price expectations.

As a result, these crops will trade off of each other. In a given year, higher corn prices might lead farmers to plant greater acreage in corn, at the expense of soybeans, cotton, or even wheat. The reduction in plantings of those crops will then lead investors and food processors to buy some of them in the futures or forward markets, in the expectation that the reduced production will push prices higher later. Similarly, weak prices in one crop can lead to weak prices in other crops, as farmers shift to them in search of increased revenue per acre. Government subsidy programs distort the markets for these crops, but these underlying relationships still apply, although government interference reduces the free market capacity for supply, demand, and price to interact.

Corn

Corn is the single largest grain crop in the world. Corn is used both for human consumption and as feed for livestock. It is grown around the world, but the United States is the largest producer and consumer by a wide margin. Corn is a staple of many people's diets around the world. It was first cultivated around 3,000 years ago in the Americas by Native Americans. Corn was brought to Europe and the rest of the world by European settlers.

Corn prices have spent most of the period since the early 1970s trading between $2.00 and $3.00 per bushel. During this time there were four spikes below this range, the worst being a drop to around $1.50 in the late 1980s. (See Figure 10.1.) The price has had more significant spikes above $3.00, although they have become less common since the 1970s and have never been sustained for a long period. Prices spiked to around $3.60 three times in the 1970s and early 1980s. Each time, prices promptly fell back into a $2.40 to $2.80 range. Corn then spiked to around $4.86 in 1996 because of concerns about a major drought, but fell back to around $2.80 within two months. By 1998 prices had dropped to $1.78, their lowest level since 1987. Prices then remained mostly below $2.40 until late 2003,

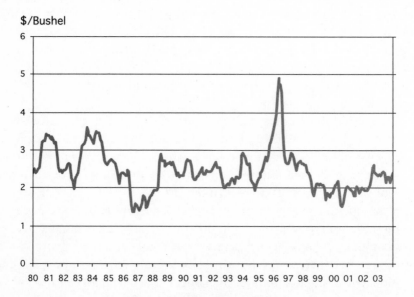

Figure 10.1 **The Price of Corn**

spiking up to around $2.60 at one point in September 2002. Prices broke above this range in 2004. Corn rose to around $2.70 in the middle of 2004, faded lower later that year, rose back to $2.75 in the middle of 2005, and then declined once more. While corn had found support around $2.35 in late 2004, prices fell to $2.00 in late 2005. Prices recovered to around $2.10 to $2.20 by early 2006.

Corn's price decline in late 2005 was due to large crops in the United States and China, as well as smaller increases in crops in other countries. Demand growth may have slowed as well. Exports from the United States were weaker in late 2005 than the market had been expected, boosting domestic inventories at a time when world corn inventories also were rising sharply.

> *While corn had found support around $2.35 in late 2004, prices fell to $2.00 in late 2005. Prices recovered to around $2.10 to $2.20 by early 2006.*

Supply

As previously mentioned, the United States is the largest producer of corn. U.S. corn output is more than 256 million metric tonnes per year, accounting for roughly 42 percent of world corn output. China is the next largest producer. At annual production around 114 million metric tonnes, China represents roughly 19 percent of world production.

Other major producers include Brazil, Mexico, India, Argentina, Canada, and France. Total world output reached 609 million metric tonnes in the 2003–2004 crop year, and rose further in 2004–2005. Production had reached 607 million metric tonnes in 1999, but declined sharply the following year. Production was relatively weak the following year, but began to recover in 2002–2003.

Demand

In the United States, corn is used primarily as livestock feed. Of the 7.9 million bushels of corn consumed in the U.S. market in the 2002–2003 crop year, nearly 5.7 million bushels went to livestock. Of the remaining 2.3 million bushels of domestic use, around 1.1 million bushels were distilled into alcohol. Most of this ethanol went into fuel applications, although about 12 percent of it was used in beverages and nonfuel industrial applications such as manufacturing and cleaning. High fructose corn syrup accounts for around 23 percent of U.S. corn use, with other sugars around 9 percent, corn starch 11 percent, and cereals and other food products around 8 percent. In addition to domestic consumption, around 23 percent of U.S. corn production is exported.

Outlook

Corn supply fell below world corn consumption for several years, from 1999 through the 2002–2003 crop year. (See Figure 10.2.) Production rose sharply after that, and appears to be exceeding demand as of 2005. Inventories rose sharply in 2005, both within the United States and on a worldwide basis.

Prices may subside in the near future, reflecting the increased supply and the rise in market inventories. These trends already existed in late 2004 and early 2005, however, and did not preclude sharp increases in corn prices. Investors have rediscovered corn, along with other commodities, and increased their long positions on the Chicago Board of Trade (CBOT) corn futures contract, helping to boost prices even in the face of healthy production and rising inventories. The corn market, like many

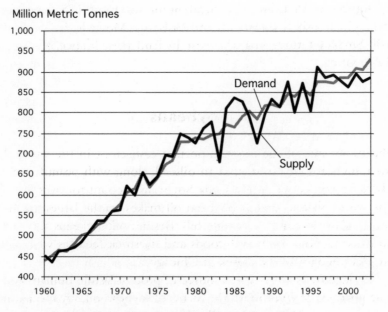

Figure 10.2 **Corn Supply and Demand**

other commodities markets, would appear to be vulnerable to investors liquidating these positions, in which case prices might fall significantly. Some of these investments in long corn positions are in commodities-indexed products, however, which may represent a solid base, less likely to be liquidated than more traditional investment positions. As such, they could represent long-term support for corn prices at higher levels than the base price levels have been in the past.

As 2006 was beginning, many corn market participants expected corn prices to drop into a range of $1.60 to $2.20, reflecting higher output, lower U.S. exports, and high market inventories. If the new wave of investors remain in the market and in fact represent a new level of price sup-

> *Prices may subside in the near future, reflecting the increased supply and the rise in market inventories.*

port for corn, prices may make a longer-term base around $1.90 to $2.00 and could trade in a somewhat higher range than otherwise might be expected.

How to Invest

Corn futures and options are traded on the CBOT. This is the largest corn futures market, and the focal point for most U.S. investors and traders. Corn also is traded on the Bolsa de Mercadorias y Futuros in Brazil. Smaller futures markets exist in Budapest, France, Korea, Japan, and Argentina.

Soybeans

Soybeans are one of the more important cash crops in the world. In the market, soybeans are considered an oilseed, along with peanuts, sunflower seeds, rapeseeds, copra, and linseeds. Soybeans account for over 80 percent of the world oilseeds traded. Soybean oil makes up the largest portion, 32 percent, of world edible vegetable oils. Besides oil, soybeans also yield soy meal (used in flour for baked goods and livestock feed) as well as whole beans. All three forms are traded in Chicago.

This legume is a very good source of protein. While humans consume sizable portions of soybeans in the forms of soybean oil, soy meal, tofu, and other forms, much of the annual soybean crop goes into livestock feed.

Soybeans are made up of 40 percent protein and 20 percent oil. Their protein content is about twice as high as the content in meat, and many people believe humans would be much healthier if they derived more of their protein directly from soybeans and less through meat consumption. The soybean seeds removed from the hull are consumed as whole beans or are crushed, with or without the hull, to produce soybean meal and soybean oil. The crushings are used as a surrogate measure of demand, although this is not an accurate measure of full consumption of soybeans, since some beans are consumed without crushing, while other beans are used as seeds for the following year. Soybean meal is primarily used as feed for livestock. Soybean oil is used in an array of products, from ice cream and salad dressings to soap and explosives.

Soybeans started as a wild plant in East Asia, first domesticated in eastern China sometime between the eleventh and seventeenth centuries. Soybeans were introduced in the United States in 1804. Today it is the second most important cash crop in the world, providing everything from protein for a hungry world to a basic chemical feedstock used in numerous products and processes.

As mentioned earlier, soybeans, soy meal, and soybean oil are all traded on the Chicago Board of Trade. This section will focus only on the prices for soybeans themselves. Many traders and investors will trade what is called "the crush," which is the spread among soybeans, oil, and meal. These spreads vary based on physical market conditions, including demand from various soybean using sectors, export expectations, and soybean crop and export conditions in other exporting countries such as Brazil and Argentina.

Soybeans are vulnerable to soybean rust, a crop disease that plagues crops around the world. The U.S. soybean industry avoided rust until 2004, when it first appeared here. It was not clear how the rust came to the United States, but some suggest that it was carried here on hurricane winds from the Caribbean. Soybean rust had reduced the yields of every other major producing country prior to its appearance in the United States. Fungicide applications for the disease have increased production costs by an estimated $25 per acre since 2004.

Soybeans are also one of the crops involved in controversies related to genetically modified (GMO) seeds. Beginning in the late 1990s some nongovernmental organizations (NGOs) began to express concern that GMO food stocks could disrupt natural crops and plants, and present an environmental risk. Concern has also been expressed over the potential health risks to humans, although there has been no evidence to confirm such risks. Anti-globalization groups also raised the issue that growers would become dependent on a few large seed suppliers if they become too closely involved in using GMO seeds. A group of European governments and NGOs spread these concerns throughout Africa and other parts of the world, emphasizing that U.S. seeds and crops were genetically modified while their own crops were not. They encouraged these countries, some of which were facing massive malnutrition and starvation problems, to reject U.S. food aid since the presence of these GMO grains in their countries could lead to contamination of their crops, even though the method in which such contamination would occur was extremely improbable.

Prices

For most of the period from the early 1970s through 1998, soybean prices fluctuated above lows around $5.20 to $5.50 per bushel, with spikes to around $9.00. This pattern was most prevalent in the 1970s and 1980s. By the 1990s soybeans moved into a less volatile price pattern, trading between those same lows and peaks that were around $6.20 or $7.00. There was a sharp rise in soybean prices from 1995 into the second quarter of 1997, when prices reached $8.78 on a monthly average basis and approached the peaks last seen in 1988. (See Figure 10.3.)

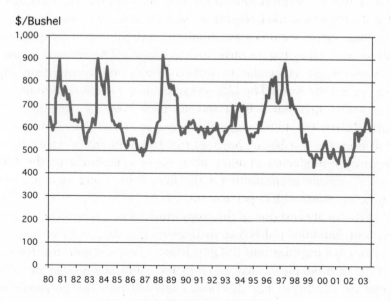

Figure 10.3 **The Price of Soybeans**

Prices then blew off, and dropped as low as $4.25 in 1999. Prices traded between this low and $5.40 until the second half of 2002. This reflected, in part, strong growth in soybean production in various countries; output doubled in Brazil and tripled in Argentina. It was also a time when investors and speculators were abandoning commodities markets en masse.

As mentioned earlier, soybeans are planted annually, giving farmers great flexibility from year to year as they decide whether to plant them. Thus, when prices are low, as they were from 1997 into 2002, farmers can shift away from soybeans to other crops. However, this did not happen during that period, because the prices of other crops the farmers could plant were weak as well, and soybeans, for all of their price weakness, continued to look like a relatively more attractive crop to plant.

Prices rose above $5.40 in the third quarter of 2002, rising to trade between $5.20 and $6.40 for most of the period from 2003 into 2005. Soybean prices shot up to trade above $7.60 in June 2005, before slumping back down to trade between $5.40 and $6.20 for the rest of the year.

Supply

The United States accounts for roughly 40 percent of total world production. In the United States, soybeans are the second largest crop in terms of acres planted, following corn.

World soybean production rose to a high of 197.1 million tons in the 2002–2003 agricultural year. Production dropped 3.7 percent the following year due to a decline in the U.S. crop. Favorable weather conditions in the United States during the 2004–2005 harvest contributed to a recovery in output to an estimated record U.S. production of 85.5 million tons.

In the United States, soybeans are largely cultivated in Midwest and Southern states. The top five soybean producing states are Iowa (17 percent), Illinois (14 percent), Minnesota (10 percent), Indiana (8 percent), and Nebraska (8 percent). The United States exports approximately 38 percent of its soybean production, contributing almost half of total world exports.

Brazil is the second largest soybean producer, yielding roughly 25 percent of the world production. Production in South America has increased an average of 9 percent per year since 1990, in contrast to average growth increases in the United States of 3 percent per year during this time. The third largest producer is Argentina, accounting for approximately 17 percent of the world production. China is the fourth largest producer, contributing to roughly 8 percent of the world supply. India and Pakistan each supply about 2 to 3 percent of the world's production output. Other countries make up the remaining 5 percent in production.

Demand

Soybeans are crushed to produce soybean meal and soybean oil. In the year 2003–2004, 70 percent of the total world supply was consumed in crushing demand. The United States is the leading crusher of soybeans, processing roughly 25 percent of the total world crushings. This is followed by Brazil, China, Argentina, and the EU, which crush approximately 17 percent, 16 percent, 15 percent, and 8 percent, respectively. Indian, Mexico, Japan, Taiwan, and other countries also are significant soybean processors.

Production in South America has increased an average of 9 percent per year since 1990, in contrast to average growth increases in the United States of 3 percent per year during this time.

China is the largest importer of world soybean supplies, taking in 30 percent of total world imports. China's demand for soybean meal as feed for poultry and livestock, and for soybean oil used in cooking, has been amplified by rapid income growth in recent years. The second largest importer is the European Union, receiving roughly 26 percent of total world imports.

The Crush

As mentioned earlier, some traders and investors trade what is called the crush, which is the spread between soybeans and soy meal and soybean oil. This spread is based on the physical fact that much of the soybeans produced each year are ground up to produce meal and oil. The crush thus is a physical process. There is a financial counterpart to it, reflecting the typical and range of yields of meal and oil contained in soybeans. The oil content and yield varies with crops and harvests.

The crush value is a dollar amount determined by the price of soybeans relative to the combined price of soybean meal and soybean oil. This value is traded in the cash or futures market based on expectations of future price movement of soybeans versus the components. A typical bushel of soybeans weighs roughly 60 pounds; when crushed, it might yield 11 pounds of soybean oil and around 44 pounds of soybean meal, with another 5 pounds going to waste.

The soybean trade uses the *gross processing margin* (GPM) formula to express the difference between the prices for the meal and oil and the price of the soybeans themselves. The GPM is the price of 48 percent protein meal (the standard on the Chicago Board of Trade), in dollars per ton of meal, times 0.022, plus the price of soybean oil (in cents per pound) multiplied by 11, less the price of the underlying soybeans that were purchased to make the meal and oil. Farmers, traders, grain elevator operators, and investors will arbitrage this ratio in the physical market with the ratio in the futures markets. They will also trade differentials among the three soy contracts on the CBOT based on variations from the basic underlying price relationship.

Outlook

Soybean prices may find support above $5.40 in the years ahead. Prices could rise to test the $7.60 high of the middle of 2005, but sharp increases in prices are not predetermined. Demand for soybeans has been rising worldwide, as more people shift to higher consumption of meats, leading to increased use of soybeans for livestock feed. But supply also is rising. (See Figure 10.4.) Countries are becoming more competitive on an inter-

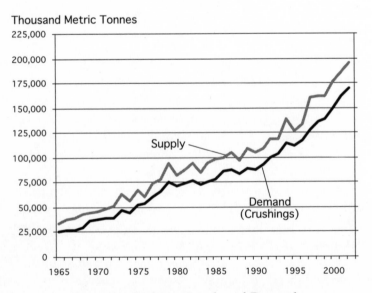

Figure 10.4 **Soybeans Supply and Demand**

national basis, and worldwide inventories of soybeans have risen to record levels in recent years. From 1987 through 1996 world soybean inventories, at the end of each crop year, averaged less than 11 million metric tonnes. These stores fell to as low as 7.8 million metric tonnes at the end of the 1996/97 crop year. They rose sharply after that, averaging 28.8 million metric tonnes from 1997 through 2002. Such large inventories can help limit any price increase based on either actual increases in demand for soybeans or investor buying based on expectations of rising demand.

Exports of soybeans, by the United States and other countries, is an important factor to watch in trying to fathom soybean price trends. In the 2004–2005 crop year U.S. exports were off significantly from expectations. Brazilian exports rose, though not as much as U.S. shipments fell below expectations. This suggested that soybean inventories were rising and would likely lead to some further price weakness. Prices were expected to drop to test support around $5.40, and maybe even drop to $5.00. While prices have been stronger since 2003, many farmers remember the extended period of lower prices that preceded this period and remain cautious about expectations that prices could stabilize around $6.00 per bushel.

How to Invest

Soybean futures are traded primarily on the oldest commodity exchange in the United States, the CBOT. Other markets for soybean futures are located in Brazil, Argentina, China, and Tokyo. Futures and options are traded on soybeans, soybean meal, and soybean oil.

The CBOT separates soybeans into three quality categories. CBOT futures contracts call for the delivery of 5,000 bushels of yellow soybeans No. 2. Futures contracts of yellow soybeans No. 1 are traded at a $0.06 premium, while No. 3 soybeans are traded at a $0.06 discount.

Wheat

Along with corn and soybeans, wheat is a major food crop. First cultivated in southwestern Asia in prehistoric times, wheat has been a major source of nutrition for humans throughout history. About 20 percent of the world's caloric intake today comes from wheat, primarily in the form of flour used in baked goods. It is grown around the world, with Russia and China being the largest producers. It is consumed around the world as well.

Wheat is a type of grass. Several varieties are grown for consumption. Most wheat grown in the United States is winter wheat, planted in the autumn or winter for harvesting in the spring. Perhaps three-quarters of U.S. wheat production is winter wheat. There is also summer wheat, planted in the spring for harvesting in the autumn.

Wheat prices traded between $2.50 and $4.50 per bushel for most of the period from the early 1970s until 1998. (See Figure 10.5.) There were a few spikes above this range, in 1974, 1980, and 1996. Prices also dipped down to nearly $2.00 in 1977. In 1998 wheat prices dropped below $2.50, moving into a low and narrow range from $2.00 to $2.50 for four years, into the middle of 2002. Prices then rose suddenly, to around $4.10 in September 2002. Prices came back off, dropping to around $3.00 in the middle of 2003. Since then prices have risen back to around $4.00, in late 2003, only to sell off once more. Wheat traded between $3.20 and $3.90 for most of 2004 and 2005, dropping back to around $3.05 in December 2005 as reports of large wheat crops in many countries hit the market, and inventories of wheat rose sharply both in the United States and around the world.

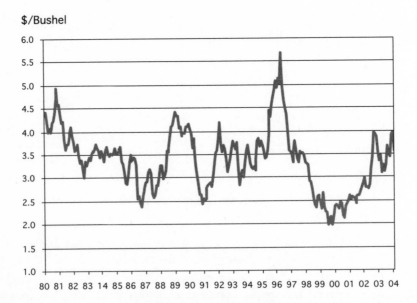

Figure 10.5 The Price of Wheat

Supply

World wheat production peaked in 1997 at 609.2 million metric tonnes. From then until 2004 it declined, to around 551.8 million metric tonnes in the 2003–2004 crop year. World wheat production rose sharply the following year, although final data are not available while this is being written. It appears that world wheat output may have risen nearly 13 percent in the 2004–2005 crop year, to a level surpassing the 1997 crop year level. The world wheat crop may have totaled 623.8 million metric tonnes in that crop year.

China is the largest producer of wheat, harvesting around 86.0 million metric tonnes in the 2003 crop year. India is the second largest producer, at 69.3 million metric tonnes.

The United States was third in that year, at 63.6 million metric tonnes. It is estimated that U.S. production declined in subsequent crop years. U.S. wheat production may have dropped around 8 percent in 2004. The U.S. crop represented nearly 12 percent of the 2003 worldwide harvest, but the U.S. market share declined to around 9 percent the next year, as U.S. production fell while world output rose sharply. The United States nonetheless represents a much larger share of the export market for wheat, shipping roughly half of its wheat harvest overseas and accounting for more than a quarter of world wheat exports.

Other large producers include various European countries, including France, Germany, Poland, and the United Kingdom. Russia, Australia, Canada, Pakistan, Turkey, and Argentina also are significant producers.

While production has more than rebounded to levels surpassing the previous peak in 1997, world ending stocks (the amount of wheat in inventories at the end of each crop year) are lower than they were in the late 1990s. Stocks declined sharply between 1999 and 2004, as world consumption of wheat was exceeding wheat production in each of those years. As a result, world inventories declined roughly 30 percent from 208.9 million metric tonnes in 1999 to around 136.8 at the end of the 2004–2005 crop year. Even so, inventories remain high, representing nearly three months' worth of worldwide wheat consumption at present. Around one-tenth of world wheat inventories are held in the United States. Wheat inventories were estimated at about 143 to 147 million metric tonnes at the end of 2005.

Demand

Demand for wheat has grown steadily over the past 45 years, reflecting the steady growth in the world's population combined with increased consumption of wheat for many people. (See Figure 10.6.) Worldwide wheat consumption may have totaled 605.2 million metric tonnes in the 2004–2005 crop year. This estimated demand level was 2.2 percent higher than the 592.0 million metric tonnes consumed the year before.

The world's largest wheat consumer is China, which accounts for around 17 percent of annual wheat demand. Other large consumers include Russia, India, Europe taken as a whole, and the United States.

Outlook

Wheat consumption exceeded annual wheat production consistently for four years, from 2000 through 2003. Production shot higher in the 2004 crop year, and appears to have generated a surplus relative to consumption for that year. This may have been reflected in the decline in U.S. wheat prices to lows around $3.10 per bushel in December 2005. The increase in wheat output, the rise in world and U.S. wheat inventories,

> *The world's largest wheat consumer is China, which accounts for around 17 percent of annual wheat demand.*

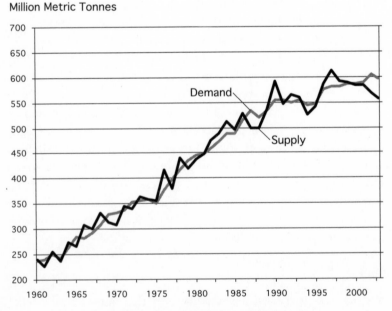

Million Metric Tonnes

Figure 10.6 **Wheat Supply and Demand**

and a reduction in U.S. wheat exports estimated to have been close to 10 percent all contributed to this price weakness.

Wheat consumption is expected to continue to rise in 2006 and the years ahead. The world's population is growing, and the rise in income in many parts of the world is being reflected in increased purchases of wheat-containing foods. There was a slowdown in wheat consumption due to a low-carbohydrate diet fad in the United States and Europe in 2003 and 2004, but those fad diets appear to have faded and wheat demand has risen once more.

Wheat production meanwhile will likely remain strong. It may decline somewhat in 2006 from the record levels of the 2004–2005 crop year, reflecting producers' desires not to overproduce but to keep output in line with growing demand.

The difficulty in matching supply and demand may contribute to some further price weakness. Prices may test $3.00 more severely at times. However, there appears to be long-term support around $3.00, and again around $2.75 to $2.80. These levels may represent a base for wheat prices in the future. Similarly, prices may find resistance around $4.00. The price of wheat has the capacity to rally to this level in the future. It has shown the capacity to spike even higher at times, to $4.50 and even to $7.00. Such spikes do not appear to be sustainable for wheat prices though.

On the positive side for prices, demand is rising. Also, as discussed regarding corn, the rise of investor long interest in wheat, especially by more passively oriented commodities-index investors, could lend additional support to wheat prices, if not provide them some upward momentum.

How to Invest

The largest volume futures and options contracts for wheat are traded on the CBOT. Wheat, in various varieties, is also traded on numerous exchanges around the world, including two exchanges in Kansas City and Minneapolis, and exchanges in Sydney, Australia; Brazil; Hungary; France; and Winnipeg, Canada.

11

Base Metals

The base metals covered in this chapter are copper, lead, and zinc. Each one is important to construction, transportation, and power systems in various ways. Copper formerly was the largest base metal market, although aluminum has supplanted it. Copper and aluminum are traded on the New York Comex. The aluminum contract is not well traded or very liquid; the copper market is much more liquid. For both metals the volumes are much more substantial on the London Metals Exchange (LME). Lead, zinc, tin, and nickel are not traded on U.S. futures exchanges, but only on the LME.

Steel is not a base metal, but it is an interesting commodity. Steel is such a large and diverse market that a viable futures exchange has not developed. That may seem strange, but the diversity and the economic interests of some steel market participants have actually hindered the emergence of a steel futures market. That may change in the near future, as the LME and other exchanges are considering opening a steel market.

In addition to these metals there is a wide range of specialty metals and minor metals, ranging from titanium, beryllium, and lithium as light metals to metals like cobalt, bismuth, selenium, germanium, and gallium. These are extremely specialized metals markets. They trade among professional trading companies, producers, refiners, and users. By and large, investors avoid these markets directly, although acquiring shares of metals producing companies can be an interesting way to buy exposure to some of these metals.

Copper

Copper is a major metal used in electrical, electronic, plumbing, and other applications. Copper is used in transportation systems, housing, commercial construction, and appliances. The average American home has something like 30 or 40 electrical motors in it, running everything from the refrigerator to the cassette recorder (if any of those have not been replaced by a CD player and a digital music player). Every one of those motors has copper wires wound around inside the motor. Copper is also used in plumbing; in automobiles, trains, and planes; and most other things that have either electricity or water coursing through them. Of course, copper has been around for a long time, at least since the bronze age, since bronze is an alloy of copper and tin. Copper was one of the first commodities I studied intensely in the 1970s.

The copper market experienced a long period of lower supply while demand continued to rise. This was a consequence of an earlier period of lower copper prices. Copper prices had a pretty clear price pattern from the early 1970s until late 2005. During this time copper traded between 60 cents and a high of $1.40 to $1.60. Strong economic growth would fuel copper use, pushing copper prices higher. The copper price would rise to levels above $1.00 per pound. It happened in 1974, in 1979–1980, in 1988, and in 1994–1995. The spike in prices would stimulate a surge in mine production and scrap recovery from old electrical and plumbing equipment. The increase in supply typically would take a year or two to kick in, due to the lead time needed to ramp up production at mines, by which time economic conditions would be softening and fabrication demand would be waning. The increased supply and softening demand would lead to a decline in prices. Prices would fall to around 60 cents, a level at which scrap recovery efforts would slack off and mines would be shuttered. This happened with relatively good predictability four times over the 1970s, 1980s, and 1990s.

There were permutations, each time, of course. History repeats itself, but always with twists to trip up the more mechanically minded followers of trends. For example, the balance between copper supply and demand moved into a deficit in 1982 or 1983. At that point a number of copper market analysts became bullish on copper. They were early, however, because during the recession of 1980 to 1982 a massive (for that time) amount of copper had built up in inventories. These stocks hovered over the market, helping to keep the price down for several years. By 1987 these stocks had been drawn down to relatively low levels. By this time the economic expansion had run for five years. People were beginning to expect a recession, although it turned out that a recession was still three years away. By 1987 a number of copper market observers who had turned bullish in 1982 and 1983 and had stayed bullish through the ensuing years were giving up their hopes that copper prices would ever rise. (We turned bullish in the first quarter of 1987, due to our observation that stockpiles had fallen to low enough levels that they would no longer restrain prices.) Copper prices began rising around the first quarter of 1987. We held our bullish view even after the U.S. stock market plummeted in October of that year, based on our analysis at that time that the stock market sell-off was not a precursor to a recession, monetary and fiscal policies still were stimulative, and a recession was probably three years away.

The cycle was repeating itself in the late 1990s. (See Figure 11.1.) Following the run-up in copper prices to around $1.40 at the end of 1994, there was a surge of production increases, scrap rose, and demand softened

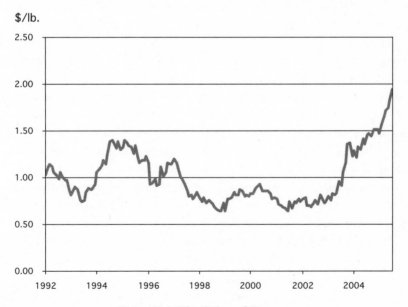

Figure 11.1 **The Price of Copper**

a bit. These fundamental conditions were enough to start the copper price declining. Copper fell initially to around 95 cents, and then it dropped more sharply. It traded between 62 cents and 88 cents for most of the period from 1997 until the fourth quarter of 2003.

In the early phase of this period of horizontally moving prices, copper inventories registered against positions on either the LME or the New York Comex rose from around 300,000 metric tonnes in July 1998 to around 923,000 metric tonnes in March 2000. This was a sign of overproduction and surpluses in the market, as unsold metal was put into warehouses. Inventories then fell back to around 393,000 metric tonnes in December 2000. The market took this as a bullish sign, and copper prices began to recover. It was a false start, however, as weak economic conditions around the world led to a slump in fabrication demand even as copper supplies jumped higher in 2001. This led to a massive increase in inventories to record levels. Copper inventories registered against these two exchanges peaked at 1.3 million metric tonnes in May 2002, and stayed above 1.2 million until February 2003.[1] The increase and maintenance of copper inventories at such high levels was seen as extremely bearish for the copper market, and prices subsided to the lower end of that 62- to 88-cent range.

Starting in 2003 these inventories began to fall. While the market still behaved as if a worldwide recession was under way, industrial output of a number of copper-using items started to rise sharply. The recovery began to emerge in the second half of 2002 but really took hold in the second quarter of 2003. Demand started rising. Supply meanwhile was off, reflecting the effects of the lower prices. (See Figure 11.2.)

By the start of the fourth quarter 2003 it was clear that demand was rising sharply and that copper fabricators were drawing down inventories. Copper inventories registered with the LME and Comex had dropped to around 800,000 metric tonnes by the start of the fourth quarter, a level that various copper market participants, including some of the largest producers, had staked out earlier as being a critical signpost on the path to copper price recovery. Copper prices moved above 90 cents in October 2003 and past $1.00 in December.

Prices kept rising over the course of 2004 and 2005. Initially it looked

---

[1] A third exchange in Shanghai now has become an important trading center, and its data increasingly needs to be taken into consideration in copper market analyses.

Thousand Metric Tonnes

Figure 11.2 **Copper Supply and Demand**

as if the copper price was going to peak around $1.50 to $1.60, as it had in past cycles. Prices approached that level in September 2004, and a ceiling around $1.48 to $1.54 held until June 2005. The price broke through this ceiling and moved to $1.60 in June, and then above $1.70 in August. By December 2005 copper was trading around $2.00 to $2.05, record levels.

Some copper market observers were suggesting that copper prices may have moved out of their historical range, between 60 cents and $1.60, and might move into a new, higher range of perhaps 90 cents to $2.00. It is too soon to know whether this new range will hold.

By the start of the fourth quarter 2003 it was clear that demand was rising sharply and that copper fabricators were drawing down inventories.

Much of the bullishness in the copper market had focused on Chinese demand, in line with conditions in most commodities markets from 2003 through 2005. Demand for copper has been strong in China, but it has also been strong in the United States, Japan, India, Brazil, and many other countries. There did seem to be a firm base of fabrication demand, as opposed to investor or speculative buying, supporting some of the price increase. Much of the move from $1.70 to $2.00 may prove to have been a combination of technically driven speculation and year-end inventory building by fabricators concerned about supplies and price. That being the case, coupled with the information in the next paragraph, it is possible that copper prices may decline significantly in 2006 and beyond.

In the fourth quarter of 2005 a scandal hit the copper market related to a large short position that a Chinese copper trader was alleged to have built up in the copper market, centered on the LME. There was some covering of these positions, by purchasing copper, and there was a wave of speculative buying based on the supposition that the Chinese government would have to buy copper to cover its short position. In the end this did not seem to happen. Worse for the copper bulls, it turned out that the Chinese government had pretty large copper inventories of its own, which it could use to cover the short positions. This not only suggested that there was metal around to meet future needs, but it confirmed that much of the strong demand that had sucked up copper inventories from the market and fueled the price rise in 2004 and 2005 was buying for inventory, and not for current consumption.

Added to the potential of less buying going forward is the prospect that mine production will increase significantly in 2006 and beyond. A number of mines that were shut down or cut back during the period of low prices from 1997 through 2003 have been restarting. Their production did not appear in 2005 output, due to various hiccups in the restarting process, but they can be expected to supply significant amounts of copper going forward.

The copper market has moved from a period in 2004 of enormous deficits of newly refined metal entering the market relative to fabrication demand, to a time when supply and demand are much more closely aligned. A surplus in supply over demand may reappear in 2006, adding to price weakness.

Supply

Copper is produced around the world. Mine production totaled around 14.5 million metric tonnes in 2004, up from 13.6 million in 2003. Further increases were expected in 2005, as the mining industry responded to rising prices and tight supplies. However, there were various labor interruptions and physical problems at individual mines, which limited the expansion in 2005. Even so, several projects are under way that will increase production. Chilean production declined in 2005, due to a range of problems. Production meanwhile increased 11 percent in Australia, 86 percent in Brazil, 39 percent in Indonesia, and 8 percent each in the United States and Papua, New Guinea.

The production increases are expected to show up more forcefully in the copper market in 2006 and beyond. As a result, the period of tightness in copper's market balance, and consequently higher prices, may persist a bit longer.

The major copper producer in the world today is Chile. Chile accounts for more than one-third of world copper mine production, or roughly 5.4 million metric tonnes in 2004. The United States has been the second largest producer, mining around 1.2 million metric tonnes in 2004 and 2005.

> *The production increases are expected to show up more forcefully in the copper market in 2006 and beyond.*

Production is rising once more, as mines come back online and some new projects are developed. Other producers include Peru, Poland, Russia, Uzbekistan, and the countries previously named. Zambia and the Congo (formerly Zaire) used to be major producers but have declined in importance. There are efforts to revitalize the copper mines in both countries, but the recoveries are being slowed by a number of political, economic, and other obstacles.

Interestingly, copper reserves are estimated to be around 470 million metric tonnes. That represents around 32 years' worth of copper production at recent output levels. Resources, meaning copper in the ground that either has not been proven up to the point of being considered mineable reserves or is not economically mineable at recent price levels, total another 940 million metric tonnes, or another 65 years' output at recent rates. So the world has nearly a century's worth of copper in the ground in terms of reserves and resources, which compares favorably to those estimates from the early 1970s that we would run out of copper by the late 1970s.

One also must not forget China as a copper producer. At present the country is refining more copper than any other country. Its refineries are fed by domestic ores, imported mine concentrates, and scrap. China itself is mining around 620,000 metric tonnes per year of copper, but the figure is rising rapidly as new mines come online. While China has been seen as a source of demand for the copper market, some of the more farsighted market participants are considering the day when China becomes a supplier of copper to the world market.

In addition to copper mine output, a significant amount of copper is recovered from scrap each year. Perhaps 10 percent of total refined metal supplies each year comes from recycled materials. This percentage is expected to increase in the coming decade, as efforts to recover metals from old automobiles and electronic products are increased around the world.

Demand

The major use of copper is in building construction, which accounts for 48 percent of world copper use. This includes wiring, plumbing, heating, air conditioning, and ventilation systems. Copper is used in most electrical and electronic products, for everything from the wiring to the motors. These products take around 21 percent of annual copper usage. Trains, planes, and automobiles—transportation systems—take another 10 percent of copper use, while industrial machinery and equipment takes 10 percent and household and consumer goods take another 11 percent. There are some smaller chemical and medicinal uses of copper as well.

Copper use has been expanding at a compounded annual rate around 3.6 percent per year over the decade from 1995 through 2004. This marked an acceleration from the long-term growth rate seen in the 1970s and 1980s, reflecting stronger growth in many parts of the world and increased use of copper in the construction of infrastructure around the world. Demand has been rising in China, India, and other countries in which economic development has accelerated since the early 1990s. This trend toward increased copper usage is projected to continue over the coming decade, with the amount of copper being used each year growing at an even faster pace than has been the case in the previous 10 years.

Outlook

Earlier I mentioned that many copper market participants have begun to wonder aloud whether the old paradigm of copper trading between 60 cents and $1.60 has been replaced with a new, higher range of likely copper prices. The view is that copper might find a base around 90 cents in future periods of weakness, and that the new ceiling may be closer to $2.00 than $1.60.

There are a lot of reasons to believe that this may be the case. In fact, this is my company's long-term outlook for copper prices. One point that should be made is that if copper prices bottom out around 96 cents per pound over the coming decade, while inflation continues around the 3 percent per annum that has been seen since 1984, the inflation-adjusted copper price would be around 75 cents at the base, not so far above the previous bottoms. In other words, if one thinks of 60 to 70 cents as the inflation-adjusted floor for copper prices, a nominal price floor around 90 to 95 cents seems reasonable.

This trend toward increased copper usage is projected to continue over the coming decade, with the amount of copper being used each year growing at an even faster pace than has been the case in the previous 10 years.

It is always dangerous to assume that a change signals the end of a long-term pattern, whether in prices, supply, or demand. That said, something clearly has changed in the world. More people have more money than before, and they want to use it to buy more things, including houses, cars, and electronics. All of these things use copper, so copper demand ought to be expected to remain strong. In the words of an economist, the demand curve for copper has shifted upward, perhaps on a permanent basis. That means that copper prices may well find support at higher levels than otherwise might be expected. Nevertheless, prices around $2.00 do not seem sustainable, nor do prices below 90 cents.

How to Invest

Copper futures and options are traded on the New York Comex. Copper is also traded on the LME, along with other base metals.

In addition to copper futures and options, some investors buy equity and equity options of copper mining companies. Many U.S. copper mining companies have been absorbed into other companies over the past two decades, but Phelps Dodge remains a major copper producer with a significant portion of its revenues still coming from copper. As a result, many investors trade Phelps Dodge's stocks and options as surrogates for copper. Many other copper producing companies are large and diversified mining companies, such as Rio Tinto and BHP Billiton. As such, their revenues and share prices do not track copper as closely. There are some newly emerging, smaller copper mining companies as well.

Lead

Lead is one of those basic metals that seemed to serve mankind well for several millennia. Perhaps because it is relatively malleable and has a somewhat low melting point, lead was identified early as a useful metal in many applications. It was used to fashion containers and pipes for water and other liquids. It was used in paints, pigments, and cosmetics. It was used in solders to hold metal products together. Unfortunately, lead is toxic for humans and animals, and the use of lead in many products has been banned or discouraged in recent years for health and environmental reasons. Lead pipes and solders formerly were used in plumbing, but lead leaching into the water supply was slowly poisoning people.

Today, lead remains a vitally important metal. Other metals have been substituted for many of its uses, but lead is still critical to transportation due to the use of lead-acid batteries for cars and other vehicles. Because of the decline in lead use in other applications, today batteries account for about 70 percent of worldwide lead use and about 85 percent of U.S. lead use.

Most lead is mined in conjunction with zinc and other metals. Many ore bodies that contain lead also contain silver, gold, and sometimes copper, and often other vital by-product metals such as bismuth, cadmium, and many others. Lead mining occurs around the world. The major producing nations are China, Australia, the United States, and Peru. A very large amount of lead is recovered and recycled from spent batteries each year as well.

Lead prices have had a rockier road than those of other base metals, perhaps reflecting the move to substitute other metals for lead. (See Figure 11.3.) Lead prices rose sharply through the 1970s, to around 58 cents per pound in 1979 and 1980. Prices then plunged to 18 cents by 1985. Prices recovered in an erratic pattern to 52 cents around 1990, only to fall back to 32 cents within a year or so. Prices rose once more, touching 52 cents again in 1996, then dropped back to around 38 to 43 cents from the end of 1998 into 2003. Prices then began rising, and lead traded between 40 and 45 cents on the London Metals Exchange for much of 2004 and 2005 before moving toward 49 cents in late 2005. U.S. producer prices moved toward 52 cents in late 2003, and then to levels around 65 cents in late 2005.

Lead prices have had a rockier road than those of other base metals.

Cents/lb.

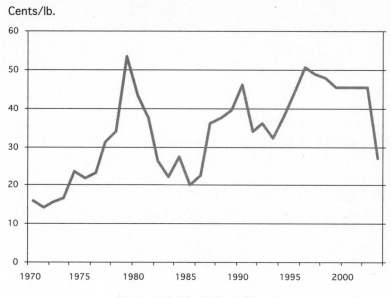

Figure 11.3 **The Price of Lead**

Supply

Around 3.3 million metric tonnes of lead are mined each year at present. The largest producer is China, which mines around 950,000 metric tonnes per year. China has also established a major lead and zinc refining industry, importing mine concentrates and scrap from around the world for refining. China may account for more than one-third of world refining of lead at present, up from around 5 percent a decade ago. Today China exports a significant amount of refined lead, perhaps around 450,000 metric tonnes per year.

Australia produces around 680,000 metric tonnes of lead per year, while the United States produces around 440,000 annually. Peru mines around 300,000 metric tonnes per year, and additional lead is produced in Mexico, Kazakhstan, Sweden, and other countries.

In addition to mine production, around 55 percent of annual refined lead supply comes from recycling, especially from batteries. In the United States there is only one primary lead refinery in operation, located in Missouri. However, there are about two dozen factories that recover lead from old batteries and other scrap. These plants may supply around 84 percent of total lead supply in the United States. Worldwide, the proportion of total supply that comes from recycling is not that high, but the share of lead supply that comes from scrap is greater than it is for probably any other metal.

Demand

As previously mentioned, most lead today is used in lead-acid batteries in cars, trucks, and other transportation systems. Lead batteries also are used in backup power systems, load-leveling systems, and other battery applications.

World lead use was around 7.5 million metric tonnes per year in 2005, rising steadily. Lead use may have risen 3.9 percent in 2005 alone. Despite the substitutions for lead in most applications, the world is using more lead than it used to. Not only that, but the rate of growth in demand is accelerating. This growth and acceleration represents the increases in the auto population worldwide. Lead use was rising at a rate of 2.1 percent per annum from 1960 through 1990. The pace has quickened since then, as the rate of purchasing automobiles has accelerated. From 1990 through 2004 the annual growth rate for lead use has been 3.4 percent, more than 50 percent faster than the old rate. (See Figure 11.4.)

Given the fact that lead-acid batteries are the primary use for lead, the demand for batteries for use in automobiles exerts a strong influence on this metal's price. As a consequence, there is a bit of seasonality built into lead prices, insofar as a cold winter in the northern hemisphere, where most cars and trucks are driven, can lead to the failure of batteries and an increase on a seasonal basis in demand for replacement batteries. Consequently, cold weather spells in Europe and North America are sometimes reflected in a speculative blip up in lead prices. Sometimes lead prices will rise going into the northern hemisphere's winter, as investors and speculators build long lead positions on the LME in advance of the winter. If the winter turns out to be a mild one, these speculative positions will be sold off and prices will fall back.

Other uses include paints and pigments, although in this area lead has been engineered out of many paints and nonindustrial coatings. Lead still finds some use in paints and pigments, which incorporate about 12 percent of the world's annual lead supply. Lead is also still used in sheathing and shields against radiation and electrical charges. Perhaps 3 percent of annual lead use goes into sheathing for electrical cables, to protect against stray electrical charges and interference.

Lead was used as an additive to boost the octane in gasoline for many

Thousand Metric Tonnes

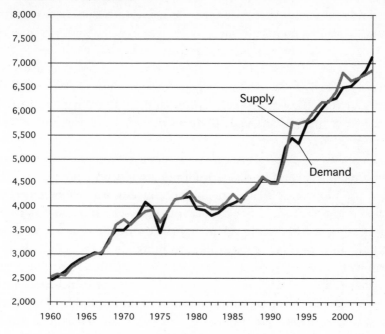

Figure 11.4 **Lead Supply and Demand**

decades but has been phased out of most fuels now. Lead traditionally was heavily used in brazing alloys and solders, but tin, silver, bismuth, and other metals are being substituted for lead in these materials. Lead shot is still used in ammunition, although a growing number of jurisdictions are requiring use of steel, bismuth, or other shot in place of lead, especially in hunting waterfowl.

Regionally, Chinese lead use has been rising sharply for several years. It may have increased around 20 percent in 2005. The rate of increase may slow to around 9 percent in 2006. European use meanwhile continues to decline, as factories shift away from Europe to Asia. U.S. lead use has been rising around 1.5 to 2.0 percent per annum in recent years, reflecting steady increases in battery output.

Outlook

Demand for lead is likely to continue to expand. Chinese demand may rise around 9 percent in 2006 and may keep close to that pace in future years.

U.S. use may be around 2 percent per annum going forward. Demand in other developing countries should be expected to rise, being only partially offset by weak lead use in Europe as the site of manufacturing continues to shift. The key factor behind lead use is the continued rise in the world auto population, and this trend does not appear likely to reverse for many years to come. There is little likelihood of a substitution away from lead–acid batteries in vehicles, meanwhile, so this market will likely continue to use lead for years to come. Overall, demand may increase around 3.0 to 3.5 percent in 2006.

As recently as 2001 the consensus seemed to be that lead demand would remain weak, lead prices would remain low, and zinc prices would have to rise to levels sufficient to maintain operational profitability at lead and zinc mines, since lead could not be expected to carry its fair share of the need to generate revenues. This analysis overlooked the importance of the steady and continual growth in auto production and sales, which has contributed importantly to strong fabrication demand support for prices.

Mine production will continue to rise. The pace of increase may be relatively slow in 2006, but expansions and new mines are under development in numerous countries. Refined supply will probably rise around 3.4 percent in 2006, which may be sufficient to close a portion of the gap between newly refined lead output and fabrication demand. The market may remain in deficit, however, which could help support prices, if not move them higher, in the near term. The rate of output increase is projected to quicken in 2007 and 2008 when a few new, larger lead and zinc mines are started.

Demand has exceeded supply since 2003, leading to a steady reduction of market inventories of lead. Over time mine production, and refined output including metal recovered from scrap, will catch up with demand. It may well be 2008 before this happens. Until that time, lead prices may show a level of strength that would have surprised the market even a few years ago.

How to Invest

Lead is traded primarily on the LME; it is not traded on any U.S. futures or options exchange. London Metals Exchange contracts may be purchased by U.S. investors through various brokerage companies that provide this service.

Doe Run Company, the one major U.S. lead company, is privately owned and not publicly traded. Other lead producers tend to be diversified metals companies, such as BHP Billiton, and their share prices tend not to reflect lead price changes per se.

Zinc

Zinc is most often mined in conjunction with lead. The major producing nations are China, Peru, Canada, Australia, and the United States. Nearly half of zinc use is in galvanizing steel. Zinc actually has many uses, including a variety of metal alloys, as a component in brass and some bronzes, and in a wide range of chemical compounds used for everything from paints and pigments to agricultural chemicals.

Zinc prices were more restrained than prices for copper, lead, and other metals in the 1970s. Prices did rise, from around 15 cents per pound in the 1950s and 1960s to around 30 to 40 cents in the 1970s, but the increase was neither as dramatic nor as volatile as those of other metals. Prices drifted into a range between 35 and 50 cents in the first seven years of the 1980s. Zinc prices moved upward more sharply in the late 1980s, when prices shot from around 49 cents in March 1988 to 95 cents in March 1989. (See Figure 11.5.) Fabrication demand for zinc rose about 4.5 percent that year. That was not a particularly large amount, but it was a strong increase compared to the previous year's growth rates.

Prices steadily declined after 1989, moving to around 45 cents once·

Figure 11.5 **The Price of Zinc**

more by the third quarter of 1993. Prices rose back to 60 cents by late 1994, and traded between that and 50 cents until early 1997. Zinc rose to 80 cents over the course of 1997, only to fall back to trade between 47 and 60 cents for much of the next four years. In the second half of 2001 zinc prices fell sharply, dropping to 37 cents. Prices began rising in late 2003, along with the prices of other base metals, as investors moved into these markets and fabrication demand was relatively strong. Prices stayed around 45 cents until the end of 2004, when they began to rise once more. Zinc traded up to 68 cents in the first half of 2005, before staging another upward move in the final months of 2005. By December 2005 the price had risen to around 82 cents.

China has been a major producer of zinc in recent years. It has been an exporter of this metal for much of that time, as it has been mining and refining more zinc than it could use domestically. This reversed in 2004 and 2005. After being a net exporter of zinc from 1988 through 2003, China is estimated to have been a net importer of zinc in 2004 and 2005. This shift in China from being a net supplier to being a net buyer was one of the factors behind the sharp increase in zinc prices during 2004 and 2005. Zinc demand was strong in other countries as well, adding to the upward pressures on prices. Market inventories were drawn down during this time.

Supply

Zinc mine production totaled around 9.1 million metric tonnes in 2004. Production is estimated to have risen further to 10.1 million metric tonnes in 2005. Refined metal production, including metal from scrap, was around 10.1 million metric tonnes in 2004 and around 10.25 million in 2005. The increase in mine production represents expansions of existing mines and new developments in Australia, China, and India. China is the largest producer, accounting for more than 20 percent of world mine production and an even larger share of zinc refining. Peru, Australia, and Canada also are major producers.

After being a net exporter of zinc from 1988 through 2003, China is estimated to have been a net importer of zinc in 2004 and 2005.

Demand

Galvanizing steel takes about 47 percent of the 10.5 million metric tonnes of zinc used annually in 2004 and 2005. The next largest is in brass and bronze used in plumbing, electronics, and other metals castings. Brass and bronze account for about 19 percent of world zinc demand. Other zinc alloys use another 12 percent of zinc supplies, while zinc chemicals take around 9 percent. The remaining zinc demand is spread across a number of smaller uses, including pigments and paints.

In the early 1990s a trend developed to galvanize sheet steel used in automobile body panels and other applications on both sides with zinc. Prior to that time, galvanized steel was often galvanized, or plated, with zinc only on one side. Simple math made it obvious that this would double the use of zinc in many galvanizing applications. Galvanizers announced a round of plans for new galvanizing plants to accommodate this increased demand. Some market observers and participants mistook the collective galvanizing capacity of these factories as an indication of future demand. In fact, the galvanizing industry was building far more capacity than demand would warrant, and some market participants were disappointed when demand did not rise as much as they had expected.

Ignoring the overexpectations in the market, the move to double-dipped galvanization in steel nonetheless boosted zinc use tremendously. Figure 11.6 clearly illustrates the 37 percent rise in zinc use from around 5.4 million metric tonnes in 1992 to 7.4 million metric tonnes just three years later, in 1995. Zinc use was growing at 2.5 percent per annum from 1960 through 1990. From 1990 through 2004 it was growing at a rate of 5.1 percent. A large part of that increase was reflected in the jump in the early 1990s due to the advent of double-sided galvanizing. Even after that one-time jump, the annual rate of increase in zinc use from 1995 through 2004 was at 3.9 percent per year, substantially higher than the pace of growth in demand prior to 1992.

Outlook

One of the points made in this book is the fact that commodities are individual investments. While prices for many commodities move broadly in line with each other, not all commodities prices move together, and the trend within each commodity's prices varies significantly from the others. People look at gross movements and get the impression that the commodities involved are moving together, when in reality there are significant differences among the commodities in question. Supply and demand trends for each commodity dictate the price trends of each one. Some metals are already seeing increases in production in response to increases in

Thousand Metric Tonnes

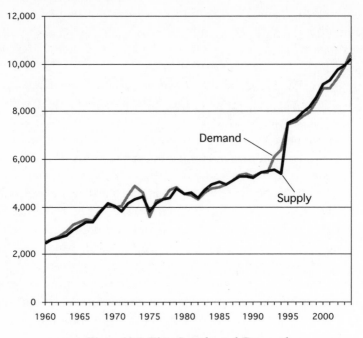

Figure 11.6 **Zinc Supply and Demand**

prices since 2002, while others will experience a longer lag before production increases. Thus, some metals may have more positive price outlooks than others.

Zinc is one beneficiary of this distinction. There are several major and smaller zinc mines under development around the world, but the bulk of the increases in output will not be seen until 2007 to 2009. Thus, zinc prices may remain stronger relative to other metals for a longer period of time. Mine production will be rising in the years ahead, but much of the increase may be a few years away. Demand meanwhile continues to rise at rates above the historical trend prior to the 1990s.

Newly refined zinc supplies have fallen below fabrication demand levels over the past two years, 2004 and 2005. This has led to the drawing down of inventories. This period of large deficits of zinc supply relative to demand is expected to continue through 2006, and maybe even into 2008. In this environment, zinc prices may be very strong for a time, and may well blow right past the 1989 record prices around 95 cents.

How to Invest

Like lead, zinc is traded primarily on the LME and not on any U.S. futures or options exchange. London Metals Exchange contracts may be purchased by U.S. investors through various brokerage companies that provide this service.

Most zinc producers tend to be diversified metals companies, such as BHP Billiton, and their share prices tend not to reflect zinc price changes per se. Apex Silver Mines is a company that is developing a major mine in Bolivia. I tend to consider Apex a silver mining company, and the market seems to treat its shares that way. When its San Cristobal mine opens in 2007 it will be a major producer of silver, but it will also be one of the larger zinc mines in the world. Some investors treat Apex as a zinc mining company and invest accordingly.

> *In this environment, zinc prices may be very strong for a time, and may well blow right past the 1989 record prices.*

12

The Fundamentals Still Apply

If I have succeeded in my goal for this book, you now are much less certain and more introspective about investing in commodities than you were at the outset. I presume you were already interested in investing in commodities—otherwise you would not have bought the book and read it. So that puts you into one of several categories. One category of potential readers includes the general investors who have heard all the hype about the easy money to be made in the commodities supercycle now under way and who are seeking some guidance as to whether to believe the sales pitches, and, if so, how to approach investing in commodities.

There is no easy money to be made, in the long run, in financial markets. There are wins and losses, and it takes a lot of hard work, careful analysis, and experience to develop the seeming intuition that allows an investor to stick to his convictions at times, and to take the profits and liquidate positions at other times. I hope this book has put some fear of losing money into the hearts and minds of some investors who had bit into the commodities supercycle pablum hook, line, and sinker.

Voiced another way, there is an old Taoist saying that the wise person is full of anxiety in undertaking anything, and so he is always successful. In other words, do your homework. Study hard. If something sounds too good to be true, it probably is false. If someone says that commodities bull markets last 17 years, ask to see the data. If someone says he has had an un-broken string of financial wins in commodities, or any other markets, ask to see the independently audited records.

I have reviewed what commodities are, as investments, as markets, and as significant components in the world economy. I have shown how commodities prices have been declining most of the time since the Industrial Revolution began, and discussed the real economic reasons for this, including lower costs of production, increased unit production through mechanization, increased discovery and development of mineral and energy deposits, and other reasons.

> *The wise person is full of anxiety in undertaking anything, and so he is always successful. In other words, do your homework.*

It Starts with the Fundamentals

When I chose the title for my summary chapter, I hit a stumbling block. Obviously the fundamentals still matter in determining commodity price levels and trends. That said, what else is left to say? But, surprisingly, many people do not seem to understand or believe this. Given the lack of information, knowledge, and understanding prevalent in commodities markets, there are great opportunities for thoughtful investors to profit in commodities, by sifting through the chaff for the grains of truth in the markets, and by using these basic truths as the basis for a methodical approach toward investing.

In the long run, fundamentals of supply, demand, and inventories clearly exert strong influences on prices. Short-term price trends are strongly influenced by other factors and shorter-term developments, but supply and demand fundamentals still assert themselves. These short-term factors, which include exogenous trends and speculative forces, actually can be defined as fundamentals, if one understands the dynamics of these markets.

The problem is not that fundamentals do not apply and do not affect prices. The problems lie in the definition and measurement of these fundamentals. As I see it, there are three basic stumbling blocks to understanding commodities investment:

1. Many analysts and other market participants do not fully understand what the fundamentals are in each commodity market, and there is a great deal of misdefinition.

2. The measurement of these fundamentals is much poorer than most analysts and observers realize.

3. The relationships of various fundamentals, exogenous variables, and price movements themselves are extremely complex and do not lend themselves to simple, univariate explanations and analyses.

Let's step away from the commodities markets for a metaphor. Everyone knows that money supply affects inflation, but no one seems to be able to accurately construct an econometric model that details how this relationship actually operates over various periods of time and monetary policies. So, too with the commodity markets: You simply cannot say that A leads to B and expect such a simple explanation to accurately portray a multivariate, interactive market dynamic.

None of this is new. Nor is it limited to precious metals or even commodities markets. These are universal problems in the realm of market analysis. The systems, the markets, that mankind has developed are complex and interconnected. They do not lend themselves to easy explanations and analyses.

Given this, there are two issues worth discussion. First, what are the definitions of fundamentals? Second, why would people consider it legitimate to ask whether the fundamentals still affect commodity price trends?

Defining Fundamentals

First, what are the definitions of fundamentals? Simply put, they are supply and demand. You must also add in investment demand, especially for physical commodities, although one can argue that paper transactions are in many ways fundamentals of these markets.

Earlier in this book, in the discussion on gold, I mentioned the various markets for gold and of the importance of knowing which gold market you are talking about. If the amount of gold being traded in London, New York, Dubai, Mumbai, Shanghai, and other market centers is 60, 100, or 200 times as much as physical supply and demand, do these trades not constitute a very important part of the fundamentals of that market? I have sometimes referred to these trades as a very fat tail that wags the dog. If you try to exclude these trades from your fundamental analysis, that analysis is put at a severe disadvantage. You will be trying to explain the price patterns of a multibillion-ounce gold market based on the fluctuations of

110 million ounces of physical supply and demand. Are all those other trades inconsequential or illegitimate? Do they matter less, or more, than the amount of gold being sold into the market by miners and scrap refiners, or the amounts of gold being purchased by jewelers and electronics manufacturers? Clearly, these billions of ounces of gold trades each year have little to do with the fundamentals of supply and demand in the physical market. Who is it that trades so much gold, and why?

All of these are legitimate questions related to the fundamental structure, mechanics, and operations of the gold market. To ignore them and focus solely on physical gold flows is to severely handicap one's analysis.

The converse also can be a problem. Some analysts who do not understand these paper transactions add some of them into their physical market balances, suggesting that every time a mining company locks in a price for future production and commits to sell at a forward price, there is somehow a physical ounce of gold bought and sold behind that transaction. That simply is not true. Forward transactions, from currencies and bonds to oil, copper, and gold, are based on credit and do not involve physical stocks of these assets changing hands until such time as the forwards are unwound. However, in the gold and silver markets, unlike in any other commodity markets, some people mix these paper apples with physical oranges, further confusing their fundamental analyses.

Obviously the turnover in international markets is a fundamental. To argue that these trading patterns are not a fundamental part of the market is absurd. To concentrate on only the new supply and demand, to expect to be able to explain price movements based only on new supply and demand, is equally ludicrous. That said, most commodity analysts concentrate only on new supply and demand, and ignore the larger spectrum of market transactions.

You also must add in inventories, and changes in inventory levels. We have conducted research that shows the importance of inventory levels not only in silver but also in copper, uranium, and other commodities, and used the findings of these studies to improve our price models for these commodities.

Fundamentals often are defined too narrowly, excluding important fundamentals. For example, many metals analysts still exclude secondary supply—the recovery of metal from scrap—from their precious metals balance sheets, even though these sources of recycled material consistently account for 10 to 30 percent of total annual newly refined supply.

More significantly, many analyses exclude investment demand as a fundamental. We segregate investment demand from fabrication demand because the factors that drive each of these market segments are so different, and the effects of each of these market segments on prices are quite different. But we include investment demand as a fundamental factor. In fact, investment demand is the single most important variable affecting gold prices. It has been for decades, and it continues to be so today.

Another recent problem that has contributed to the sense that fundamentals may no longer explain price changes has been the use of wildly unrepresentative data streams as statistics of supply and demand. Using these extremely bad statistics as estimates of supply and demand leads to

> *Investment demand is the single most important variable affecting gold prices.*

the cursory conclusion that there is no relationship discernible between the fundamentals, so misrepresented, and price developments. It is not that the fundamentals are not reflected in prices, but rather that the data do not represent the fundamentals.

There is a sparse amount of real data and research available on many commodities markets. In gold, there are two groups, CPM Group and another, that undertake any field research programs, collecting statistics and developing data series on supply and demand. The same is true in silver and platinum group metals.

There is also a problem with made-up data series. Many people simply make up statistics to support their preconceived conclusions, or rely on truly twisted forms of illogic to bend and contort the available data to meet their needs. Others rely on trade data showing imports and exports, and often wind up double- and triple-counting metal because of the numerous transactions in which a single ounce of metal is employed.

All of what we do should be directed at projecting prices accurately. Otherwise, it most likely is beside the point. One often hears analysts suggesting that the price of a financial asset or commodity is out of line with the fundamentals of that market. I do not doubt that the prices can vary from what fundamentals dictate in the short run, and that the short run can persist for a long time, but more often than not, what really is happening is that the analysts' fundamental analysis is inaccurate.

If I am faced with a situation in which the data suggest one market outcome but the market behaves differently, I am more likely to assume that the data are wrong than I am to assume that the market, the price, is wrong.

In March 1986 my company was still part of Goldman Sachs. At that time, we issued a buy recommendation on gold. It was the first time since early 1983 that we felt the intermediate-term outlook for gold—two or three years forward—was positive, that prices seemed more likely to be higher in two or three years than they were at that time. Our view was based on signs of stronger, rising investment demand for gold.

At the time, Consolidated Gold Fields mining corporation still existed, and we had a close cooperative relationship with the analysts in their research operation. In fact, we shared several consultants with them. I met with their two analysts in March 1986, when I was in London circulating our new gold buy recommendation to Goldman's clients. One of Consgold's analysts said he saw no evidence of rising investment demand, and he asked us to support our opinion. I cited the usual figures on coin sales and the like, but added that the strongest evidence was the 10 percent or more increase we had seen in gold prices over the previous 12 months. Gold prices had been rising, by a somewhat healthy pace. Why? Because investors were buying. The price forecast was based, in part, on an analysis of the fundamentals, as reflected in the price.

This is in line with a famous quotation of John Maynard Keynes. When someone complained that economists were always changing their opinions, he responded that when he received new information, he took it into account in his thinking. "What do you do, Sir?" he asked. The bottom line is that many people have been doing woefully inadequate research, or pseudo-research, on precious metals and other commodities for years.

There is one fellow who publishes a newsletter of sorts on gold. In late 1992 he railed against CPM Group, which was saying that central bank gold sales had risen sharply and were likely to remain high for years to come. His view was that we were lying to sell research, that central banks were not large sellers, and that the price of gold would "adjust" to $800 as soon as the market "realized" this reality. Shortly thereafter the Dutch and Belgian central banks both announced that they had sold large amounts of gold. Our estimate was that total net gold sales in 1992 were around 12 million ounces, and that the Dutch and Belgian deliveries, in early 1993, would boost net sales that year to around 22 million ounces. This fellow then came out with a report that said the gold price had been restrained by massive central bank gold sales, which he put at around 50 million ounces, a ridiculous number. As soon as these sales ended, as they surely would, he said, gold prices would have to rise sharply, to around $800.

The shocking part of this story is not that such people exist, and can live with themselves. It is not that they can get away with publishing such rubbish. The shocking part is that anyone, much less mining and investment professionals, listens to them.

When the markets do not live up to their preconceived or ill-conceived notions of what prices ought to be, such people resort to complaining that the data are wrong, or that there is a conspiracy to distort the markets. There certainly has been a spate of conspiracy theories circulating related to precious metals and copper markets lately. More often than not, there is no conspiracy, and it is simply a matter of people not having the gumption to admit to the errors of their analysis.

This leads to a corollary: If your analysis based largely on fundamentals and macroeconomic variables consistently projects long-term price trends with a reasonable degree of accuracy, it just may be that your analysis and the underlying statistics are correct. If that is the case, one need not resort to conspiracy theories to explain market behavior.

I like to stress the fact that it is possible to accurately project metals prices without having accurate data or an effective market model. Never underestimate the occurrence of coincidence.

In 1998 I was asked why gold prices had dropped from around $400 to around $300, at a time when fabrication demand for gold, in jewelry, was reported to be rising strongly. Clearly fundamentals were not at work, I was told. Actually, the gold price was falling expressly due to fundamentals in the physical gold market.

On the surface, narrowly defined fundamentals did not seem to support this conclusion. Broader fundamentals did through. Fabrication demand had been rising sharply while supply, as traditionally defined, seemed relatively stable. This would not have seemed to point to declining prices. Remember, however, that prices have a greater influence on fabrication demand than fabrication demand has on prices: The decline in prices contributed to the rise in fabrication demand, since fabrication demand is negatively correlated to prices.

However, the two fundamentals that exert the strongest influence on the price of gold were changing dramatically in a way negative for gold prices at that time. Investment demand was falling, since there were no good reasons for investors to abandon stocks for gold, at least until the middle of 1998. Central bank sales meanwhile were high and rising. Investment demand has a greater price-setting role than do central bank sales, and it was our view that the decline in demand from this segment of the market was behind the drop in gold prices.

Why Do People Ask This Question?

Turning now to the second issue, why anyone would even think it worth asking whether fundamentals still apply, I suppose there are several reasons this question gets asked in the commodities markets. One is that so many analysts and investors have been dead wrong so often about commodities. Gold and commodities were pronounced officially dead as investments and assets in 2001 and early 2002, roughly one year after the current bull market rally began and just before the increases in prices began to get interesting. Banks and dealers that had spent tens of millions of dollars to build commodities desks just after the last big peak in 1980, and then had spent tens of millions more to carry these loss-making operations for two decades, were slashing staffs, closing operations, and cutting back on their exposure to commodities. These sorts of dead-wrong conclusions about commodities are far too common. When people consistently get things wrong, they look for good reasons for their mistakes. One rationale that people will believe for getting commodities consistently wrong is that these markets defy analysis, since the fundamentals do not seem to matter to price directions.

The second reason the question gets asked is that the markets in fact have changed. One of those changes has been the more prominent role of various types of institutional investors and proprietary traders. A third reason has been the diminution of fundamentally based research groups in the financial community and at mining companies. A fourth is the increased reliance on technical, chart-based, and computer-based price patterns and momentum indicators as the bases for the increased volume of short-term trades occurring in the interbank and paper markets.

When I began in this business in the late 1970s few people used technical analysis. I studied the Dow theory and other technical programs because I wanted to know when and where technically based speculators, traders, and others should be expected to enter and exit the markets. When I went to Wall Street in 1980, no one at the trading company I joined did technical analysis. I began providing a weekly technical "heads-up" report for our traders so they would know what to expect from the technical crowd. My superiors warned me not to distribute or advertise this technical analysis very prominently, as it would lead to no good. Today, that trading company is an adjunct to the foreign exchange desk at Goldman Sachs, and no one at it trades based on fundamentals. In fact, my estimate is that virtually all of its metals trades are investment-oriented, for its own managed accounts, and that they are entirely based on technical and momentum indicators. They are not unique. If there are more than 6,000 commodity trade advisers and commodity pool operators registered with the National Futures Association, probably fewer than two dozen of them are fundamentally driven metals-oriented operations.

In 1980, probably fewer than 10 percent of all commodities transactions were based on technical patterns. Today, probably more than 95 percent of the transactions by volume are technically based. In 1980, most of the trades were of intermediate-term duration; today, most are extremely short term.

This change is not limited to commodities. In 1980 the majority of foreign exchange trades reflected international trade. Today, more than 80 percent reflect capital flows.

> *If there are more than 6,000 commodity trade advisers and commodity pool operators registered with the National Futures Association, probably fewer than two dozen of them are fundamentally driven metals-oriented operations.*

Let's take the case of silver as a closing example. We wrote in our reports for some time in the 1990s that there were tremendous inventories of bullion which would keep prices down, even in the face of a current-account deficit of newly refined supply relative to demand. The view we expressed throughout the 1990s was that at some point these inventories would reach critically low levels, and this, combined with developments in the investment demand sector, most likely would contribute to a period of higher prices. For most of the period from 1991 into 2003 we have reiterated the view that one should not expect silver prices to rise until these fundamental developments emerged. Many others in the silver market ran ahead of prices, expecting rising prices because of this current account deficit, ignoring the effects of inventories and net investor sales. Until 2003, at least, they were repeatedly disappointed. In this case, it was not that the fundamentals were not affecting silver prices. Rather, it was too narrowly defined fundamentals on the part of some observers, and mismeasurement and misuse of statistics on the part of others.

Such errors are not limited to precious metals. Around 1983 the copper market moved into a current account deficit. Many analysts turned bullish, even though reported market inventories of refined copper were at record high levels. Over the next four years copper prices languished. By 1987 and 1988 inventories had been drawn down to extremely low levels, at which time prices responded by rising. Nominal copper prices rose from an annual average of 61.45 cents per pound in 1986 to $1.15 in 1988. By then, however, many analysts had given up on the possibility of higher copper prices.

Conclusion

Putting all of this together, my view is that the commodities markets are extremely interesting markets for investors. Commodities are an asset class. They represent a legitimate place for investors to put their money with a fair expectation of profiting from their investments. There are profits to be made in commodities. They may not be the ones that many people think are there for the taking. There is no supercycle. Profits will be made on both the long and short sides of individual markets.

The fundamentals of economics still apply: Higher commodities prices already are leading to reduced demand for a number of commodities and are stimulating the largest production expansion program for commodities in history. These basic economic facts of life will limit the rally, which is already quite mature for a peacetime rally in commodities prices in the modern economy.

Commodities remain vitally important to the world economy. As more people move up the economic ladder, they will want more food, better housing, better transportation, and more electrical and electronic goods. This will help increase demand across a wide range of commodities; it is already having a major effect, and it will continue to do so. The effect will not be one-way or immediate, but rather will occur over many years. It will also be countered by the increases in supply mentioned in the previous paragraph. Those people who view China's emerging consumer class solely as customers for commodities and goods manufactured overseas are wrong. China already is emerging as a major source of many commodities, as well as a major consumer. It is converting itself from being a net importer of steel and other commodities into a net exporter of these. That trend will continue, and will spread to other commodities.

The future of commodities as investments thus is neither necessarily boom nor bust. It is a combination of these factors. These are complex markets, and any simple analysis is doomed to lead to bad investments. Investors need to do their homework. They need to be skeptical of what people marketing investment products and ideas tell them. Commodities are like any other financial market—they lend themselves to honest analysis, and such honest work can be rewarded with handsome returns.

Index